CHILDREN OF POVERTY

Studies on the Effects of Single Parenthood, the Feminization of Poverty, and Homelessness

edited by

STUART BRUCHEY
Allan Nevins Professor Emeritus
Columbia University

T0352799

FAMILY EMPOWERMENT

ONE OUTCOME OF PARENTAL PARTICIPATION IN COOPERATIVE PRESCHOOL EDUCATION

KATHERINE M. DUNLAP

Taylor & Francis Group

LONDON AND NEW YORK

First published 2000 by Garland Publishing Inc.

Published 2018 by Routledge
2 Park Square, Milton Park, Abingdon, Oxon OX14 4RN
52 Vanderbilt Avenue, New York, NY 10017

First issued in paperback 2018

Routledge is an imprint of the Taylor & Francis Group, an informa business

Library of Congress Cataloging-in-Publication Data
Dunlap, Katherine M.
    Family empowerment : one outcome of parental participation in cooperative preschool education / Katherine M. Dunlap
        p. cm. — (Children of poverty)
    Includes bibliographical references and index.
    ISBN 0-8153-3378-1 (alk. paper)
    1. Education, Preschool—Parent participation—North Carolina—Charlotte Case studies. 2. Socially handicapped children—Education—North Carolina—Charlotte Case studies. I. Title. II. Series.
LB1140.35.P37D86 1999
372.21—dc21   99-28531

ISBN 13: 978-1-138-96956-8 (pbk)
ISBN 13: 978-0-8153-3378-4 (hbk)

To my parents, Katherine and James Dunlap.

Contents

If you've made up your mind
You can do anything,
You are absolutely right.

The human mind doesn't care what you plant --
Success or failure --
But it will return
what you plant.

A great pleasure in life
Is doing what
People say you cannot do.

Archie Allen
March 1993

Acknowledgements

This book evolved from a doctoral dissertation of the same title. As with any dissertation, many people contributed to the finished product. Without the guidance of the Reverend Dr. Charles A. Summers, pastor of Seigle Avenue Presbyterian Church, I would never have understood the power in empowerment. In 1989, Dr. Summers led a study of the McKnight article, "Why servanthood is bad." As a social work educator, I squirmed as residents of the low-income housing project criticized the role of social work in their lives, but this dialogue taught me that community change is contingent on the empowerment of people.

I extend hearty thanks to the children, parents, staff, and volunteers of Seigle Avenue Preschool Cooperative. Now, in early 1999, the preschool is in its eleventh year of operation. Along with the educational programs of Seigle Avenue Presbyterian Church, the preschool has moved into a new facility called the Hope Building. This structure meets all criteria for licensing, and the preschool plans to extend its hours to accommodate parents who are working or enrolled in school. The parents' program is still going strong under the leadership of a new parent coordinator who continues the tradition of empowering parents through training and support. In addition, Seigle Avenue Preschool has helped five new preschools develop similar, family-centered empowerment programs.

From the beginning, members of the preschool Board of Directors have been committed to providing quality education and to promoting opportunity for all families. They have developed tracking methods and sponsored research efforts which are unusual in a program of this size. Invariably, boards and staff have encouraged my efforts and implemented my suggestions. From the parents, I gained insight and wisdom. For reasons of confidentiality, I will not name them here, but they know who they are—for they taught me, among other things, to cook green beans and fry chicken Southern style.

My teachers at the Mandel School of Applied Social Sciences offered direction. Once my chair, Dr. Wallace J. Gingerich, realized that parental outcomes are as important as outcomes for children, he helped me capture the richness of these stories. Dr. Kathleen J. Farkas inspired me to speak in my own voice, and Dr. Pranab Chatterjee gave me a sense of history and the tools of qualitative research. Dr. Richard L. Edwards, dean of the Mandel School at that time, deserves a special mention; without his influence, the part-time doctoral program would not have existed.

At UNC Charlotte, Dr. Roslyn Mickelson introduced the theories of Pierre Bourdieu in a breakthrough moment. The librarians at UNC Charlotte procured material from across the country, expediting every request.

At the University of North Carolina at Chapel Hill, Dean John B. Turner believed in my potential and pushed me into doctoral studies. Dr. Gary L. Shaffer offered encouragement and practical advice. Dr. H. Carl Henley, Jr., confirmed my research methods, although he would have preferred a quantitative approach! His support was invaluable.

My fellow doctoral students provided a sounding board throughout the process. Dr. George Gottfried helped me refine "the researchable question," and Dr. Kimberly Strom-Gottfried provided insight, direction, encouragement, a spare bedroom, and many recipes for fun and food.

My greatest debt is to my husband, George W. Bostian. He proofread every draft, and he suffered with me through seemingly insufferable Saturdays without relief from work. Throughout this process, he supported me at every step with persistent good humor. Without his unceasing love and encouragement, I could not have told— or lived—this story. His is the hand behind the voice.

Family Empowerment

CHAPTER 1

Introduction

Positive effects of preschool education on children have been well documented (Berrueta-Clement et al., 1984; Consortium for Longitudinal Studies, 1983, Deutsch, Jordan, & Deutsch, 1985; Lazar & Darlington, 1982). This study considers positive benefits for caregivers who participate in cooperative preschool education. Since not all caregivers are parents, the study includes grandparents who have custody of children, and kin with responsibility for kith.

HISTORICAL CONTEXT

Preschool education began in the United States during the middle of the twentieth century and flourished as the spearhead of the War on Poverty. The best-known program was Head Start, a national compensatory education project begun in 1965. However, many other disparate parent training programs also emerged. These were united by four assumptions: First, low-income families fail to prepare children for successful entry into school. Second, the early years constitute a critical period for cognitive growth. Third, negative family influences usually are not overcome by later schooling. Fourth, a "diffusion effect" transmits program gains to siblings.

Evaluation of academic preschools and the parent training model demonstrated significant and substantial long-term benefits for children; however, few studies examined changes in parents, and substantial ethical concerns were identified.

Informed by research on parent training programs, the family support movement emerged in the late 1970s. Family support programs provided emotional sustenance, information, and instrumental assistance to families within a context of empowerment. Although program focus varied considerably, common goals included enhancement of parents' child-rearing capacities; empowerment of parents as advocates for change; and brokerage of resources.

Family support programs have been difficult to evaluate; however, mounting evidence suggests that they positively affect the cognitive and social development of economically disadvantaged children. Some argue that family support programs produce positive outcomes for adults, but this has not been clearly documented.

THE THEORETICAL BACKGROUND

This study combined several research streams. First, it viewed empowerment as a process of adult development. Second, drawing heavily from the research and experience of John McKnight, it posited that lasting empowerment is situated within community. To this end, the study assumed that neither children nor parents can be "fixed" by plucking them from their environment for inoculation or enrichment. Instead, this study assumed that enduring change occurs only when people are empowered to alter the fabric of their own lives and communities as they see fit. Third, this study assumed that the process of empowerment involves acquisition of the cultural capital of the dominant class. Building on the research of French economist Pierre Bourdieu (1971, 1977) and his followers (Lareau, 1987, 1989; Ogbu, 1974, 1978, 1990; Lubeck, 1985), this study postulated that individuals can amass cultural capital and translate it into human capital without renouncing their own ethnic heritage.

FOCUS OF THE STUDY

The unanswered questions were how, when, where, why, and for whom family support programs work (Weissbourd, 1989). Weiss (1987) explained:

> It is unfortunate that there is so little pertinent research about program and parent interactions, about staff and parent attitudes toward each other, and the like, that would help in identifying the crucial features and practices of nondeficit programs and in answering the question of whether these programs are in fact

empowering. Overall, the field is now long on prescription and short on description and analysis of nondeficit partnership and multilateral program models. (p. 145)

According to Zigler and Weiss (1985), understanding how and why certain programs work for certain individuals is the most pressing need in this area. That is the focus of this exploratory investigation. Guided by a review of the theoretical literature, empirical work, and the author's extended observations, this study was based on the following presumptions: Through involvement with the family component of this preschool, caregivers acquire cultural capital. Over time, they translate cultural capital into human capital, or economic gain. This process, called empowerment, ultimately strengthens families and neighborhoods.

THE RESEARCH SETTING

In an ecological study such as this, environment is a critical element, for the setting possesses particular physical and material attributes which shape behavior; and each setting in turn is shaped by its particular history. This private, non-profit preschool, founded in 1986, serves one of the oldest public housing projects in a major southern city. It was established by and is housed in a small, racially-integrated Presbyterian church which has served the neighborhood since 1941. According to Weiss (1987), programs such as this "hold substantial promise for promoting adult development and strengthening families" (p. 154).

In order for their children to participate, caregivers must meet specified obligations, including attending semi-monthly meetings. The cooperative component automatically precluded participation by caregivers who were employed during the day.

Weiss (1988) separated family support programs into "flagships" and the "fleet." She described flagships as the large, research-driven programs usually mounted by universities or government agencies. Fleet programs are grassroots efforts established under local auspices, often driven by the vision of a few community leaders.

This preschool represented a ship of the fleet. It served one of the poorest segments of society, in a substandard facility, with minimal financial investment. However, it appeared to be effective. Because it was a ship of the fleet, it offered a significant opportunity for identification of the salient characteristics essential for replication or expansion of an affordable program.

As Rappaport (1981) explained, "Most professional advice is drawn from a very limited set of personal or professional experiences in settings designed and controlled *by* professionals *for* others. Researchers can learn much if they are willing to observe the process of empowerment when it is taking place, even if that is in settings such as churches which are typically ignored" (p. 19). Zigler and Weiss (1985) also advocated for programs that benefit not only the child but also the family and community.

The evolution of the caregivers' program at this preschool paralleled national developments as an indigenous worker transformed parent training into family support. The next family coordinator took the program one step further. Rather than viewing empowerment as a by-product, she identified empowerment as a program goal. Similar actions have not yet been reported by other programs.

THE PURPOSE OF THIS INVESTIGATION

The goal of the investigation was twofold: first, to contribute to the knowledge base by generating information about the process of empowerment; and, second, to promote replication by identifying salient characteristics of an effective family empowerment program.

The Methodology

This naturalistic inquiry was based on two types of analysis: participant observation of the caregivers in the current cohort, and case studies of caregivers who completed the program from one to five years ago. The project presumed that caregivers acquired cultural capital through involvement in the cooperative component of the preschool. Caregivers translated cultural capital into human capital; and this process, called empowerment, benefited caregivers, their families, and their neighborhood.

The naturalistic method was chosen for its utility. As Weiss (1987) explained:

Qualitative assessments, including intensive interviews and ethnographic observations about program processes, are useful in at least four ways: they can reveal unanticipated positive and negative consequences of the intervention; they help capture practical knowledge; they address the question of whether the program was implemented as designed; and they can help explain the pattern of quantitative program outcomes. (p. 153)

Social Significance

Marian Wright Edelman (1989), president of the Children's Defense Fund, eloquently proclaimed, "If it is to save itself, America must save its children" (p. 27). This is a worthy mandate, but helping children is not the direct focus of this project. Children cannot mature and prosper if dissevered from their families and communities. In order to save children, we must redeem the fabric of society in which they grow and are nurtured. This study contributes to that endeavor.

Edward Zigler (1978), the founder, administrator, and evaluator of Head Start, similarly concluded that long-term effects of early intervention depend, at least to a great extent, on "the degree to which parents are involved in the training of their children" (p. 73). Bronfenbrenner (1979) supported this approach when he speculated, "The impact of day care and preschool on the nation's families and on the society at large may have a more profound consequence than any direct effects for the development of human beings in modern industrialized societies" (p. 165).

Overview of Contents

The first section presents a historical overview and examines the current context for early childhood intervention. Chapter 2 reviews the history of preschool education in the United States from its earliest beginnings through the period of rapid proliferation in which parent training programs emerged. This section examines the three causal theories that dominated the intellectual field during that time—genetic inheritance, cultural deprivation, and economic difference. Chapter 3 examines research findings that impelled the transformation of parent training programs into the parent support movement. This chapter includes a discussion of the ecological approach, the role of community, and the process of empowerment. The fourth chapter reviews current conditions in the United States and examines the sociology and function of education as proposed by Pierre Bourdieu (1971, 1979).

These chapters are followed by a section on methodology. In Chapter 5, the research question is posed. Chapter 6 explicates the methodology, and Chapter 7 analyzes the setting in which the research took place. Chapter 8 describes the participants, and Chapter 9 discusses entry and data collection.

Data are presented in the third section. Chapter 10 describes salient features which attracted caregivers to the preschool; the family program; roles of staff and board members; and programmatic barriers to empowerment. Chapter 11 presents caregivers' reports of changes in parenting skills and family relationships. In Chapter 12, the roles of cultural and human capital are explored and the process of empowerment is delineated; further, each concept is illustrated by a case summary. Neighborhood impact is the subject of Chapter 13. Finally, conclusions and recommendations for further study are included in Chapter 14.

CHAPTER 2

Parent Training

This chapter reviews the history of preschool education in the United States from its earliest beginnings through the period of rapid proliferation in which parent training programs emerged. Three causal theories are presented and evaluated: genetic inheritance, cultural deprivation, and economic difference. The chapter concludes with a consideration of ethical issues which tainted early parent training programs.

EARLIEST ENDEAVORS

The first kindergarten, transplanted from Germany, opened in a private home in Watertown, Wisconsin, in 1855. Kindergartens proliferated under religious and philanthropic patronage, for this was a period of national awakening to social problems. "The tides of immigration brought to American shores peoples difficult to assimilate and slow to accept American ideals and standards of living. Slums were in process of formation. They became sources of disease, crime, delinquency and industrial disorders" (Braun & Edwards, 1972, p. 74).

Preschool education became the great hope for regeneration of society; and young women, trained in normal schools, entered the work with "rare enthusiasm and consecration to the cause. No neighborhood was too criminal, no family too degenerate, no child too bad" (p. 75). The kindergarten teacher taught in the morning and spent afternoons finding work for the unemployed and medical care for the ill. According to Braun and Edwards, family assistance may well have been the most important contribution of pioneer kindergartens.

In the early 1900s, Maria Montessori established *Casa di Bambini*, a school for deprived children in a slum dwelling in Rome, Italy. Humanitarian Margaret McMillan founded a similar "open air" nursery in the slums of England. Both these experimental schools achieved considerable success, although their influence on American education was minor until the 1960s (Consortium for Longitudinal Studies, 1983).

The first parent cooperative preschool was established in 1915 at the University of Chicago by a group of faculty spouses. Called the Chicago Cooperative Nursery School, it fostered children's total development; however, the pupils were primarily from middle- and upper-class homes. After the establishment of the Chicago school, a number of other colleges began laboratory schools that were important in expanding knowledge about children's development. By the 1930s, early childhood education had attained professional status in the United States (Gordon & Browne, 1985).

During the Second World War the Kaiser Child Care Centers opened in Portland, Oregon, to serve the children of women needed in war-related industry. This was the world's largest and most comprehensive child care agency; however, it closed after the war ended because women were no longer needed in the labor pool.

There were few additional gains in early childhood education until 1957, when Sputnik I, the first Soviet satellite, was launched. This event inspired a re-evaluation of the educational system (Weinberg, 1979). The publication of J. M. Hunt's *Intelligence and Experience* in 1961 challenged stereotypes about fixed intelligence (Paget & Bracken, 1983). This was followed by the civil rights movement, which focused attention on the plight of the poor after decades of benign neglect (Halpern, 1988). Under the leadership of President Lyndon B. Johnson, poverty as a political issue was rediscovered, and the War on Poverty was engaged (Bromley, 1972). Policymakers and educators passionately embraced cognitively-oriented preschool programs for poor children (Consortium for Longitudinal Studies, 1983).

ACADEMIC PRESCHOOLS

The spearhead of the War on Poverty was Head Start, a national compensatory education project begun in 1965. Initially, Head Start provided summer programs for economically disadvantaged four- and five-year-old children. The goal of Head Start was to "forestall the developmental deficiencies characteristic of disadvantaged children" through early intervention (Karnes, Teska, Hodgins, & Badger, 1970, p. 925). Intervention was presumed to impart immediate benefits so that "class differences would be eliminated by the time of school entry" (Zigler & Berman, 1983, p. 895).

When it was established, Head Start represented a radical departure from the prevailing ethos. Most childcare professionals and middle-class parents considered group day care an unacceptable alternative to home care for children younger than age three (Caldwell & Smith, 1970; Foster, Berger, & McLean, 1981).

Although Head Start was the largest and most visible program, it was not the only early intervention project established during this period. Many, such as the Perry Preschool Project, the Verbal Interaction Project, and the Mothers Training Program, were established as demonstration or model projects; and research reports proliferated in a fertile political environment. Henniger (1979) compiled a bibliography of over 1300 titles produced from 1970 to 1978, and published in periodicals ranging from popular works such as *Ebony* and *Parents Magazine* to more academic journals spanning education, psychology, psychiatry, counseling, child welfare, community psychology, pediatrics, and law.

CAUSAL THEORIES

The long-term goal of these programs was to eliminate social problems associated with poverty. To accomplish this ambitious goal, programs sought explanations for the root causes of poverty and inequality. Three distinct causal theories reigned: genetic inheritance, environmental deprivation, and economic difference. These explanations, although originally focused on the children of the poor, were extended to parents and caregivers by association.

Genetic Explanations

There is overwhelming empirical evidence that in the United States, African American children generally score lower than whites on standardized measures of intelligence or IQ tests (Bronfenbrenner, 1975;

Ogbu, 1978; Scarr & Weinberg, 1976). The most controversial explanation for this phenomenon was provided by Arthur Jensen (1969) in his famous discourse on inheritance of intelligence. Referring to Head Start, Jensen began his treatise with the pronouncement, "Compensatory education has been tried, and it apparently has failed" (p. 2). He refuted the argument that IQ differences result from environmental differences and culturally biased tests; and, after carefully defining the intelligence quotient (IQ), he reviewed the concept of heritability.

Jensen concluded that genetic components are far more significant than environmental factors in determining IQ; and he maintained that about 80% of a person's IQ is inherited while only 20% is attributable to environment. According to Jensen, environment acts as a threshold variable. "Below a certain threshold of environmental adequacy, deprivation can have a markedly depressing effect on intelligence. But above this threshold, environmental variations cause relatively small differences in intelligence" (p. 60).

Jensen hypothesized two distinct types of ability; and he suggested that whites exhibit both, while blacks demonstrate only the more basic type. Further, he concluded that since black and white students exhibit different capabilities, schools should employ different instructional strategies with the two groups. He encouraged educators to use other strengths in children. "Diversity rather than uniformity of approaches and aims would seem to be the key to making education rewarding for children of different patterns of ability" (p. 117).

Many authors have refuted Jensen's position (Scarr-Salapatek, 1975; Gould, 1981). Bronfenbrenner (1975) agreed that "genetic factors play a substantial role in producing individual differences in mental ability" (p. 97); however, he presumed a multidirectional correlational relationship between heredity and environment. In order for genetic potential to be realized, the environment must be appropriately complex and stimulating. Further, Bronfenbrenner maintained that the potential of heritability could be enhanced by improving the environment.

Ogbu contested Jensen with extensive argument (1974, 1978). In a controlled study, Lee, Brooks-Gunn, and Schnur (1988) asked whether participation in Head Start for one year eliminated the relative cognitive difference between children who attended and those who did not. The authors found significant Race x Background interactions. Head Start appeared to be most effective for African American children in the below-average ability group; and the authors concluded that initial deficits were *not* due to genetic factors. Rather, children were capable of learning when exposed to the dominant culture as represented by the outcome measures. The authors inferred that "The indication that the program worked especially well for the most cognitively disadvantaged children suggested that a preschool program especially designed for such children would be most likely to correct the specific deficits of those who come from a cognitively depressed environment" (p. 220).

More recent behavioral genetic research suggested that genetic influence on individual differences was usually significant and often substantial (Scarr & Weinberg, 1976, 1978; Weinberg, 1989). In an overview of recent research in this field, Plomin (1989) concluded that there is a genetic influence in intellectual ability—including IQ—and in specific cognitive abilities, academic achievement, reading disabilities, mental retardation, personality factors, psychopathology, and delinquent and criminal behaviors. Plomin noted that "genetic influence is so ubiquitous and pervasive in behavior that a shift in emphasis is warranted: Ask not what is heritable, ask what is not heritable" (p. 108).

Zigler (1978) and Zigler & Trickett (1978) claimed that conjectures regarding heredity were essentially irrelevant. "The IQ reaches its maximum efficiency as a predictor of everyday performance when it is employed to predict school performance" (Zigler & Trickett, 1978, p. 791). However, performance is greatly influenced by a variety of personality and motivational variables that have little to do with formal cognitive and achievement variables. In a ten-year study of Canadian children, Fotheringham and Creal (1980) concluded that achievement is shaped by a number of family variables, including genetic inheritance, opportunity, reinforcement, and expectations.

Plomin (1989) supported this view with a second message which he considered as important as his first: The data which supported heritability also provide the best available evidence of the importance of environment. Non-genetic factors may be responsible for more than half of variance for most complex behaviors (Plomin, 1989; Rowe & Plomin, 1981; Plomin, Loehlin, & DeFries, 1985). McCall (1983) supported this position by speculating that environmental variation within families accounts for as much as 15% to 25% of the variation in

IQ. Willerman (1979) suggested that environmental differences may account for 22% of the variance among genetically-related individuals.

Environmental Explanations

Proponents of environmental explanations were propelled in large measure by their desire to refute theories of genetic heritability. The cultural deprivation model, sometimes referred to as the social pathology model, was based on the premise that there are essential deficits in certain children, their families, and their cultures. Hunt (1967) provided a technical definition: "Cultural deprivation may be seen as a failure to provide an opportunity for infants and young children to have the experiences required for adequate development of those semi-autonomous central processes demanded for acquiring skill in the use of linguistic and mathematical symbols and for the analysis of causal relationships" (p. 284).

Hess and Shipman (1965, 1966) defined three tenets of the cultural deficit paradigm. First, the behavior that leads to social, educational, and economic poverty is learned. Second, this behavior is promoted by lack of meaning in the mother-child communication system. And third, it is perpetuated by family systems which offer predetermined solutions and few alternatives (p. 870). Deutsch (1963) explained the significance of this phenomenon: "The lower-class child enters the school situation so poorly prepared to produce what the school demands that initial failures are almost inevitable. . . ." (p. 380).

Proponents maintained that deficits could be remedied through compensatory education. Schools were designated as the primary change agent responsible for exposing low-income and minority children to a set of experiences that their culturally-deprived families were unable to provide.

Much of the research and development that shaped the conceptual basis for the cultural deficit model drew strongly from Basil Bernstein's (1960) theoretical formulations. In contrast to those who sought a biological explanation of social class and ethnic group differences, Bernstein looked at environmental explanations. He proposed that middle- and lower-class parents employ different child-rearing techniques which result in different patterns of language and thought. According to Bernstein, middle-class parents instill the values of order, rationality, stability, planning for long-range goals, and the control of emotions. Their elaborated code, as he terms middle-class language, promotes superior abstract-reasoning abilities and permits complex and subtle intellectual activity. Bernstein maintained that lower-class parenting lacks these characteristics (Laosa, 1983, p. 333). This hypothesis was supported by a series of studies of mother-child interaction conducted at the University of Chicago by Brophy (1970) and Hess and Shipman (1965, 1966).

Oscar Lewis (1966) also provided support for this premise through his study of Puerto Rican families in New York City. Lewis proposed that about twenty percent of those officially certified as poor live in a culture of poverty. According to Lewis, the poor perpetuate poverty. They share traits, habits, values, and hopes that are transmitted to their children in the same way other cultural patterns are conveyed.

Lewis (1966) identified seventy traits, which he described along four systemic dimensions: "the relationship between the subculture and the larger society; the nature of the slum community; the nature of the family; and the attitudes, values and character structure of the individual" (p. 21). Lewis maintained that the culture of poverty was both a reaction to, and an attempt to cope with, marginal position in a "class-stratified, highly individuated, capitalistic society" (p. 21). The individual who grows up in the culture develops a "strong feeling of fatalism, helplessness, dependence, and inferiority" (p. 23). Though members may talk about middle-class values and even claim some as their own, they do not live by middle-class canons. They exhibit a strong present-time orientation with little disposition to defer gratification and plan for the future. Families are matriarchal, and childhood is not cherished. Thus the culture of poverty is predicated on negative qualities or pathology within the culture: family disintegration, personal disorganization, fatalism, and resignation.

The concept of a culture of poverty was extended to include African American families by the Moynihan Report (1965). It reads, "At the heart of the deterioration of the fabric of Negro society is the deterioration of the Negro family. It is the fundamental source of the weakness of the Negro community at the present time" (p. 5). Acknowledging three centuries of injustice, the report concluded, "The policy of the United States is to bring the Negro American to full and equal sharing in the responsibilities and rewards of citizenship" (p. 48).

Although the intent was to define the "problem" as a prelude to national action, the report was interpreted as further proof of cultural deficits in the black community.

Economic Explanations

The assumptions of the culture of poverty theory were challenged by Piven and Cloward (1971), who argued persuasively that poverty serves the economic order in the United States. Cheap labor and economic racism confine blacks to low-skilled jobs, low wages, and economic uncertainty. This economy requires the poor to devise ways to cope with chronic crises, catastrophes, and events totally beyond their control.

The economic explanation was coupled with a perspective which viewed black and white families as different but equal. Proponents argued that low-income and minority groups were not deprived of culture but rather were developing cultures different from those of the white middle class. Citing the retention of African mores and behaviors, the cultural variance model encouraged scholars to judge black families by black culture and values (Baratz & Baratz, 1970).

William Ryan (1976) maintained that the cultural deprivation model "blamed the victim." The child was seen as the source of the problem rather than as the victim of inequality and racism.

In a landmark publication, Hill (1971) countered the preoccupation with pathology by focusing on strengths in black families. From an analysis of census data, he identified and analyzed five assets: adaptability of family roles, strong kinship bonds, strong work orientation, strong religious orientation, and strong achievement orientation. Hill decried the practice of equating class lifestyle with operational indicators such as income, education, or occupation, maintaining that these indicators are only correlates of class lifestyle and values. In other words, many lower-income people have middle-class lifestyles, while many middle-income people have lower-class lifestyles. The merger of lifestyle and operational indicators, although common, creates unwarranted class images (p. 29).

Stack (1974) studied strengths of black families in the field. She spent three years conducting an ethnomethodological study of an urban Midwestern community comprised of African American immigrants from the south. Her intent was to understand the residents' interpretations of their own life experiences. Stack did not find the unstable, disorganized, matriarchal, fatherless society postulated by the culture of poverty. Instead, she discovered "extensive networks of kin and friends supporting, reinforcing each other—devising schemes for self-help, strategies for survival in a community of severe economic deprivation" (p. 28).

Stack (1974) concluded that African Americans had developed highly adaptive structures such as swapping, fostering, and reciprocity in order to survive. These strategies "comprise a resilient response to the social-economic conditions of poverty, the inexorable unemployment of black women and men, and the access to scarce economic resources of a mother and her children 'on aid'" (p. 124).

EMERGENCE OF PARENT TRAINING PROGRAMS

The earliest Head Start programs plucked children from their families and plunged them into activities to promote compensatory education. As researchers extracted new or revised theories, programs were modified to reflect these changes in perspective. For example, Head Start was moved from a summer schedule into the school year; and several optional formats were tried, including home visits, part-week, and part-day participation for preschoolers, and an adolescent curriculum for older students (Harmon & Zigler, 1980). One of the most significant changes was the emergence of parent training programs.

Head Start policymakers, program administrators, and child-development specialists agreed that parents should be included in the evolving programs; however, they held different—often conflicting—notions about the appropriate form of parent involvement. Gordon (1970) suggested five possible levels of participation: audience or observer; teacher of the child; volunteer; trained worker; and decision-maker. Historically, parents have usually served as audience or observer and as classroom volunteer, especially through parent-teacher associations. A few parents have been decision-makers through participation on Boards of Education and other advisory boards (Davies, 1978).

The majority of Head Start leaders defined parent participation as parent training. "Parents had to learn *with* their children, particularly how to *be* parents" (Valentine & Stark, 1979, p. 297). This approach usually combined didactic instruction in home economics and parenting skills with a focus on parents as teachers in the home. It arose from the belief that the poor perpetuate poverty. "They share traits, habits, values, and aspirations that they transmit to their children in the same way other cultural patterns are transmitted. In this way a 'cycle of poverty' is established" (p. 299).

This view was supported by experts in early childhood education for whom successful education meant individual change, fostered by appropriately supportive parents (Taylor, 1967). These experts maintained that the culture of poverty could be eradicated by exposing children and adults to middle-class experiences. Laosa (1983) described the process through which parents were expected to become agents of change. ". . . Poor and ethnic minority parents are taught child-rearing techniques that are considered to produce children with the intellectual skills and attitudes necessary for successful academic competition with their middle-class peers" (p. 333).

A minority of planners defined parent involvement in terms of parental control over the local Head Start program (Caliguri, 1970). Parental participation varied considerably across sites. In some centers, parents governed with total self-determination. In others, parents were included on Parent Advisory Committees, but their influence was moderated by other committee members. The focus on parental control arose from the alternative understanding that poverty has less to do with cultural or psychological factors than with unequal distribution of resources and opportunities. The concomitant solution was to increase scarce resources and make institutions more responsive to those they are designed to serve.

A few researchers went so far as to eliminate parents entirely from early intervention programs. They used college students (Rickel, Smith, & Sharp, 1979; Jason, Clarfield, & Cowen, 1973), paraprofessional aides (Durlak, 1979; Cowen, Dorr, Trost, & Izzo, 1972; Rickel & Smith, 1979; Weissberg, Cowen, Lotyczewski, & Gesten, 1983), and even siblings (Cicirelli, 1972) to influence children's behavior. All found improvements in behavioral indicators.

Within Head Start, the majority opinion prevailed; and the educational framework for parental involvement became parent training, rooted in the cultural deficit model of poverty (Valentine & Stark,

1979). Each site was encouraged to develop independently, however, and program quality varied tremendously. Although the policies set forth in the 1975 federal guidelines included both educational and political definitions of parental involvement, most sites emphasized parent training over parent control (Zigler & Seitz, 1982).

CHARACTERISTICS OF PARENT TRAINING PROGRAMS

Parent training programs have several features in common. First, they are developed by professionals. Second, their goal is to teach parents how to instruct their own children. Third, the target of their intervention is school-relevant skills.

Goodson and Hess (1975, 1976) studied twenty-eight parent training programs which had formal evaluations. The authors extrapolated three assumptions that undergird parent training programs. These assumptions were confirmed by Zigler and Berman (1983). The first, labeled the "home deficit assumption," maintained that homes in low-income communities failed to prepare young children for successful entry into first grade of public school. This assumption emanated from the research showing that the environment in lower-income homes was different from that in middle-income homes on a number of variables, including type and pattern of stimulation, language style, pattern of parent/child interaction, and motivation.

The second assumption, drawn from research on critical periods, concluded that the early years were particularly important influences for cognitive growth. The third assumption reflected a belief in the culture of poverty. This assumption maintained that the impact of family influences was not usually overcome by later schooling. This was drawn from research indicating that family influence was not greatly modified by school experiences (Coleman et al., 1966; Hess, 1969; Jencks, 1972).

Following the work of Cicirelli (1975), Clarke-Stewart and Apfel (1978) added a fourth assumption: the presence of a "diffusion effect" through which program gains were transmitted to younger siblings. This assumption implied that parent training programs were more cost-effective than remedial programs in which professionals must reach every child.

Parent training programs employed a number of different strategies. The primary methods included didactic instruction (Radin, 1972), demonstration (Burgess, 1982), home visits (Levenstein, 1970; Strom & Johnson, 1974; Gordon, 1970), and group meetings (Rose, 1974). Many programs combined several approaches (Brim, 1959; Harman & Brim, 1980). Although Bronfenbrenner (1974a, 1974b) counseled programs to involve neighborhood and community leaders, there is no evidence that this recommendation was implemented in any substantive way.

Although parent training programs were created to meet the educational needs of low-income children, the middle class often adopted their strategies (Wenig & Brown, 1975). Major media groups promoted education-oriented toys, books, and television programs oriented toward middle-class families (Goodson & Hess, 1976).

EVALUATION OF PARENT TRAINING PROGRAMS

Changes in Children

In hindsight, Edward Zigler, the architect, administrator, and evaluator of Head Start, concluded that the parent training model was infused with a naive optimism about what services could do to eliminate poverty (1982, 1983). The primary outcome measure was the child's intelligence, as measured by standardized IQ tests. These tests have many positive qualities: they are well-developed, available, easy to administer, and are positively correlated with academic achievement measures (Zigler & Seitz, 1980). However, standardized IQ tests measure only one aspect of school success (Iscoe, 1973; McClelland, 1973; Scarr, 1981).

The Westinghouse Report, one of the first and most widely cited evaluations of the Head Start project, was designed to provide a quick statement about the long-term effects of the project (Westinghouse Learning Corporation, 1969). The study has been criticized for a number of major methodological flaws, including lack of a control group; absence of standardization among programs at different centers; a dearth of adequate measures for cognitive ability; total omission of measures of affective and motivational development; and the small size of the sample of children involved in the full-year program (The Consortium for Longitudinal Studies, 1983). Nevertheless, the report indicated that early gains in academic aptitude—measured by IQ—faded after several years. This information was used to restrain the expansion of Head Start and to shift the focus from numerous supplemental summer activities to a few full-year programs.

A number of educators realized that a rigorous longitudinal study was necessary to determine the effectiveness of preschool education programs. In 1975 the Consortium for Longitudinal Studies (originally known as the Consortium for Developmental Continuity) was formed by a group of independent investigators involved with early childhood education programs since the early 1960s. The goal of the Consortium was to facilitate an accurate, independent evaluation of the effectiveness of preschool education.

Findings of the Consortium were significant and substantial. The Consortium concluded that preschool programs improve school competence; increase individual scores on standardized intelligence tests; and boost achievement scores in reading and math. Further, preschool graduates are less likely to be placed in special education or remedial classes; and they have higher self-esteem and they value achievement more than their controls. Mothers of program graduates are more satisfied with their children's school performance (Lazar & Darlington, 1982). Students who participate in a preschool experience are more likely to hold jobs during later adolescence and the early adult years. They also found less delinquency, less use of welfare, and a lower incidence of teenage pregnancy (Berrueta-Clement, Schweinhart, & Weikart, 1983; Consortium For Longitudinal Studies, 1975, 1983). At age nineteen, students who participated in preschool education between 1962 and 1967 demonstrated increased high school graduation rates, enrollment in post-secondary programs, and employment (Berrueta-Clement, Schweinhart, Barnett, Epstein, & Weikart, 1984; Schweinhart, 1987).

Becher (1986) and Honig (1982) also reviewed the research on parent training programs and drew two conclusions: First, through naturally occurring behaviors, parents play a crucial role in facilitating the development of intelligence, competence, and achievement in their children. Second, parent training programs have been effective in improving the intellectual functioning of children. These results were maintained across a variety of program models including home visitation, parents as classroom aides, parent group meetings, mothers as models, and a toy lending program. These findings have been confirmed by others (Bronfenbrenner, 1974a; Goodson & Hess, 1975, 1976; Irvine, Horan, Flint, Kukuk, & Hick, 1982; Lee, Brooks-Gunn, & Schnur, 1988; McKay & McKay, 1983; Mistry, 1983; Ryan, 1974; Schaefer, 1972; Zigler, 1978).

Changes in Parents

Few studies examined changes in parents (Gordon, 1978, 1979; Harman & Brim, 1980; Parker, Piotrokowski, & Peay, 1987). For example, Becher's comprehensive review of parental involvement in education included no substantive discussion on the impact of participation on students' parents (1986). The Consortium (1973) speculated that its results were due in large measure to parent/child interaction. However, their studies were designed and implemented before the importance of parent involvement was suspected, and their data did not address parental change. In a review of multiple programs, Clarke-Steward and Apfel (1978) concluded, "Maternal behavior change has usually been assumed, and then ignored, in program evaluations" (p. 83).

Several studies of parents included limited outcome measures. McKinney examined the extent of involvement in parent training programs by measuring attendance at meetings (1978, 1980); and Raim (1980) noted improved parental reading skills as a serendipitous artifact of a tutoring program.

A number of evaluations considered changes in parental sentiment. Clarizio (1968) and Wohlford (1974) both used short-term, therapeutic-like treatments as parent participation variables. Clarizio compared three groups: mothers who attended small group meetings led by Head Start staff; mothers also assigned to individual counseling with a school social worker; and a control group of mothers who did not participate in a group but whose children were in Head Start. He found no significant differences in maternal attitudes toward education.

Wolhberg (1974) reported that parents who participated in a language development group demonstrated more positive attitudes than parents who participated in a sensitivity discussion group, but no data analysis was reported. Several studies found that parent training increased self-esteem (Donofrio, 1976; Greenwood, Breivogel, & Bessent, 1972; Lombard, 1981; Strom & Johnson, 1974) or satisfaction with the school (Herman & Yeh, 1980). In addition to increases in self-esteem, Adams found vast changes in economic status for eleven of the thirteen most intensely involved Head Start participants (1976).

A nationwide study of parent participation in twenty Head Start centers in forty-eight states was mounted by Midco Associates (Bromley, 1972). Hypotheses linked two types of participation—parents as decision-makers and parents as learners—to specific outcomes. Although few programs supported parents as decision-makers, strongest results were observed when parents were highly involved in both roles. Parent participation was related to personal growth, beneficial outcomes for children, and institutional change. The study relied on retrospective parental self-report and self-selection. Citing the dearth of evaluative information about parent involvement in Head Start, the author recommended further study of staff characteristics, involved and uninvolved parents, and community impact.

Only six of the twenty-eight programs evaluated by Goodson and Hess (1975, 1976) examined changes in parental behavior. Five of the six documented some changes in developmental expectations of personal power, although the results were not always statistically significant; and the authors determined that no conclusions could be drawn.

Only a handful of researchers directly addressed the issue of class structure and education. In a conceptual paper, Kohn analyzed parent-child relationships from a social structure, rather than a psychodynamic, point of view and concluded that values mediate between class and behavior (1975). Differences in the behaviors of parents in four social status groups were noted by Brophy (1970), who attempted to identify some of the mechanisms through which cultural disadvantage was transmitted. Bee, Egeren, Streissguth, Nyman, and Leckie (1975) used an empirical model to evaluate teaching strategies of middle-class and lower-class mothers. Their findings supported the theory of cultural deprivation. Gordon (1969) captured the dilemma concisely: "Parental involvement becomes a way for parents to learn social rules and social skills so that they can modify the system. . . . Who is going to teach the parents? What social rules should be learned? Which social skills?" (p. 13).

The lack of consistent, positive results may be attributed to several factors. First, researchers have not adequately defined participation. Measures have often been subjective, global, or unspecified, obscuring the nature and extent of actual parental participation in training programs. Second, outcome measures have not been conceptually linked to participation variables. Third, outcome measures have been restricted or incidental.

Goodson and Hess (1976) expressed concern about the paucity of programs evaluating their impact on parents. "If parents display no new behavior or attitudes, it is difficult to dismiss the alternate hypothesis that the program staff has a direct influence on the child" (p. 49). Zigler (1978) agreed, "The real lever that produces these effects may turn out to be what the program stimulates the mother to do with the child" (p. 73).

ETHICAL ISSUES

Significant ethical concerns were associated with early parent training programs. First was the difficulty of defining socially competent parenting in a pluralistic, complex, and rapidly evolving nation that exhibits "diversity among and within groups, and the variation is perhaps widest in the beliefs, attitudes, and behaviors surrounding family life and especially the rearing of the young" (Laosa, 1983, p. 337). Yet program sponsors and professionals planned, initiated, administered, and evaluated parent training programs based on *their* assessment of need, usually without regard for the ethnic or cultural traditions of the parents involved. Content was modeled largely on an ideal image of the middle-income family in the dominant culture. Valentine and Stark (1979) maintained that "self-determination is not only an important component of quality education but the link between education and the material and social progress of the poor." In practice, however, the parent usually became a passive recipient of professional expertise (p. 311). The only decision available was whether to participate. The consequences of the parent training movement, when directed by the dominant class, represented an attempt to eliminate all other subcultures (Laosa, 1982).

Tulkin (1972) noted two additional ethical issues: the cultural deprivation theory did not advance the knowledge base because it did not "focus attention of how specific experiences affect developmental processes"; and the theory ignored political realities (p. 326).

Though contested by Zigler (1980), Schlossman (1978) also maintained that parent training programs shifted the burden of accountability from professionals, often sponsored by governmental agencies, to parents, usually poor mothers. In Ryan's terms, parent training programs blamed the victim for the original problem and for the fact that the problem was not remedied by brief interventions (1976). Schlossman concluded, "But to the extent that such programs hold poverty mothers mainly responsible for the children's later failures, I believe they do a grievous disservice. It is no sport at all to increase the burdens of the poor" (p. 808).

These ethical concerns were addressed by the next generation of programs which arose across the nation: the family support movement. This movement is described in the next chapter.

CHAPTER 3

Family Support

Research findings impelled the transformation of parent training into a family support movement. The new approach was undergirded by ecological theory, a renewed awareness of the role of community, and an emerging understanding of the process of empowerment. This chapter discusses these influences and evaluates the effectiveness of family support programs.

THE RE-EXAMINATION OF PARENT TRAINING

The overarching goal of compensatory education was to "fix" children so that they could escape the cycle of poverty enslaving their parents. This strategy proved too simplistic and idealistic, and it ignored those remaining in poverty—parents, aunts, uncles, grandparents, and even children of the children.

Urie Bronfenbrenner spurred both a re-examination of the role of family in education and a rededication to family issues (1974c). The secondary analyses by Bronfenbrenner (1974a) and Goodson and Hess (1975) tentatively concluded that early intervention programs with parent components produced more successful outcomes. Bronfenbrenner's work, in particular, had a major impact on subsequent programming (Zigler & Weiss, 1985). Consequently, family support gradually replaced parent training in academic preschool education.

FAMILY SUPPORT PROGRAMS

Weiss (1988) succinctly described the underlying premise of family support programs as they emerged in the late 1970s:

> These programs are predicated on the assumption that the
> provision of information, emotional support, and instrumental
> assistance to families will help parents reduce stress and enhance
> their coping and child-rearing capacities, and thereby positively
> affect the child's development. (p. 5)

Family support programs—sometimes called family resource
programs—provide emotional sustenance, information, and
instrumental assistance to families. Although they usually include an
educational component, they maintain an ecological focus wherein the
parent is both a recipient and a provider of resources (Zigler & Weiss,
1985). Further, they build on strengths rather than deficits (Weissbourd
& Kagan, 1989).

Family support programs represent increased understanding of
contextual factors and a commitment to empowerment. In addition, they
reflect concerns about dramatic demographic and political changes in
this country (Weiss, 1989). Working mothers, changing family
structures, increasing mobility of families, growing poverty among
children, and reduced federal intervention conjoined to alter the fabric of
society. Most traditional social institutions were slow to respond to
these changes, creating a climate ripe for an entirely new type of
program. Family support emerged as a "cohesive and unifying
approach" (Weissbourd & Kagan, 1989, p. 27).

Family support is not new. It existed in the colonial communities
described by Cremin (1978) and Getzels (1978). However, as the welfare
state emerged, well-intentioned policies often produced contradictory and
counterproductive results detrimental to families. The current movement
attempts to strengthen families by using the past "in a manner that
respects the autonomy, diversity, and strength of the American family"
(Weissbourd & Kagan, 1989, p. 30). What is new is the acceptance of
diversity within family structure, the need for support, and the
movement away from a focus on social pathology or personal deficit
(Kagan & Shelley, 1987).

Administratively, the evolution from parent training to family
support is characterized by a shift from attempting to install fully
specified program models into communities to a recognition that
detailed programming is inevitably and best shaped at the community
level (Halpern & Larner, 1988). Although the first programs focused
exclusively on adults in their roles as parents, current programs often

span the life cycle. Most programs operate through direct intervention with adults; however, some also offer indirect support such as information and referral.

The scope of family support programs varies. Some are comprehensive, while others offer a single service such as a telephone hotline or parenting classes. The constituency also varies, for some programs serve an age-specific population while others nurture people throughout the life span. Many assist families through particular life events such as pregnancy, divorce, or family relocation (Weissbourd, 1983). Some Head Start programs have evolved into family support programs (Parker, Pietrkowski, & Peay, 1987).

Family support programs may be staffed by professionals, paraprofessionals, volunteers, or a combination of all three. Cooperative groups are organized and led by parents. Auspices may be public or private; and some programs are well funded while others struggle to survive (Weissbourd & Kagan, 1989). In some states, universal programs have been established. While these may reduce the stigma associated with social services, they increase competition for limited resources (Weiss, 1989).

Given this diversity of scope, what are the common elements that define family support programs? Weissbourd and Kagan (1989) list three goals: enhancing parents' child-rearing capacities; empowering parents as advocates for change; and providing a community resource for parents.

Rooted in the ecological approach, these programs evince the tenets of empowerment: the focus is on strengths rather than pathology; structure and content are flexible; participants generally determine activities; the role of staff and volunteers is collaborative; and activities reflect the communities in which family support programs exist (Weissbourd & Kagan, 1989).

The relationship between the family support movement and its theoretical foundations has not been linear. Emerging programs were informed by research hypotheses, which in turn shaped and revised theory. Evaluators focused on the ecological approach, the role of community, and the process of empowerment, described in the next sections.

THE ECOLOGICAL APPROACH

Renowned Cornell University professor Urie Bronfenbrenner first articulated the ecological approach, which builds on the field theory of Kurt Lewin (1951). The basic premise is straightforward: behavior evolves as a function of the interplay between person and environment, expressed symbolically by Lewin's classic equation, $B = f(PE)$. Bronfenbrenner stressed the dynamic qualities of the individual; the reciprocity, or two-directional interaction, between person and environment; and the multiplicity of settings (1986). Using Lewin's terms, he described the ecological environment "topologically as a nested arrangement of concentric structures, each contained within the next" (Bronfenbrenner, 1979, p. 22). Like Lewin (1949, 1951), Bronfenbrenner considered not only objective qualities of the environment but also the ways in which the environment is perceived by those who interact "within and with it" (p. 23).

Bronfenbrenner (1979) identified four levels or structures within the environment. The smallest, the microsystem, is the immediate setting or place where people readily engage in personal interaction. Homes, schools, and churches are all microsystems. The second level, the mesosystem, is a system of contiguous microsystems. It includes two or more settings in which a person participates. For a child, the mesosystem may be home and school. The third level, the exosystem, affects a person but does not include the person as an active participant. For example, a child's exosystem might include parental employers, activities of the local school board, and a sibling's network of friends.

The fourth and largest system, the macrosystem, refers to consistencies among the first three systems that exist—or could exist— at the level of culture or subculture. This definition includes belief systems and ideologies. To explain, Bronfenbrenner noted that preschool programs in France resemble each other, though they differ from their counterparts in the United States. Further, relationships between school and home in France differ from relationships between school and home in this country. Bronfenbrenner emphasized the connections among these systems, noting that each shapes human development in a particular context.

For Bronfenbrenner, the primary function of the family is to nurture future generations; and he stressed that parents—not professionals—are best able to rear their children. Bronfenbrenner

(1978) decried public policies that neglect or undermine parents and families. After careful analysis of the disintegration of the American family, he asserted, "The issue is not who cares for the children but *who cares for those who care*" (p. 777). Summarizing findings from an evaluation of multiple academic preschool programs, Bronfenbrenner explained:

> When the breadwinner was unemployed, the family income below the poverty line, many children crowded into a small space, and only one parent present—he or she without much schooling—all, or even just two or three, of these conditions occurred together, no intervention program, whatever the strategy employed, was able to be very effective. (p. 779)

Bronfenbrenner (1978) continued, "The critical factor is the conditions under which the family lives" (p. 779); and he chastised a society "in which it is more difficult to sustain a family than to dissolve it" (p. 782). Bronfenbrenner linked individual responsibility and work (1974, 1986); and he strongly advocated national adoption of a Curriculum for Caring in which children, under careful supervision, learn to care by ministering to older adults, the sick, younger children, and the lonely in schools, neighborhoods, and the community at large. Bronfenbrenner maintained that caring activities teach future generations to make human beings human.

Bronfenbrenner was a forceful advocate for children and families. His theories prompted researchers to examine more closely the reciprocal relationship between children and adults (Anglin, 1988; Houts, Shutty, & Emery, 1985). One of the most important consequences of his work has been a refocusing on the role of community in human development (Hobbs, 1978). Another significant contribution has been the refocus on process (Cochran, 1988). The next sections examine the role of community and the process of empowerment in family support.

The Role of Community

Getzels (1978) suggests that the term "community" is so familiar that its meaning is often taken for granted. In fact, the term is used in multifarious ways. In 1955, Hillary found no fewer than ninety-four definitions of community in the sociological literature alone. At an abstract level, Getzels defined community as a group of people conscious of a collective identity characterized by common norms and values (p. 681).

The linkages among community, school, and family have changed since the founding of the United States (Comer, 1984, 1986). According to Lawrence Cremin, a noted educational historian, in colonial times the community was essentially a group of families, with the church and school serving as institutions for articulating and implementing extrafamilial policies. The family was central to every aspect of life. The church, a powerful force of consensual regulation and instruction, consisted of a cluster of families voluntarily joined for mutual purposes, including mediation of knowledge, values, attitudes, skills, and sanctions (Cremin, 1978).

Schools during the colonial period were an extension of the family, rather than a surrogate for it. Where schools were established, there were generally strong, abiding family linkages derived from overlapping sponsorship, support, control, and management—other words, from shared purposes. Schools reflected the values of the families that supported them; therefore, blacks, the working poor, and other alienated groups received no formal schooling. Nevertheless, blacks in the antebellum south received informal instruction from the church and from black peer groups. In other sections of the country, immigrants established mutual benefit societies to sustain their ethnic subcultures and to strengthen their ties with the dominant culture (Cremin, 1978).

Getzels (1978) noted that these early, geographically-localized, self-contained, autonomous communities have been replaced by geographically-extended, loosely knit, overlapping communities. Children, families, and schools are embedded in a variety of communities—"communities within communities"—whose impact fluctuates throughout the lifespan (p. 672). At one point, the greatest impact on the child may come from the family, while at another point the greatest influence may be wielded by the school or church. Schools are no longer an extension of the family. Today, the character of education offered by the school and the education acquired by the child are a function of multiple communities.

Getzels developed six categories that define community in relation to education. The categories include local community (based on geography); administrative community (derived from political systems);

social community (established through interpersonal relationships); instrumental community (based on mutual concern); ethnic, caste, or class community (founded in nationality, race, or culture); and ideological community (subsumed from historic, conceptual, or sociopolitical consciousness).

This concept of community stresses the interdependence of systems and multiplicity of interactions among them (Leichter, 1978). For example, the school derives its cognitive and affective expectations from the communities that support it, while children derive their cognitive and affective expectations from the communities that rear them. When expectations of these communities do not coincide, conflict erupts (Getzels, 1978; Kagan, 1987).

Conflict also arises when communities lack tangible or intangible resources. In their pioneer work on child abuse and neglect, Gabarino and Sherman (1980) explored the relationship among families and community by studying the "neighborhood effect." They concluded that socially impoverished neighborhoods rob families of enduring supportive relationships and place high- risk families at even greater risk for abuse and neglect of children.

Conflict also emerges when two communities espouse different norms, values, or expectations (Kagan, 1987). For example, conflict may arise when teachers expect parents to supply additional resources while parents expect schools to provide all materials. Conflict can occur when teachers and parents differ in their expectations regarding appropriate behaviors for students. Entry into school represents a time of social discontinuity when the potential for conflict is especially high (Leichter, 1975). Parent programs can serve as a bridge between communities during such transition periods.

Using the traditional epidemiological paradigm, Cassels (1976) stressed the need to strengthen communities. He observed, "throughout all history, disease, with rare exceptions, has not been prevented by finding and treating sick individuals, but by modifying those environmental factors facilitating its occurrence. . ." (p. 121). Cassels urged policymakers to prevent the development of social problems by identifying and modifying sources of extra-personal stress; and he exhorted community mental health professionals to strengthen the social milieu.

Services Integration was the response of the federal government. In 1971, Elliot Richardson, then secretary of Health, Education, and

Welfare, defined Services Integration as "a process aimed at developing an integrated framework within which ongoing programs can be rationalized and enriched to do a better job of making services available within existing commitments and resources" (Kusserow, 1991a, p. 1). As with parent training programs that attempted to impose middle-class values on poverty-level parents, Services Integration attempted to impose external regulations on community social services. The goal of Services Integration was to ensure that benefits reached those for whom they were intended by reducing interagency barriers, inefficiency, and duplication of efforts. Although Services Integration made programs more accessible to individual clients, it had little institutional impact. Despite twenty years of well-funded, comprehensive initiatives, Services Integration failed to change the fabric of society (Kusserow, 1991b).

Crane (1991) offered a theory of community that helps explain the lack of success of Services Integration. He expanded the epidemiological approach with his premise that social problems are contagious, suggesting that "ghettos are communities that have experienced epidemics of social problems" (p. 1226). The epidemic theory was predicated on the assumption that social problems are spread through peer influence; and Crane maintained that behaviors leading to substance abuse and teen pregnancy are likely to increase sharply as neighborhood quality decreases. Neighborhood quality cannot be improved by mandating mental health. Wholeness is restored by decreasing individual susceptibility to peer pressure and by reducing negative peer pressure. Theories of empowerment offer methods of accomplishing these goals and improving the quality of community life.

Empowerment

Rappaport (1987) defined empowerment as "a process, a mechanism by which people, organizations, and communities gain mastery over their affairs" (p. 122). "It expresses itself at the level of feelings, at the level of ideas about self-worth, at the level of being able to make a difference in the world around us, and even at the level of something more akin to the spiritual"(Rappaport, 1985, p. 17). Zimmerman (1986) found a single consistent dimension of empowerment which combined beliefs and actions and which integrated individuals into community. According to Rappaport (1987), "This dimension was described by a sense of civic duty, political efficacy, and perceived personal competence, and was negatively related to alienation and positively related to willingness to be a leader" (p. 136).

The concept of empowerment emerged in the United States during the early 1970s in response to the social and economic struggles of the previous decade (Cochran, 1987). Martin Luther King, Jr. explained in his last address to the Southern Christian Leadership Conference in 1967:

> The problem of transforming the ghetto, therefore, is a problem of power—confrontation of the forces of power demanding change and the forces of power dedicated to preserving the status quo. Now power properly understood is nothing but the ability to achieve purpose. It is the strength required to bring about social, political, and economic change. (Washington, 1986, p. 246)

Empowerment is an ecological theory which considers the person and the environment, including roles, relationships, resources, costs, and benefits (Rappaport, 1987). Although the term has been used differently by different groups, the concept of empowerment is predicated on the acceptance of the cultural differences/strengths model. In social work, empowerment is one element of the strengths perspective (Saleebey, 1992; Weick, Rapp, Sullivan, & Kisthardt, 1989).

Proponents of empowerment maintain that the cycle of poverty can be broken by empowering adults to change their social milieu, thereby creating a matrix in which poverty cannot survive. Empowerment enables people to change the communities in which they reside (Arnstein, 1971). The focus is on individual strengths, not pathology. This is not a top-down, hierarchical decree like Services Integration; it is an effort by individuals to endorse and work for the changes they desire.

The concept of empowerment is not a model or a paradigm. Rather, it is a collation of principles, ideas, and techniques (Saleebey, 1992). Empowerment is rooted in traditional social work principles, including a belief in the dignity and worth of the individual and the right to self-determination. John McKnight, a vocal advocate for empowerment of individuals as a way to change communities, stresses the capabilities available even in the poorest communities (1980, 1987a, 1987b;

McKnight & Kretzmann, 1990). The use of the agency as resource echoes the functional school of social work thought (Saleebey, 1992; Hasenfeld, 1987).

A key element is the tenet that individuals understand their own needs better than others understand them (Cochran & Woolever, 1983; Rappaport, 1981). This tenet is followed by the corollary that people should have the power to act on their understanding (Baker-Miller, 1982; Pinderhughes, 1983). The professional helper serves as facilitator, collaborator, and colleague rather than as expert or advisor (Gutierrez, 1990; Rappaport, 1987).

Rather than viewing help as a scarce and costly resource, the empowerment perspective assumes that help is infinite. Each person who is in need of help can also be a provider of help to others. The need to understand people from *their* frame of reference is a driving force. According to Saleebey (1992), "Work should focus on what the client has done, what resources have been or are currently available to the client, what the client knows, and what aspirations and dreams she may hold" (p. 47). Thus, empowerment of a teen-age parent living below the poverty level may not resemble the empowerment of a middle-aged, blue-collar worker.

Empowerment resembles help, as defined by Keith-Lucas (1972), in that it cannot be given. Those who are empowered can "provide the conditions and the language and beliefs that make it possible to be taken by those who are in need of it" (Rappaport, 1985, p. 18). These conditions emerge through dialogue and collaboration. From his work with oppressed peoples, Paul Freire (1973) is convinced that helpers can overcome barriers of distrust, paternalism, and oppression through humble dialogue and a willingness to accept what others have to offer. Ultimately, however, empowerment is a response that must be chosen by those in need of it.

Membership is important to the process of empowerment, for people who are alienated are extraordinarily vulnerable (Bronfenbrenner, 1974, 1986; Saleebey, 1992). A synergistic perspective assumes, as do Lewin and Bronfenbrenner, that the whole is greater than the sum of its parts. Thus the small group is a powerful tool of empowerment. When people are brought together, they create new and unexpected patterns and resources for solving patterns (Gutierrez, 1992). Dr. King recognized this phenomenon in a posthumously published essay entitled *A Testament of Hope*. He said, "The summer poverty programs, like most other government projects, function well in some places and are totally ineffective in others. The difference, in large measure, is one of citizen participation; that is the key to success or failure" (Washington, 1986, p. 325).

Empowerment is not only an individual construct; it is also an organizational, political, sociological, economic, and spiritual phenomenon (Rappaport, 1987; Gottlieb, 1992). Rappaport explains, "Our interests in racial and economic justice, in legal rights as well as human needs, in health care and educational justice, in competence as well as in a sense of community, are all captured by the idea of empowerment" (p. 130). The extent of need influences the type of empowerment strategy required (Alter, Deutelbaum, Dodd, Else, & Raheim, 1992). Consequently, the manifest content of empowerment differs across peoples, cultures, settings, organizations, and communities.

Rappaport (1987) lists three additional assumptions of empowerment theory relevant to this study. First, historical context is a critical variable in any examination of empowerment. Since operating conditions strongly influence outcomes, accurate description of historical context is essential to understanding and generalization. This includes systematic specification of personal, programmatic, and organizational factors. Cultural context is a second critical variable that must be described fully. Diversity is protected by respecting and revealing the variety found in cultural contexts.

Rappaport's third assumption involves language. Word choice is crucial, for terminology carries connotative and denotative meanings that shape assumptions. Rappaport (1981) explained that it makes a great deal of difference whether an individual is viewed as a parent or a client, for people are likely to conform to assigned roles. Cummings (1986) underscored this assumption through an analysis of the school failure of minority students who spoke English as a second language. He examined three factors—reinforcement of cultural identity, active collaboration with parents, and meaningful use of language in preschool—and concluded that all these are associated with high levels of conceptual and linguistic skills in both the primary and secondary languages.

THE PROCESS OF EMPOWERMENT

Differences in the definition of empowerment involve whether empowerment is a state or a process. Berger and Neuhaus (1977) suggested that empowerment is a state like wealth or anger. This was consistent with the earlier analysis of power developed by French and Raven (1959). However, most authors now consider empowerment as a process (Baker-Miller, 1982; Barr, Cochran, Riley, & Whitham, 1984; Gutierrez, 1990; Vanderslice, 1984).

Perhaps both definitions apply. In a stratified society with an unequal distribution of resources, some people possess power. They may not be aware of this attribute; in fact, they may take it for granted. However, these people do not need to become powerful, for they are already powerful. They possess the means to evoke change in themselves, their families, their neighborhoods, and their communities. For these fortunate people, empowerment is a state. Dr. King stated, "The powerful never lose opportunities—they remain available to them" (Washington, 1986, p. 598).

Others do not possess this faculty. They are barred from normal development by obstacles such as social class structure, structural differences engendered by gender or race, and perhaps the influences of bureaucracies. In King's words, "The powerless, on the other hand, never experience opportunity—it is always arriving at another time" (Washington, 1986, p. 598).

Cochran (1987) suggested that empowerment becomes germane when such barriers are encountered, "the removal of which are beyond the present or future capacity of that person as an individual" (p. 11). Removal of these obstacles is the basic purpose of the empowerment process. In an early study of group empowerment conducted before the term was coined, Zurcher (1969) and colleagues attended 174 meetings of twelve neighborhood action groups over a nineteen-month period. The community groups, established by the Office of Economic Opportunity, were intended to be pivotal components in a local anti-poverty program. Zurcher noted that these task groups represented a radical departure from the therapy, training, and laboratory groups common at the time. He identified seven stages of development within the groups: orientation, catharsis, focus, action, limbo, testing, and purposive. Groups moved through these stages at different rates, but the stages were epigenetic. In analyzing why some groups were more effective than others, Zurcher stressed the importance of trust, collaborative participation, indigenous leadership, and membership. These elements are critical components of empowerment as it is currently being defined.

Women who were adolescents when their first children were born may be especially vulnerable to truncated development (Furstenberg, Brooks-Gunn, & Chase-Lansdale, 1989; Furstenberg, Brooks-Gunn, & Morgan, 1987; Scott- Jones, 1990). Card and Wise (1981) maintained that adolescent child-bearing disrupts the normal route to adult achievement by reducing the number of years the mother would ordinarily spend in school; and Miller reported similar findings (1983).

Family Matters, a family support program begun at Cornell University in 1976 by Bronfenbrenner and Cochran, was one of the first to study the process of individual empowerment. The study involved 160 families with three-year-old children in the city of Syracuse, New York. Families were evenly distributed across neighborhoods, and they represented a broad spectrum of income levels. About one third of the families were African American and one third were single-parent families. The original research design involved two approaches: families either received home visits by paraprofessionals who reinforced family strengths, or they participated in activities with clusters of other families. After nine months, the two programs were merged. Neighborhood workers spent more than two years helping families identify strengths and needs and work toward improvement in their life circumstances (Cochran, 1987, 1988).

Though they did not use the term "empowerment" in early descriptions, researchers with *Family Matters* identified a systematic and invariant series of steps or stages in the process of change (Cochran, 1987, 1988). Since mothers entered the program at different points in their own development, they were affected by the program in different ways; however, all proceeded along the following continuum.

The first stage identified by *Family Matters* involved a change in self-perception. Mothers began to believe in and care for themselves. This provided a framework for the second phase, altered relations with members of the household. Mothers initiated new efforts to reach out to others—children, spouse, relatives, neighbors, and friends. In the third stage, mothers established new relationships with distant relatives and friends. In the fourth stage, mothers gathered information related to broader community action. The fifth and final stage was characterized by change-oriented community action; that is, mothers took some social action on behalf of their children (Cochran, 1987, 1988).

According to Cochran's (1987) definition of empowerment, the capacity to change the balance of power between families and controlling institutions is the goal of empowerment. Although *Family Matters* influenced parental perceptions, it did not stimulate collective organization. Moreover, the assessment of *Family Matters* did not examine whether parents gained the ability to influence key individuals (employers, teachers, or welfare workers) or institutions (schools, local government, or human services agencies). Cochran concluded that the empowerment process promoted and evaluated by *Family Matters* was therefore incomplete.

Since *Family Matters* was a time-limited project, it may be that program design truncated the process. Community and institutional change takes time; and it is possible that parents accomplished the final phase of empowerment after the formal conclusion of the project.

In a review of the empowerment literature, Vanderslice (1984) summarized five actions that contributed to personal empowerment: recognition and valuation of one's skills, knowledge, and resources; development of additional abilities; broadening of networks to obviate isolation; belief in the legitimacy of needs and opinions; and successful interaction with the environment to reinforce self-efficacy and confidence. Unlike Cochran (1987), Vanderslice observed that these actions were not necessarily sequential.

Kieffer (1984) expanded the process view by proposing that empowerment is a long-term process of adult learning and development. In a retrospective, ethnographic study of fifteen grassroots community organizers, he found that each was provoked into action by a "mobilizing episode," an event which was "never of such objective force or magnitude that it would predictably energize others" (p. 19). According to Kieffer, this event was followed by a year or more of reactive engagement and exploration that Kieffer called the "era of entry." During the next phase, the "era of advancement," mentors and peers were critical as subjects began to understand social and political relations. In the third phase, the "era of incorporation," individuals matured in self-concept, strategic ability, and critical comprehension; and they developed leadership skills and survival strategies necessary for enduring community involvement. During this period, the need to resolve multiple role conflicts was especially frustrating for women. In the final stage, the "era of commitment," individuals searched for viable and meaningful ways of applying their newfound abilities.

Kieffer's (1984) four stages were predicated on two elements: constructive conflict and praxis. By constructive conflict, Kieffer meant not only the realization that something was not right but also the willingness to become involved in the solution. By praxis, he meant a circular relationship of experience and reflection through which actions evoke new understandings, which then provoke new and more effective actions" (p. 26). Like Cochran (1987), Kieffer found a consistent progression of development stages as individuals moved from seeing themselves as helpless victims to their personal acceptance of themselves as assertive and efficacious citizens.

In a reassessment of the ecological approach, Bronfenbrenner (1988) described two sources of change:

> The first is intervention from the outside; the second, of equal importance and necessity, is the initiative taken by an active living organism whose basic impulses are directed toward survival, constructive action, and psychological growth. (p. xi)

Under what conditions does empowerment occur? Although there is little concrete information about the sources of change that beget and succor empowerment, this review suggests a number of elements that should be considered. First, individuals must be free from acute environmental or personal stress. As Bronfenbrenner (1978) explained, no intervention is likely to succeed when parents are struggling to provide food, shelter, and clothing. Along the same lines, empowerment is not likely to occur while individuals are actively involved in substance abuse or other destructive behaviors.

Second, a number of personal characteristics seem to be linked to empowerment. Individuals must perceive the need for change; and they must be willing to work toward their goals. This is the constructive conflict described by Kieffer (1984) in which leaders recognized a problem and were willing to become involved with the solution. Additionally, individuals must demonstrate self-awareness and a propensity to engage in personal reflection, or praxis. Individuals also need specific skills and knowledge, often learned as part of the empowerment process.

Opportunity constitutes the third element. Empowerment is unlikely in a school that bars parental participation or in a neighborhood from which transportation to employment is unavailable. Professional helpers and community leaders can support empowerment by creating opportunity.

Empowerment appears to be enhanced by social support that extends beyond the bounds of nuclear family to include friends and relatives. Working together, individuals increase self-esteem, create positive peer pressure, ward off harm, contribute to family wellbeing, and encourage change (Dunst & Trivette, 1988, 1990). Family support programs promote social support by offering opportunities to give as well as to receive (Weiss, 1990).

EVALUATION OF FAMILY SUPPORT PROGRAMS

Because of their diversity and fluidity, family support programs have been difficult to evaluate (Weissbourd & Kagan, 1989; Zigler & Black, 1989). In fact, Seitz (1985) suggests that the most successful programs may not be evaluated due to the ethical implications of assigning families to a no-treatment control group.

Zigler and Black (1989) have documented two primary reasons that evaluations of the family support movement have been sparse. First, adequate evaluations are costly and funding has been scarce. Secondly, there are many difficulties related to design. Weiss (1988), in an excellent discussion of design problems, asserts that measures relating to parents, child-parent interactions, family functioning, community change, and social competence have not been developed. The only well-established outcome measure available is an assessment of children's cognitive abilities, notably IQ. Researchers are reluctant to conduct evaluations based on such a narrow measure which may be unfair and which could jeopardize credibility. Halpern (1990) adds that flexibility, a program strength, is an evaluation weakness.

Self-selection and high attrition rates also present problems for evaluators (Cochran, 1988; Powell, 1988). For example, Powell reported that almost one-half of the eligible families chose not to participate in a community-based, peer-oriented intervention program. Although the neighborhood appeared homogeneous according to demographic descriptions, ethnographers found three distinct groups of potential participants. Powell concluded that an evaluation of recruitment issues may be as important as the investigation into program effects.

Extant research has not yet addressed the "black box of treatment" (Weiss, 1988). In particular, evaluators need to examine program participation data, for there are few indicators regarding recruitment and retention to particular programs. According to Weiss, this information is needed to inform policy debates about such issues as whether parent support is effective with low-income families. In addition, program planners need information about social networks, personal and environmental factors which condition program participation, and personal characteristics that affect participation. Both program planners and managers need pragmatic information about staff recruitment, training and supervision, outreach, staff burnout, and use of volunteers.

Despite these wide gaps in knowledge, evidence is mounting that family support can positively affect the development of economically disadvantaged children (Weiss, 1988, Weissbourd & Kagan, 1989). For example, documented benefits of the Child and Family Resource Program, a family support program implemented in eleven locales in the United States, include better preventive health care and nutrition for young children; rapid assistance to families during crisis; correction of problems through referral; and a general improvement in the overall quality of life (Zigler & Seitz, 1980, p. 365).

Equally important, family support programs are forcing conventional service delivery systems to re-examine their programs and make them more efficient and more responsive to the needs of consumers. According to Weissbourd and Kagan (1989), the educational system offers an example of such changes as many states incorporate services for children from birth through age five. The state programs acknowledge the importance of the early years of development as well as the primary role of parents.

Some researchers have argued that family support programs produce positive outcomes for adults as well as children. The Yale Child Welfare Research Project suggested that the major contribution of the program was its long-term impact on family patterns, including limitations on family size, educational attainment, economic self-sufficiency, and quality of life (Seitz, 1987; Zigler & Weiss, 1985). Parker, Piotrkowski, and Peay (1987) found modest gains in the psychological wellbeing of mothers who participated in supportive activities of a Head Start program. More evidence is necessary to support this hypothesis; however, if confirmed, it could have far-reaching policy implications (Weissbourd & Kagan, 1989; Weiss, 1987; Seitz, Rosenbaum, & Apfel, 1985; Zigler & Weiss, 1985).

There is widespread agreement that families play a pivotal role in child development. There is also consensus regarding the importance of community in supporting families. The unanswered questions are which family support programs work; and how, when, where, why, and for whom (Weiss, 1988). A review of economic theory in the next chapter suggests some answers to these questions.

CHAPTER 4

Family Empowerment

After the Moynihan Report (1965) was published, analysts avoided an examination of urban social problems, partly to avoid stigmatizing ghetto residents and partly from fear of providing fuel to racist arguments. Although family support programs proliferated, there was little systematic research into the problem of poverty for more than a decade, until Wilson (1987) tackled the issue. This chapter discusses Wilson's premise and describes the function of education using theories proposed by Pierre Bourdieu. Applications delineate family empowerment; and the section concludes with a review of implications.

THE CURRENT CONDITION

When research into the causes of poverty resumed, a number of authors extolled the strengths and virtues of black families (Baumrind, 1972; Hale-Benson, 1986; Logan, Freemen, & McRoy, 1990; McAdoo & McAdoo, 1985). Ghetto families were represented as resilient networks able to adapt to a hostile society. According to Wilson (1987), these researchers shifted the focus from "discussions of the consequences of racial isolation and economic class subordination to discussions of black achievement" (p. 9). Little attention was paid to internal differences within the black community or to the fact that theories of cultural strength actually encouraged stereotypical thinking (Frisby, 1992). Consequently, energy was diverted away from appropriate amelioration of the "dreadful economic condition of poor blacks" (Wilson, 1987, p. 9). There was little public recognition that the success of both black and white citizens is inextricably bound.

William Julius Wilson (1987) broke the silence by refuting the notion of a culture of poverty and the impact of race (and thus by association, IQ) in an analysis of the poorest groups in the United States. Wilson maintained that all African American families—irrespective of class—lived together in one community before the civil rights movement commenced. All African Americans sent their children to the same schools, shopped at the same stores, and attended the same churches.

After the Civil Rights Act of 1964 opened housing, vertical integration prompted a mass exit from traditionally black neighborhoods. This exodus dissolved the monolithic black community, for only those who could not move were left behind. Wilson (1987) explained, "Today's ghetto neighborhoods are populated almost exclusively by the most disadvantaged segments of the black urban community, that heterogeneous grouping of families and individuals who are outside the mainstream of the American occupational system" (p. 8). He referred to the remnant as the underclass.

According to Wilson (1987), poor, urban neighborhoods lost the social buffer provided by working and middle class families; and the results were overwhelmingly negative. Ghetto youth rarely encounter stable marriages; and they almost never see men and women engaged in steady employment. The relationship between education and employment takes on new meaning; for youth who see no connection between the two make little effort to acquire the knowledge and skills required by a mainstream economy. With few individuals working outside the neighborhood, crime and teen-age pregnancy increase, social isolation ensues, and segregation based on economic class emerges.

These are the conditions found in the neighborhood under consideration. The following sections discuss the role of individuals within a market economy, the function of education, and the significance of social segregation.

HUMAN CAPITAL AND THE MARKET ECONOMY

Concurrent with the Civil Rights Movement, economists and educators, guided by Nobel Laureate Theodore W. Schultz, began to recognize the economic importance of human beings in the manufacturing and production processes of a market economy (Johns,

Morphet, & Alexander, 1990). Schultz (1961) called this personal factor "human capital." Today, the idea seems obvious; however, when first proposed, it was considered revolutionary.

> The mere thought of investment in human beings is offensive to some among us. Our values and beliefs inhibit us from looking upon human beings as capital goods, except in slavery, and this we abhor. . . . Hence, to treat human beings as wealth that can be augmented by investment runs counter to deeply held values. . . . By investing in themselves, people can enlarge the range of choice available to them. It is one way free men (sic) can enhance their welfare." (1961, p. 2)

Gary S. Becker (1962, 1975), a student of Schultz and the 1992 winner of the Nobel Prize in Economic Science, explained that growth of physical capital accounts for a relatively small part of the growth of income in most countries. "The search for better explanations has led to improved measures of physical capital and to an interest in less tangible entities, such as technological change and human capital" (1962, pp. 9–10).

Webster's Electronic Thesaurus defines *capital* as one's total property, including real property and intangibles. Synonyms include means, assets, resources, and wealth. Although human capital is frequently associated with earnings and wages, Schultz (1961) contends that the general theory includes both qualitative and quantitative dimensions.

According to Schultz (1961), much consumption constitutes investment in human capital. Schultz elaborated by identifying five categories of activities which improve or increase human capital: health services; on-the-job training; formal education; adult education; and migration of individuals and families to adjust to changing employment opportunities. Ben-Porath expanded the discussion to include family influences (1980). Essentially, there are many ways to expand human capital, including those listed by Schultz, "But all improve the physical and mental abilities of people and thereby raise real income prospects" (Becker, 1962, p. 9).

An investment in human capital can be measured not only by the cost of production but also by the yield, or benefit. After an extensive, albeit preliminary, analysis of the economic effects of education and other investments in human capital, Becker (1975) concluded that profits from educational investments outweigh costs. Further, he found that education benefits not only the individual but also society. The concept of human capital helped "sell" social programs for families and children to policy makers, business executives, and community leaders (Weiss, 1990). Pacesetters understood that, in order to succeed in the economic sphere, people must possess and demonstrate a particular type of personality, persistence, and intelligence, as well as knowledge and skills. Although these attributes may not be measured by conventional tests, they can be inculcated through education and training (Becker, 1962, p. 45).

Tutelage of the underclass is a primary goal and function of the family support movement. As Moock (1974) explained, "Parents who have been deprived of adequate human capital investment themselves from birth cannot impart the cognitive skills necessary for the scholastic and economic success of their children" (p. 104).

The concept of human capital clarified the relationship between economics and education; and it expanded the rationale for investing in people, particularly those from the underclass (Moock, 1978). As Becker (1962) noted, "An emphasis on human capital not only helps explain differences in earnings over time and among areas but also among persons or families within an area" (p. 45). Nevertheless, the general theory does not explain the differential rates of return on investments in education. This is the province of the theories of Pierre Bourdieu.

EDUCATION AND CLASS STRUCTURE

Social class is a useful concept because it captures the complex interplay of a number of variables such as educational level, occupation, and family connections (Kohn, 1963). Pierre Bourdieu, a French philosopher and critic of higher education, maintained that educational systems maintain social class structures.

Bourdieu (1971, 1977) studied the French policy of expanding educational opportunity in order to reduce social inequality. He concluded that educational expansion actually creates new forms of social stratification which perpetuates poverty and impedes progress toward equality (Swartz, 1990).

Bourdieu began his research on education in France during the 1950s, when General Charles de Gaulle was consolidating his political power, absorbing the lessons of Algiers, and reconstructing or modernizing French society (Robbins, 1991). Although his work is just beginning to filter into the English-speaking realm, Bourdieu's educational theory is similar to that of Bowles and Gintis (1976), which explains social inequality in economic terms. Concerned with class structures, Bourdieu drew from the work of Durkheim, Marx, Bernstein, and others. He has been criticized for his difficult expository style, his circular approach to explanation, and his conceptual ambiguity; however, Bourdieu has built a "theoretical system that may be the most comprehensive and elegant since Talcott Parsons" (DiMaggio, 1979, p. 1462).

Theoretical Constructs

A number of concepts generated by Bourdieu's analysis of scholastic institutions are germane to educational research. These include field, cultural capital, habitus, and symbolic violence.

Field

Like Bronfenbrenner, Bourdieu was inspired by the vector psychology of Kurt Lewin (Bourdieu, 1971a). According to Bourdieu, the concept of field refers to the totality of actors and organizations involved in an arena and the dynamic relationships among them. This is similar to Bronfenbrenner's nesting of systems; however, Bronfenbrenner concentrates on levels of systems, while Bourdieu focuses on activities between fields. Like Lewin, both stress the importance of individual perception in the determination of reality.

The concept of field is useful, for "it suggests that hierarchy and conflict are at the base of even ostensibly neutral cultural enterprises and permits provocative comparisons among such fields as art, science, and religion" (DiMaggio, 1979, p. 1463). For Bourdieu, every field is an arena of conflict. The goal is to obtain capital; and the educational system is the primary locus of this activity in contemporary societies. Schools do not facilitate upward mobility; they multiply initial inequalities among classes, consigning the poor to failure and ensuring the success of the middle class. The concept of "habitus" undergirds this process.

Habitus

Bourdieu coined this term to references ideas rather than place. "Habitus" refers to "a set of relatively permanent and largely unconscious ideas about one's chances of success and how society works that are common to members of a social class or status group" (Swartz, 1990, p. 72). Family is the privileged site for the most profound inculcation of the habitus, as it provides the child's first definitive framework for the systematic imposition of the group's values and ideologies. When the child reaches school age, the educational system takes over, both sharing and contending with the family in the refining and entrenchment of the habitus (Shirley, 1986, p. 98).

Bourdieu (1971a) explained the role of educational institutions in creating habitus: "What individuals owe to the school is above all a fund of commonplaces, not only a common language and style but also common meeting grounds and grounds for agreement, common problems and common methods of tackling them" (p. 182). People may hold differing opinions on a topic, but they agree to quarrel about particular subjects. "What attaches a thinker to his (sic) age, what situates and dates him (sic), is above all the kind of problems and themes in terms of which he (sic) is obliged to think" (p. 183).

Habitus leads to self-fulfilling prophecies. Thus, whether a student remains in school depends on his or her perception of the opportunity for success. School work becomes meaningless to students who do not believe that individual effort can break the cycle of economic and political disenfranchisement. Further, students with limited aspirations are unlikely to pursue academic excellence. Consequently, many minority youth and members of the underclass drop out of school. Calabrese (1988) claims that the social response blames the victim, for it is not the school but the student who is renounced for failure.

Cultural Capital

Educational attainment is also affected by differences in "cultural capital." Culture is more than accumulated knowledge. Generally the term refers to "the values, beliefs, and norms which have been passed down from generation to generation, albeit with frequent modifications, throughout the history of society" (Goslin, 1990, p. 30).

By "cultural capital" Bourdieu meant linguistic style, manners, patterns of behavior, modes of leisure and arts consumption, knowledge, and titles such as degrees (Shirley, 1986). The term also includes verbal facility, general cultural awareness, information about the school system, and general knowledge about the world (Swartz, 1990).

Cultural capital is derived from participation in a class, a society, and an age. "Examples are ways of thought, forms of logic, stylistic expressions and catchwords (yesterday's existence, situation, authenticity; today's structure, unconscious and praxis) which seem so natural and inevitable that they are not properly speaking the object of a conscious choice" (Bourdieu, 1971a, p. 180). Thus cultural capital is more than the instrumental skills required for social competence. It is intrinsic and elemental. Individuals do not possess cultural capital; rather, they are possessed by it.

As an asset, cultural capital can be inherited. It can also be purchased with time, energy, and money. Cultural capital can be exchanged for occupations with higher status and income, for members of one class move into another by "translating" cultural aptitudes into economically remunerative pursuits. This has been a particularly effective strategy through which dominated groups have gained access to the middle class.

Social Class

Bourdieu viewed social class as a composite of capitals: cultural capital; economic or human capital; and social capital, which he describes as family prestige and connections. Classes are distinguished from each other by differences in the volume of total capital, with the upper classes possessing greater resources than the lower classes. Differences in types of capital delineate groups within the same class. As Swartz (1990) explained, professors and industrialists are both members of the dominant class, although one trades in cultural capital while the other wields human capital.

Language and symbolic power

Symbolic power is the ability of the dominant class to establish legitimacy "both as a political power bloc and as institutional loci for the definition and monopolization of culture" (Shirley, 1986, p. 100).

Groups and classes act *as if* the dominant culture is universal and legitimate, "forgetting" that it is arbitrary and often concealed. Thus "the dominant culture is identified with culture as such (that is to say, as excellence)" (Bourdieu, 1977b, p. 115). Subcultures are defined in terms of their distance from the dominant culture, a condition Bourdieu labels "cultural deprivation" (1977b, p. 115).

Language plays a critical role in the creation and maintenance of symbolic power (Bourdieu, 1977b). Bourdieu elaborated, "What makes the power of words, the power of words to command and to order the world, is belief in the ligitimacy (sic) of the words and of him (sic) who utters them, a belief which words themselves cannot produce" (p. 117). Through control of language, the dominant group enforces its own specific dialect and its own ways of communicating (Willis, 1990).

Cole and Bruner (1971) discuss the role of language in the process of symbolic violence. "The ghetto child, who by training is likely to use an idiosyncratic mode of communication, may become locked into the life of his (sic) own cultural group, and his (sic) migration into other groups consequently becomes the more difficult" (p. 871).

Through symbolic violence, the hierarchical domination of the prevailing class is maintained. Language and communication are elements in the process of symbolic violence. Symbolic violence is fostered by educational systems that reproduce the social order. It is bolstered by the self-fulfilling prophecies of habitus, the struggle of the middle class to maintain the dominant culture, and the limited capital of the underclass.

The concepts of field, habitus, cultural capital, and symbolic power form the basis for Bourdieu's analysis of the educational systems in France. Bourdieu primarily looks at relationships between class factions rich in cultural capital and those rich in economic capital; and he highlights the connections between those richest in cultural, symbolic, and economic capital (Shirley, 1986). However, Bourdieu's theories can also be applied to differences between the dominant group and the underclass (Collins, 1990). The next section begins this application through an analysis of the sociology of education.

THE SOCIOLOGY OF EDUCATION

Cremin defined education as "the deliberate, systematic, and sustained effort to transmit, evoke, or acquire knowledge, attitudes, values, skills, or sensibilities, and any learning that results from the effort, direct or indirect, intended or unintended" (1978, p. 701). Bourdieu was less interested in education as an instrument of cultural adjustment than as a tool for equalizing economic opportunity.

Four themes emerged from Bourdieu's studies of education. First, students' academic performance is strongly related to their parents' cultural backgrounds. Second, scholastic accomplishment is related to, but not determined by, social class. Third, higher educational institutions in France are *socially* as well as academically segmented into inter-institutional tracks. Thus, the degree of success in the labor market depends not only on the *amount* of education received, but also on the *type*. Fourth, these educational institutions develop their own organizational and professional interests, which may deviate significantly from the interests of the dominant class (Swartz, 1990, p. 71).

Bourdieu initially assumed that "Working class people were the same as peasants and that the function of an educational strategy was to give these students an opportunity simultaneously to insert themselves within a modernizing society and to participate in constituting the nature of that society" (Robbins, 1991, p. 52). After a meticulous analysis, Bourdieu (1977a) supported his first assumption: working class students are disadvantaged within higher education because they have not been initiated into the culture upheld by higher education.

Bourdieu could not support his second hypothesis. Rather than finding in education an opportunity for students to acquire knowledge and skills necessary for occupational choice, he found that academic performance of individual students was strongly related to their parents' cultural background. Thus, the educational system of France reinforced a pre-existing social hierarchy. In essence, education was not a vehicle for social mobility—either upward or downward.

Bourdieu (1971a) concluded that the function of education is the conservation of the dominant culture that establishes and maintains schools. Therefore, "It follows that the educational system as an institution specially contrived to conserve, transmit and inculcate the cultural canons of a society derives a number of its structural and functional characteristics from the fact that it had to fulfill these particular functions" (p. 178).

The educational system also reproduces, rather than redistributes, cultural capital. In economic terms, this truism is captured by a transformation of the adage "It takes money to make money." Bourdieu might maintain that "It takes culture to make culture." According to Giroux, one of the flaws in Bourdieu's analysis is that culture represents "a one-way process of domination" (1983, p. 271). Further, Bourdieu minimizes the power of reflexive thought and historical agency. Paul Willis added a critical dimension to this discussion by focusing on the process of resistance, which tempers cultural reproduction (1977, 1983, 1990). In a major ethnographic study, Willis examined the ways working-class youth obtained working-class jobs. He concluded that people assume an "active and creative response, never specifiable in advance . . . to what formed and forms them!" (1983, p. 113). According to Willis, human beings are not helpless victims at the mercy of a steamroller called cultural production; rather, through the struggle of everyday life, they exercise choice and find meaning to inform their existence.

Corroborating Theories

These theories regarding education are consistent with those of other educational researchers, including anthropologist George Spindler (1974) and sociologist James Coleman (1988, 1990). Spindler suggests that educational systems transmit culture through two functions: recruitment and maintenance. Recruitment refers to the process of getting people into a cultural system and into specific roles. Maintenance is the process of keeping roles and the system functioning. People must have requisite skills—both social and vocational—for goods and services to be exchanged and for community life to endure. Like Bourdieu, Spindler stresses the role of perception. "People must believe in their system. If there is a caste or class structure they must believe that such a structure is good, or if not good, at least inevitable" (1974, p. 303).

Spindler (1974) described the transmission process. "Children seem to acquire the culture of their community best when there is consistent reinforcement of the same norms of action and thinking through many different channels of activity and interaction" (p. 300). According to this model, children from the dominant culture are likely to do best in schools created by the dominant culture to preserve the dominant culture. Where there is discontinuity among cultures and classes, children suffer.

Discontinuity in the form of conflict or stress can arise among any number of systems or fields. Occasionally, educational systems are charged with changing a culture (Goslin, 1990). Schools become intentional agents of discontinuity, usually in an effort to modernize a society (Spindler, 1974).

Discontinuity may also erupt when the school is unrelated to the community in terms of instructional methods or content. Like Bourdieu, Spindler (1974) maintained that the resulting aspirations of students become quite unrealistic. To be effective, the school must transmit the cultural capital needed by the particular society in which the individual hopes to function. For example, it is not helpful to train people to use scythes when the lawn is mowed with gasoline engine-powered machinery. It is redundant to teach shorthand in an age of computers.

According to Cremin (1978) and Hansen (1988), discontinuity often occurs when children from subordinate cultures encounter schools representing the dominant culture. Although some minority groups have welcomed the opportunity to participate in the dominant culture, conflict is inevitable when a minority group rejects the cultural capital transmitted by the educational system (Willis, 1977). A number of factors may contribute to this rejection. For example, the minority group may resent the negation of its own culture. Or, it may succumb to the apathy of learned helplessness.

The phenomenon of cultural rejection may be especially relevant for the African American community in the United States. The dynamics of education within the black subculture are similar to the dynamics of other immigrant minorities (Ogbu, 1978; Gibson & Ogbu, 1991). However, the stubborn realities of color and slavery have made it difficult—if not impossible—for African Americans to be subsumed into the dominant culture. The survival of the group has depended on the establishment of a distinct racial and cultural identity. With the current reexamination of black history, this cultural identity has become even more valued by members of the African American community (Cremin, 1978).

Coleman carefully examined minority opportunity in education (Coleman et al., 1966, 1990; Nichols, 1975) and the differences between public and private schools (Coleman & Hoffer, 1987). His current work builds on this foundation to analyze the relationships between families and schools (1987, 1988, 1990).

Coleman and Hoffer (1987) concluded, "Schools, of whatever quality, are more effective for children from strong family backgrounds than for children from weak ones" (p. 35). He explained this phenomenon using the term "social capital," by which he meant "the norms, the social networks, the relationships between adults and children that are of value for the child's growing up" (p. 36). This formulation, which included community influence, appears to be a limited application of the concept of cultural capital, although the authors did not reference Bourdieu.

Coleman and Hoffer (1987) link social capital and human capital, noting that those families that lack both have been traditionally labeled "disadvantaged." The authors suggested that creating social capital by strengthening families increases high school graduation rates and improves the human capital of the next generation.

Coleman and Hoffer (1987) also maintained that communities in which churches constitute an important domain possess social capital that aids both the family and the school in the educational process. They elaborate, "Religious organizations are among the few remaining organizations in society, beyond the family, that cross generations. Thus, they are among the few in which the social capital of an adult community is available to children and youth" (p. 37). Religious institutions may provide functional communities that nurture and sustain social capital of a neighborhood struggling to survive.

Significance

These educational theories are important for a number of reasons. First, they illuminate the dynamic interplay between scholastic institutions and class structures in society. Second, they call attention to the importance of the non-cognitive or cultural aspects of academic instruction. Third, they provide an "empowering conception of the role of cultural forces for unraveling the reproduction of class and social structures" (Shirley, 1986, p. 106).

To this end, these theories suggest a means by which individuals in the underclass can acquire human and cultural capital and move into the dominant class without sacrificing cultural identity. As Cole and Bruner (1971) reported, "The task is to analyze the source of cultural differences so that the minority, or less powerful group, can acquire the intellectual instruments necessary for success in the dominant culture, should they so desire " (p. 875). Desire is the key, for the process of empowerment precludes arbitrary domination by an arbitrary power (Bourdieu & Passeron, 1977).

Applications

Bourdieu's work is primarily conceptual in nature. A number of authors have begun to generate and test hypotheses based on his tenets. In education, researchers have used an ethnographic approach to test theories involving social class structure and the acquisition of cultural capital. This material is relatively new and spans the traditional boundaries of several disciplines, including education, sociology, social work, anthropology, and psychology. Since the theories are not widely known or understood, the following applications will be analyzed in some detail. The resulting understanding of pattern maintenance can suggest techniques for modification of those patterns.

Anthropologist John Ogbu was the first and probably the most well known investigator to acclaim the hypotheses of Bourdieu. A Nigerian, Ogbu studied education in the United States from the perspective of an outsider. In his first book, *The Next Generation* (1974), he used an ethnographic approach to examine school failure in a working-class community in California. The majority of his subjects were Hispanic or African American. After spending almost two years talking with students, teachers, community leaders, taxpayers, parents, and members of the folk system, Ogbu concluded that school failure is often an adaptation to the expectations of the dominant culture.

In subsequent ethnographic studies, Ogbu examined racial and class stratification (1990) and the role of educational systems in reproducing the social order (1978; 1991). Ogbu divided minorities into three groups: autonomous (Jews and Mormons); caste (blacks, scheduled castes of India, Burakumin of Japan); and immigrant minorities (Chinese and Japanese in the U.S.). Refuting theories of inherited differences (IQ), cultural deprivation, and unequal academic resources, Ogbu concluded that neither home nor school adequately prepared children of caste minorities to function in the dominant society.

Fordham examined the self-fulfilling prophecies of habitus through a series of ethnographic interviews with high- and low-achieving black high school students in a poor black city (Fordham, 1988; Fordham & Ogbu, 1986). Like most adolescents, the students Fordham interviewed were concerned with peer pressure. Many believed they would have to minimize their ethnic group identity to achieve vertical mobility into the dominant (white) group. For some of these adolescents this option was unacceptable; and they preferred failure to "acting white" (Fordham, 1988, p. 82).

Two authors have examined the role of teachers in reproducing the social order. Lubeck (1985) examined differences in the ways adults taught preschool students to adapt to their environments. She compared an upper-middle-class white preschool classroom and a Head Start program for low-income black children. The former was staffed by white, upper-middle-class women, while the latter was staffed by black women from working-class backgrounds. Lubeck found significant cultural differences in the learning environments created by these teachers. She concluded that the white staff encouraged values of individualism and self-expression, while the black staff reinforced collective values. In both cases, "teachers live in families very like those of the children they teach, and, in both cases they structure an environment that is consonant with their experiences outside of school" (p. 135).

Anyon (1980) examined education as an instrument of class reproduction by studying fifth grade activities in four types of schools: working-class, middle-class, affluent professional, and executive elite. The majority of students were white. All the teachers used the same math book and series; all had a particular reading program available in the classroom; and all used language arts curricula which emphasized grammar and punctuation. Despite these similarities, Anyon found distinct differences in the factors influencing non-academic learning. The author concluded that working-class children were being prepared for mechanical and routine jobs, while middle-class children were being channeled into bureaucratic occupations. Students in the affluent, professional school were gaining skills necessary to produce culture and capital. Students in the executive elite schools gave its children something that none of the other schools provided—"knowledge of and practice in manipulating the socially legitimated tools of analysis of systems" (p. 436). Their education prepared them for ownership and control of physical capital and the means of production.

Several researchers have focused on the role of parents in education (Clark, 1983; Delgado-Gaitan, 1990, 1991; Lareau 1987, 1989). Lareau observed two elementary schools—one upper-middle-class and one working-class. The exclusive use of white subjects eliminated the possibility of racial bias. Lareau concluded that both working-class and middle-class parents value education. Further, teachers in the working-class school made even more effort to involve parents than did teachers in the middle-class school. The difference between the groups, Lareau concluded, lies in class. "Social class provides parents with social resources which they 'invest' to yield social profits" (1989, p. 10).

In the working-class community, Lareau noted a separation between school and family life that paralleled the separation of work and home for these nine-to-five employees. Parents trusted teachers to provide education during the time allotted, and they rarely intervened in the educational process. In the wealthier, college-educated community, the connections between education and home paralleled the connections between professional employment and family life. Not only did parents better prepare their children for school, but they also monitored school process, intervened as they deemed necessary, and followed up with school activities at home. Lareau concluded that these parents did not see education as separate from the activities of daily living; they felt competent to assist their children; and they possessed the personal resources to do so. Perhaps most importantly, the efforts of middle-class parents were those most celebrated by the school (Mehan, 1992).

Confirming the paucity of research on parent participation in education, Delgado-Gaitan (1990, 1991) used an ethnographic approach to study Hispanic parents' involvement in literacy efforts. Like Bourdieu and Bronfenbrenner, Delgado-Gaitan maintained that "the family provides the most essential educational environment for children" (p. 58). She too determined that parents value education.

Delgado-Gaitan (1990, 1991) supported Lareau's (1987, 1989) conclusion that schools ask for very similar behaviors from all parents, regardless of background or cultural resources. She determined that the Hispanic parents in the Portillo school district often lacked necessary skills to help their children at home or to comply with school requests for participation.

Further, Delgado-Gaitan (1990) noted that requisite abilities change as children develop. In the beginning years, parents need to be able to help their children with specific tasks. As children mature, they also need to know how the system functions so that they can continue to assist their own children as they advance through the grades. Delgado-Gaitan explained, "The most important skills which the schools need to help parents acquire are those of social competence and social literacy" (p. 59). Her efforts to promote social competence moved the group she was studying from family support to family empowerment. Delgado-Gaitan's (1990) research supported the premise that empowerment is a process which occurs over time through the acquisition of cultural capital. Noting that legislative regulation can be a powerful motivator of parent involvement, she stressed the need for home-school cooperation and communication. "Literacy and empowerment presume that both the school and the home are responsible for the sociocultural changes required to benefit children's academic progress in school" (p. 61).

Implications

Each of these studies supports Bourdieu's premise that educational systems reproduce social class structures. They also suggest two conclusions: First, although social support is important, it is not sufficient as a catalyst of change. In order to promote equal opportunity, programs must also champion empowerment.

Second, the opportunity to develop cultural capital is one of the most important functions of empowerment. Through participation in a family empowerment group, caregivers gain the knowledge, values, and skills they need to enter the dominant society.

Two additional comments are significant: First, the acquisition of cultural capital does not necessarily denigrate the subordinate culture; rather, it provides an apprenticeship and a tool kit from which individuals can choose the appropriate instruments to attain personal goals. Individuals who gain cultural capital can ultimately move away from the subordinate group if they desire. Second, the freedom and ability to leave one group and join another may produce anxiety and discomfort. The family unit must assimilate the roles and norms of the new group, and the new group must change to accommodate the family. The current study, described in the following pages, attempts to illuminate the processes through which caregivers gain cultural capital and use it to strengthen the fabric of their society in a low-income public housing project.

CHAPTER 5

Study Questions

The questions that guided this study evolved from a review of the theoretical literature, from a critique of related empirical research, and from my own lengthy observations of an extant preschool program. As Kieffer (1984) noted, empowerment research in social work attempts to identify the sources and varieties of, and the means to extend, participatory competence. Moreover, participatory competence embraces two elements: personal creativity that sparks growth, and personal understanding of the sources of oppression. This investigation emphasized discovery.

The investigation was informed by the work of Rappaport (1987), who maintained that researchers should study conditions that lead to empowerment and those environments that are not conducive to it. He exhorted scientists to examine three areas: First, study empowerment as it is experienced by people who say that they are empowered; second, analyze settings which empower; and third, consider phenomena over time.

Saleebey (1992) echoed these thoughts: "Empowerment research is a cooperative enterprise toward recognizing and developing individual and community strengths and resources. It does not seek to create new and perhaps invasive technologies with which to intervene in the lives of others" (p. 160). The goal is to understand the settings in which strengths and resources exist—or might exist, and how resources are defined and used by the participants.

By combining three research streams, this project considered each of the three aspects of empowerment identified by Rappaport (1987). First, it assumed that empowerment is a process of adult development. Second, drawing from the work of McKnight (1980, 1987, 1989), it assumed that lasting change is situated within community. And third, building on the concepts of Pierre Bourdieu (1971, 1977), it assumed that individuals can become empowered by acquiring cultural capital of the dominant class. Cultural capital can then be translated into human capital, or money, which individuals can use for their own benefit and the good of their communities without betraying ethnic or cultural identity.

These three research streams guided this study, as the following application illustrates:

> Through involvement in a cooperative preschool that requires parent participation, caregivers acquire cultural capital. The process through which this occurs constitutes empowerment. Over time, caregivers translate cultural capital into human capital. Consequently, the process of empowerment benefits caregivers, their families, and their neighborhoods.

Four research questions were derived from the review of empowerment theory, from previous work in the area, and from preliminary observations of a program which appeared to promote empowerment:

1. What cultural capital have caregivers acquired through participation in this preschool?
2. To what extent have caregivers translated cultural capital into human capital?
3. What elements have facilitated this transfer?
4. What barriers have caregivers encountered?

PURPOSE AND GOAL

The primary purpose of the investigation was discovery directed by theory and previous research. As Bronfenbrenner (1979) recommended, it attempted to identify "those systems properties and processes that affect and are affected by the behavior and development of the human being" (p. 37–38).

The goal of the project was twofold: First, to contribute to the knowledge base by refining the concept of empowerment; and second, to promote replication by identifying the salient features of an effective family empowerment program.

The methodology used to investigate these questions is described in the following chapters.

CHAPTER 6

Research Methodology

This chapter reviews the research methodology that drove this investigation. First, it discusses the type of inquiry, the unit of analysis, and the initial process of gaining entrance. This is followed by information on roles, data collection, reliability, confidentiality, and data analysis. Ethical issues and an elaboration of the timeframe conclude the chapter.

TYPE OF INQUIRY

Informed by an ecological approach, this was a naturalistic inquiry. It involved two types of investigation: participant observation of caregivers in the current program at Seigle Avenue Preschool Cooperative; and case studies of caregivers who had completed this program. Taken together, these two elements formed a representative cross-section of the phenomenon under consideration.

Naturalistic inquiry was chosen for several reasons specified by Jorgensen (1989). First, little was known about the effect of preschool involvement on caregivers. Second, there appeared to be important differences between the views of outsiders—even program sponsors—and insiders, especially caregivers. Third, the phenomenon was not easily accessible. Fourth, this phenomenon had not been captured by traditional educational research. And finally, appropriate quantitative evaluative techniques were not available (Fetterman, 1988; Powell, 1987).

Since this was an exploratory study, qualitative techniques were necessary to capture site-specific phenomena, explain quantitative data, and preserve practical knowledge (Weiss, 1987; Zigler & Weiss, 1985).

Naturalistic inquiry was appropriate because time was required to learn about the culture under consideration (Leichter, 1984).

This study was particularly concerned with human meanings and interactions viewed from the perspective of insiders (Jorgensen, 1989). In Bateson's terms, the study was open to "the pattern which connects" (1978). The inductive analyses began with specific observations in order to ascertain general patterns. This strategy allowed important dimensions to emerge without presupposing critical elements in advance. Content analysis and descriptive statistics were used to summarize data (Wilson, 1977).

A sound design relies on a trained observer who uses multiple methods over a sufficient length of time (Wolcott, 1980). This study incorporated each of these elements.

UNIT OF ANALYSIS

In a cooperative preschool, learning is a process of mutual interaction and exchange, with caregivers being influenced by, as well as influencing, the systems with which they are affiliated. Although several systems were present and available for study, the primary unit of analysis in this investigation was individual people: how they were affected by the experience, how they influenced the program, and how they exported their influence to other, contiguous settings.

To study this phenomenon, the researcher observed required parent meetings for eighteen months. She then interviewed adult program graduates (i.e., caregivers of children who had previously graduated from the program) and members of the 1992–1993 cohort. Chapter 6 describes the sampling strategies and provides a comprehensive description of the individuals and groups selected for analysis.

GAINING ENTRANCE

As with all naturalistic inquiry, entry into the field involved two components: negotiation with the intended users of the evaluation and physical entry into the setting (Patton, 1990b). The first phase is described below. My physical entry into the field, my roles and responsibilities, and issues of difference are included in Chapter 9. Since there were no variables to manipulate and cooperation was freely given, gaining entry was "largely a matter of establishing trust and rapport" (p. 251).

The first phase of entry entailed securing the permission and cooperation of the stakeholders, defined by Patton (1989) as people who share an interest in the outcome of the study. For this study, stakeholders include Seigle Avenue Presbyterian Church and Seigle Avenue Preschool Cooperative.

When the proposal was presented to the Board of Directors of the preschool, the chair, Jan Swetenberg, commented, "We want to know if what we are doing is working. And if it is, we want to publicize our results so that other communities can profit from our experience." Subsequently, the Board voted to approve the research endeavor at its monthly meeting on October 9, 1991.

The staff was apprised of the project during the same week. Family Coordinator Ann Bradley confirmed the need for the study by describing her experience as a single parent in the neighborhood. She added, "This is exactly what we need to show people how our program works. It's hard sometimes. We try to give the responsibility back to the parents. And we enforce consequences. But other people don't understand. This will help." The staff agreed by consensus to endorse this project on November 7, 1991.

In the Presbyterian Church, the Session is the governing body of an individual congregation. Because of the close connection between the preschool and Seigle Avenue Presbyterian Church, the Session was kept fully informed of this project. On October 14, 1991, the Session approved the research project by acclamation.

ROLES

A number of roles are available in naturalistic inquiry, and these are usually described on a continuum. At one end is the complete participant, whose identity and purpose are unknown to those observed. At the other end is the complete observer, who watches from the outside and "participates not one whit" (Gold, 1958, p. 222).

Between these extremes are the participant-as-observer and the observer-as-participant. The latter role is most often used in rapid reconnaissance, or one-visit interviews. The former is more common in community studies, where the researcher develops relationships over time. In this role, problems of role and self commonly arise. If the researcher becomes too familiar with those being studied, objectivity is lost. If, on the other hand, the researcher does not develop meaningful relationships with participants, little information of value can be collected.

The role of participant-observer requires a careful balancing of these two extremes, but it can produce rich results. By presenting the whole, the participant-observer elaborates the significance of the parts (Bruyn, 1963). And, as if that were not enough, participant observation can also induce serendipity, or significant discoveries which were unanticipated (Whyte, 1984).

There are several limitations to participant observation. It requires a great deal of time in the field—traditionally six months or more. Some field activities can be confining or boring; and, no matter how hard they try, an observer can never fully understand what it is like to be another person (Whyte, 1989).

Despite these restrictions, the participant-observer role was chosen for several reasons. It would be comfortable for the extended period of time I planned to spend in the field exploring a phenomenon that had not been previously investigated. Because the role of participant observer could foster trusting relationships with caregivers, it appeared that this role would yield the largest and most accurate amount of information. Finally, this role offered the best opportunity to gain a realistic perspective on the total phenomenon of adult participation in preschool education.

DATA COLLECTION

The design of this study required collection of data through three processes: field observations, focus groups, and individual interviews. Each method required a different technique of data collection.

Field Notes

Written reports captured the qualitative data accrued through each visit to the field. LeCompte and Goetz (1982) recommended the use of low-inference descriptors. This term refers to the form in which field notes are kept. Concrete, precise accounts of people and events as well as verbatim reports of conversations are mandatory in naturalistic inquiry. The format used for recording field notes is included as Appendix E. The standard outline helped me collect the same type of information across diverse activities.

The first section organized basic information about the event. The narrative portion described what happened, who made it happen, and how each participant reacted to what happened; and non-verbal content. In essence, the narrative constituted a process recording of the event—a chronological report of the "he-saids" and the "she-saids."

The Comments section included my assessment of the activity and a list of new questions prompted by the experience. I also used this section to monitor my impressions, reactions, and feelings. This section created an opportunity for reflection.

Problems arise in qualitative research when field notes are not recorded immediately after an event. I vowed to avoid this pitfall. Often, I dictated notes as I drove from the preschool to the university. When this was not possible, I typed them within twenty-four hours. Only one session was lost—because I began grading my students' papers and forgot to record my notes!

Focus Groups and Individual Interviews

Focus group sessions and individual interviews were recorded using a quality microcassette recorder. Tapes were transcribed verbatim by a professional legal secretary experienced in transcribing recordings of group meetings. Appendices B and D provide protocols for these sessions.

Triangulation of Data

Although the major source of data for this study was caregivers, triangulation strengthened the design and ensured validity (Patton, 1990b). The term "triangulation" was derived from land surveying. It denotes the use of more than one technique for studying a single problem. Triangulation is educed from a basic geometrical adage: two marks make a line; three marks make a good line. In qualitative research, triangulation obviates bias and encourages confidence in the results. The ensuing conclusions are more robust and less vulnerable to method-induced error.

Denzin (1978) identified four types of triangulation: data, investigator, theory, and methodological. Each uses multiple sources to validate and confirm findings. Of these techniques, data and methodological triangulation were incorporated into this research design.

Data triangulation indicates the use of a variety of data sources, including supplementary materials (Rossman & Wilson, 1985). Program records were a primary source of ancillary data. As Allen-Meares (1990) suggested, photographs, descriptions of activities, rosters, and notes to teachers contributed to a fuller understanding of participants and their involvement with the preschool.

A second source of ancillary data was derived from oral history. Although there were few written records, there was a strong tradition of oral history. Residents remembered critical incidents that they repeated at meetings and in informal gatherings. Key community representatives were available, including the president and officers of the Residents' Organization, the pastor and staff of the Church, the activities coordinator from the Housing Authority, and the staff and board of the preschool. Each of these persons was familiar with the Preschool philosophy and program; and each had contact with caregivers in the program. All were approached during the course of the study, and all were eager to review tentative conclusions, offer explanations and interpretations, and provide supplemental information.

Use of a key informant is a third method of data triangulation. The logical candidate for this informal position was the former family coordinator, Ann Bradley. As mentioned, Bradley was knowledgeable and articulate; and her insight was invaluable. As a peer reviewer, she discussed her experiences, explained events I observed, and shared her own hypotheses.

DATA ANALYSIS

Techniques recommended by Miles and Huberman (1984) were used for analysis of field notes and verbatim transcripts of interviews. To prepare for the analysis, audiocassette tapes were transcribed onto a personal computer. To preserve the source material, the original records were write-protected and stored, and duplicates were used for the actual content analysis.

Although computer software is becoming available for content analysis, I planned to reorganize material using color-coded markers and index cards to indicate themes and patterns (Miles & Huberman, 1984). It was quickly apparent that the vast amount of data collected for this project rendered this approach cumbersome and unwieldy. Instead, the personal computer was used to reassemble information according to the categories and constructs dictated by the theory.

Data analysis proceeded through several stages. First, information was reorganized according to the questions that guided data collection. A new computer file was created for each item listed on the interview protocols (Appendices B and D). Word-processing software was used to transfer sentences and sections from the original computer files of interviews and field notes to the new files. When this was complete, the new files were analyzed for themes and patterns.

Most response sets were consistent. For example, Question 1a (Appendix B and D) asked why caregivers selected this particular preschool. Respondents routinely cited convenience and location as their primary considerations.

Occasionally discrepancies were noted within a response set; and when these occurred, they were explored in depth. For example, Question 5b on the Individual Interview Protocol (Appendix B) asked graduates about their post-preschool employment experience. Comments from the nine respondents were assembled in a new file and examined.

Four caregivers described their work. Two more said they were enrolled in high school completion programs, and one indicated she was working on a technical degree at the local community college. Although these three individuals were not currently employed, they discussed their pursuit of education as a means to employment. The remaining two caregivers unequivocally stated that they had considered education and employment but had decided not to pursue either until their youngest children were enrolled in public school. One then planned to return to college to complete the final year she lacked. The other intended to obtain a job to earn money for her family.

These responses were tested against the working hypothesis, which stated that caregivers would acquire cultural capital which they could convert to human capital. Four caregivers had clearly achieved self-sufficiency and three were making substantial progress toward this goal. At first glance, the two who were neither employed nor seeking education appeared to be exceptions, but their responses made it clear that they had each made a conscious, active choice to parent young children. Both knew that staying home meant less financial security and the delay of personal goals. Both explained that participation in the preschool had helped them understand the importance of providing positive experiences for young children. I considered their decisions within the context of the theory and concluded that all the caregivers had acquired cultural capital, although only seven of the nine were actively engaged in the process of converting cultural capital into human capital.

During my field observations, I noted differential patterns of response; and staff suggestions regarding focus group composition suggested that the cohort actually contained several subgroups. As responses to each question were analyzed, three patterns of participation became evident. During the second phase of data analysis, I explored this phenomenon. I used field notes to prepare a matrix of special events. Then I listed the activities I had observed and indicated which caregivers had engaged in each. For example, five caregivers cooked for the Valentine's Day party and five others sorted cards for the children. Three caregivers arrived in time to eat. Only the cooks stayed to clean after the event. The roster for this event listed the activities and named the participants who engaged in each.

Using the computer, I compared rosters of special events and the groupings suggested by the staff. The composition remained consistent, and I concluded that three distinct groups had emerged.

After the presence of groups was confirmed, I analyzed the composition for similarities and differences. During the field phase, I had speculated that the leadership group might be composed of older participants. This hypothesis was rejected when I learned participants' ages during the focus group sessions. I also examined levels of education, family composition, number of years of participation in the preschool, and number and ages of children; however, no clear rules for membership emerged. Several comments suggested that mothers in the uncommitted group had experienced unstable relationships within their families of origin, but this study was not designed to address early history, and not enough information was available to confirm this impression. This is an area that clearly merits further attention.

In the third phase, material was again reordered, this time according to theme. Files for individual questions were combined as patterns appeared. For example, information about relationships with significant others was included in a number of places. At this point, this material was collected and examined as a thematic unit.

Most patterns were determined by the theory itself. For example, Questions 2e and 9 on the Focus Group Protocol (Appendix D) specifically asked caregivers about events or situations that made them feel powerless. In this stage of the process, however, I also looked for examples of barriers that may have been cited in other questions. I also reviewed field notes for indications of obstacles and impediments. As the collapsed files developed, the body of the dissertation began to emerge.

The individual interviews provided a comprehensive picture of graduates, but I had only group profiles of active caregivers. While developing themes, I also restructured material by caregiver. Thus, I created individual records of the contributions of each person. This step enabled me to verify internal consistency and gave me a fuller picture of maturation and development.

During data analysis, I visited the preschool frequently to ask additional questions, review events, discuss preliminary findings, and confirm the presence and significance of themes. Occasionally I needed to clarify words such as "trifling." Although I had heard the term often during my field observations, I was not certain of its connotation, so I probed for a more comprehensive definition.

Both family coordinators and other staff were available, and I asked them to compare and contrast their experiences with mine. Caregivers, especially those in the leadership group, elaborated on their own observations of the parents' program; and community leaders shared their perspectives and affirmed my tentative conclusions. Even after the academic year ended, staff and participants were available and willing to discuss this project. In lieu of a second reader, they corroborated my conclusions.

Review constituted the fourth phase of the data analysis. Theoretical assumptions and study questions were revisited and compared with emerging outcomes. All the original interviews and field notes were re-examined for consistency; and variation, when found, was explored. As I reread the original transcripts, I noted a few comments that had not been incorporated into the current draft. When these were analyzed, most were subsumed within existing categories; however, remarks about relationships with extended family members formed an additional section.

Outside readers also contributed to the review process. Dr. Charles Summers, pastor of Seigle Avenue Presbyterian Church and community organizer Margaret Bigger read the material on setting and provided extensive feedback. Dr. Maureen Marcenko, a researcher in early intervention at Hahneman Medical College, offered substantive comments on the first three chapters. Dr. Wallace Gingerich served as a second reader by listening to audiotapes and reading transcripts from an interview and a focus group.

The fifth phase of data analysis was marked by revision as the final version was prepared. Suggestions for staff, caregivers, colleagues, and reviewers were considered and incorporated. Names and identifying information were altered to protect the confidentiality of participants. Theoretical connections were explicated; and supplementary material about caregivers was added to provide depth and clarity. The document was divided into three major sections, and chapters were revised slightly to produce a cohesive document. After numerous discussions with colleagues and a period of reflection, I extracted and compiled conclusions in the final chapter.

RELIABILITY

Reliability refers to the extent to which an experiment or study can be replicated or repeated. When compared to the stringent controls of a laboratory experiment, a naturalistic inquiry may appear to elude replication. However, careful balancing of the complex factors in a naturalistic inquiry can reduce threats to reliability.

Authors generally divide reliability into two categories: internal and external (Cook & Campbell, 1979). As LeCompte and Goetz (1982) recommend, I used triangulation, low-inference descriptors, and recording devices to assure internal reliability.

LeCompte and Goetz (1982) maintain that external reliability can be enhanced by attention to five factors: "researcher status position; informant choices; social situations and conditions; analytic constructs and premises; and methods of data collection and analysis" (p. 37). The first factor, the researcher's status, refers to the investigator's membership in the studied group, which must be explained in order for others to duplicate the investigation. This information was presented in the previous section of this chapter.

The second factor involves the choice of informants, for the selection of one constituent group may preclude access to another. The participants in this study are described in Chapter 8.

The third factor, social situations and conditions, refers to the need to specify function, structure, and features of the field site. This is addressed in Chapters 7 and 9.

The fourth factor concerns the analytic constructs and premises used by the researcher. Replication depends on careful specification of constructs, definitions, assumptions, conditions, and limitations. The assumptions for this study are clearly stated in Chapter 5. They are elaborated throughout the document and evaluated in the final chapter.

The fifth factor concerns methods of data collection and analysis. According to LeCompte and Goetz (1982), "Because reliability depends on the potential for subsequent researchers to reconstruct original analytic strategies, only those ethnographic accounts that specify these in sufficient detail will be replicable" (p. 40). Data collection is outlined in the previous section and in Chapter 8, which addresses the sample of participants.

Undergirding each of these five threats to reliability is the need for precise, comprehensive, explicit description of each phase of the research process. I have attempted to elucidate each aspect of this investigation in this chapter.

VALIDITY

Establishing validity "necessitates demonstration that the propositions generated, refined, or tested match the causal conditions that obtain in human life" (Goetz & LeCompte, 1984). According to Bronfenbrenner (1979), ecological validity refers to "the extent to which the environment experienced by the subjects in a scientific investigation has the properties it is supposed or assumed to have by the investigator" (p. 29). Questions of internal validity ask whether investigators are actually observing or measuring what they think they are observing or measuring. Questions of external validity ask whether results can be translated or compared across groups.

Internal validity may be a major strength of the naturalistic approach. The participant is immersed in the setting for a long period of time, and the data collected from informants is less abstract than that collected by instruments used in other research designs. The field setting is not contrived, and the researcher undergoes a prolonged process of self-monitoring that "exposes all phases of the research activity to continual questioning and reevaluation" (LeCompte & Goetz, 1982, p. 43).

Nevertheless, other threats to internal validity as identified by Campbell and Stanley (1963) and Cook and Campbell (1979) can be applicable to naturalistic inquiry. These include maturation and history, observer effects, selection and regression, mortality, and spurious conclusions.

"Maturation" is defined as progressive development in an individual, while "history" consists of changes that affect an entire group. Since the focus of the study was process and change, both maturation and history were present during the course of the study. I used caregivers' perception of their experiences to help me separate changes due to encounters with the Preschool from those due to other factors.

Observer effects are threats to validity posed by the presence of the observer and are comparable to effects of instrumentation in quantitative research. As the section on role indicated, no unusual observer effects were observed.

The research design precluded distortion through independent corroboration, use of key informants, and extended exposure to the field site. The choice of participants obviated problems of selection and regression, including mortality. Spurious conclusions were avoided by using low-inference descriptors; by attending to participants' perceptions of causality; by systematically analyzing the data in light of previous research in the area; and by eliminating rival explanations.

Threats to external validity are those effects which make it difficult to compare studies or translate them across groups or into similar settings. At the most basic level every setting, every person, and every event is unique; and no study can be exactly duplicated, as Cowen and colleagues have attested (1983). There is no public housing project exactly like Piedmont Courts, and there is no preschool program that completely duplicates this preschool cooperative.

Some naturalistic inquiries are so eccentric that they cannot be compared with other investigations; however, this was not true for this study. Although this phenomenon was unique, it was not atypical. All the elements—the setting, the participants, and the event—are common to metropolitan communities across the United States. The study describes the salient characteristics in a way that promotes external validity and facilitates confirmation. As Laosa (1991) indicates, the goal is to establish *generalizability boundaries* that accurately indicate the populations to which this study may apply and those for which it probably holds little meaning (p. 315).

ETHICAL ISSUES

Generally, research ethics focus on the value of human life and the rights of individuals. There are few concrete rules in naturalistic inquiry since the researcher is observing people in everyday situations. Jorgensen explains, "Participant observers are deeply concerned with ethics, but they see ethical norms as guidelines that require application in particular situations" (1989, p. 29). In this setting, ethical considerations addressed protection of human subjects, confidentiality, and the possibility of psychological stress.

Protection of Subjects and Informed Consent

The research project was approved by the Committee on Human Studies at Case Western Reserve University on April 18, 1993. Since this is an overt study, the goals and methods of the research were fully disclosed to participants and stakeholders, and their cooperation was obtained.

During the initial phase, no special consent forms were required, for my role differed little from that of the many volunteers who were involved with the preschool on a daily basis. During the second phase of the project, informed consent was obtained from caregivers participating in individual interviews and case studies. Copies of the informed consent letters are included in Appendices A and C.

Confidentiality

News travels fast in Piedmont Courts. While it was not possible to prevent others' knowing who participated in the study, it was both possible and essential to protect the confidentiality of these subjects. Field notes were written and kept at my home office. Audio tapes were transcribed by a professional legal secretary who understood the need for confidentiality and who had no connection with the site or the subjects. After tapes were transcribed, the documents were duplicated; one copy was kept at my home office, while the other was filed at my office at UNC Charlotte. Original cassette tapes and backup computer diskettes were stored in a safe deposit box at a nearby bank.

To prevent harm to participants, additional data, including rosters and demographic notations, were protected in the same way field notes were guarded. In published reports, all names, particulars, and other potential means of identification were changed to protect confidentiality.

Psychological Stress

Patton (1990b) impressively declared, "Interviews are interventions. They affect people. A good interview lays open thoughts, feelings, knowledge, and experience not only to the interviewer but also to the interviewee" (p. 353). The interview process can be very powerful. Through it, people may become conscious of previously submerged knowledge, feelings, judgments, and insights. Patton concludes, "Two hours or more of thoughtfully reflecting on an experience, a program, or one's life can be change-inducing" (p. 354).

There was no evidence that participants in this study suffered from psychological stress. They may have been changed by the experience, but the comments indicate that they enjoyed the process and considered the changes beneficial.

TIME FRAME

The investigation occurred in two phases. The first phase, observation of the caregivers' program, began in October 1992 and concluded at the end of the 1992–1993 academic year. The second phase, case studies of former participants, was conducted in May 1993. The entire project required eighteen months in the field.

Often, naturalistic inquiry continues for an unspecified period of time—ideally, until the researcher has wrung all the meaning from the experience (Gray & Wandersmith, 1980). This experience had a pre-established ending, for the caregivers' group disbanded at the end of the academic year, in late May 1993.

The next chapter describes the ecological setting for this preschool. Following that chapter is a description of the current cohort and the graduates who participated in this study. This section concludes with an analysis of the process of entry into the field and a discussion of the role of participant-observer as it was enacted in this investigation.

CHAPTER 7

Setting

In an ecological study, environment is a critical element
(Bronfenbrenner, 1975, 1979). The environment is the setting or actual
place where people readily interact with each other. Each setting
possesses particular physical and material attributes which shape
behavior, and each setting is in turn shaped by its own particular
history.

This chapter provides a dynamic description of the setting for this
study. The first section describes the region and city, and the historical
context from which they emerged. The next section describes the
neighborhood and the church, from their earliest beginnings to the
present. The final section describes the preschool in which this research
was conducted.

THE REGION AND THE CITY

Charlotte, North Carolina, named for a popular Queen of England, is
located on the Piedmont plateau, a broad, natural corridor extending
from New York to Alabama. It is flanked on the east by coastal plains
and on the west by the Blue Ridge Mountains. Climate is both
moderate and seasonal, with neither the long, cold winters characteristic
of the north nor the hot, oppressive summers of the Deep South.

The first settlers, Scotch Presbyterians, arrived around 1730. These
farmers, pushed out of Scotland as "Dissenters" under King James II and
Oliver Cromwell, migrated to the English colonies after a 100–year
"exile" in Ireland. The Scotch-Irish were followed by Methodists and
Germans of the Lutheran and Reformed traditions (King, 1954).
English, Scotch, Germans, Huguenots, and Swiss migrated up from

Charleston and the low country of South Carolina; and other English moved in from the eastern coast (Tompkins, 1903).

The early settlers, especially those from Pennsylvania, found it easiest to travel southward through the rolling surface of the Piedmont on a Native American trading path they renamed the Great Philadelphia Wagon Road (Clay & Stuart, 1990). Once established, the settlers wrested the land from its original inhabitants, Native Americans of the Catawba, Cherokee, and Tuscaroras nations. They created a prosperous agricultural region, sending hides, whiskey, and tallow to Charleston in exchange for household goods, iron, and salt (Leach, 1976).

The immigrants brought few slaves with them, and slavery did not flourish until after Mecklenburg County was established in 1762. As Tompkins (1903), an early historian, explained, "When a farmer had accumulated enough money to buy a slave, he would go to Charleston to buy what the first slave lists called a 'Negro wench' or a 'Negro man'" (p. 85). Most slaves were imported from the West Coast of Africa, probably Gambia (Rev. Charles A. Summers, personal communication December 21, 1992).

Presbyterians, the dominant sect, banded together in groups of twenty or more families "in order to have teachers and preachers of their own choosing" (Tompkins, 1903, p. 75). All their offspring received some instruction so that they might read the Bible. Boarding schools were rare, but available for boys. In 1773, a committee petitioned King George III for a chartered college, but the request was refused because the King feared the Presbyterians would encourage dissension from the Church of England. Nevertheless, the school opened and operated without a charter until it could be incorporated in 1777.

According to local historians, Mecklenburg County declared independence from Britain on May 20, 1775, a year before Thomas Jefferson wrote a similar document for the nation. The region earned the sobriquet "Hornets' Nest" during the ensuing Revolutionary War. Most of the colonial militia surrendered to the British at Charleston on May 12, 1780, and another local troop was lost in Camden, South Carolina in August. However, a few soldiers escaped to return home, determined to defend their families from the British General Charles Cornwallis, who occupied the town. Tompkins writes:

> These intrepid soldiers did all in their power to harass the British, and succeeded in impeding their progress considerably. They

captured sentries and spies, and so alarmed Cornwallis by
capturing small foraging parties that he would not send out less
than a regiment for that purpose. Every step of the British march
was greeted with a rifle shot from the woods and the determined
persistent opposition did much to dishearten the conquering army.
(1903, p. 61)

By 1786, the town claimed 276 residents and the county claimed
9,000. Of the townspeople, 69 were white women, 84 were white
males, and 123 were blacks. Although a few had been freed, most
African Americans in the region were slaves who attended worship with
their masters but sat in different sections of the sanctuary (Dimensions,
1974). Industries included a sawmill, flour mill, and blacksmith shop.
There were tavern keepers, merchants, tailors, weavers, hatters, and a
rifle maker. A United States Post Office was established in 1792.

In the last decade before 1800, the largest slave owners in the
county owned eight, nine, and ten slaves respectively. It was rare that
African Americans were taught anything except farm work. In part, this
was to inhibit their running away. It also limited competition with
poor whites (Tompkins, 1903).

The patent of the cotton gin in 1794 kindled rapid and steady
growth in the cotton industry and an increased demand for slave labor.
By 1814, there were five stores in Charlotte, and 228 African
Americans, primarily living on farms outside the city limits. In 1819,
William Davidson, the richest man in the county, owned twenty-three
slaves and 18,354 acres of land; and his total assessed property
amounted to $10,700 (Tompkins, 1903, p. 93). By 1860, thirty
Mecklenburg planters owned more than thirty slaves each; and slaves
totaled about one-third of the county's population (Kratt, 1992).

Gold was discovered in the early 1800s, making Charlotte the gold
mining capital of the United States until the California Gold Rush of
1849. In the mid-nineteenth century, the town became a major railroad
junction connected with nearby towns, the state capitals of North and
South Carolina, and the coast. The rail lines had far-reaching economic
impact, although agriculture continued to dominate the region for many
years.

The public school system was established in 1841 by a county
vote of 950 for and 578 against. Schools were funded by local and state
taxes, although during the Civil War these monies were redirected to the

war effort. Schools generally consisted of one-room buildings serving grades one through six or seven; and teachers taught all subjects to pupils of all ages (Dimension, 1974).

The North Carolina Ordinance of Secession was signed unanimously in Charlotte on May 20, 1861. Rebels claimed that states, not the federal government, had the right to regulate slavery. Between 1860 and 1865, the county furnished more than 2,713 soldiers to the Confederacy and mounted a home guard of 12,500, including all able-bodied men between eighteen and fifty. After the surrender of General Lee to General Grant at Appomattox, Virginia on April 9, 1865, the city was occupied by Northern troops. Although elections—won by Democrats—were held in 1865, troops did not evacuate the town until December 18, 1867.

The Civil War, often called "The Great Divide," split religious denominations by North and South. One result was that Northern churches sent missionaries to the former slaves, encouraging them to form their own congregations. By 1875, the pattern of segregated churches was well established with five "Negro" and nine "White" churches in the county (Dimensions, 1974).

The effect of emancipation was immediate and revolutionary. African Americans were generally idle, for they had no land to work and no skilled trades to ply. Tompkins comments, "Negroes manifested interest in politics for a while, but quit it when they found that would not get them 'forty acres and a mule'" (1903, p. 145). However, two of the three delegates to the Republican State Convention in 1867 were black. The city supported eight police, two or three of whom were black; and several of twelve aldermen were also black. There was no Ku Klux Klan organization in the county and little racial unrest during this time.

In language of his day, Tompkins explained, "The whites were not accustomed to farm work and could not hire the negroes to work and the result was that attention was diverted to something else" (1903, p. 151). That something else was trade. By June 1866 there were 66 stores in the county; and in the first six months of 1867, 12 more were built. During the decade after the Civil War, both wealth and population doubled in the county and trebled in the city (p. 153). Reconstruction ended with the political campaign of 1876, when county whites outnumbered African Americans by 375 voters. By 1880, entrepreneur and erstwhile historian D. A. Tompkins was actively promoting the 'Great Cotton Mill Campaign,' a drive to "bring the factories to the fields" (Kratt, 1992, p. 100).

During the last decade of the century, business in the city and county expanded faster than that of the state or the nation. Farms grew in size and decreased in number; and textile mills, driven by abundant electrical power, proliferated. Roads were improved using convict labor. Electric lights replaced gas lights in 1887, the same year street cars began to run. Physicians, clergy, and attorneys were plentiful, stimulating development of the first suburb, Dilworth, which opened land sales on historically significant May 20, 1891. Dilworth was quickly followed by prestigious Myers Park, designed by city planner John Nolen and landscape architect Earl Draper. Education was strengthened, and by 1902 there were 141 public schools in the county. Sixty-one served 7,927 African American students; and 80 served 10,869 white students.

In the hundred years following the Civil War, more people moved out of the region than into it. Most of the émigrés were African Americans and undereducated rural farm workers seeking economic opportunity. By the beginning of World War II, Charlotte, though a growing town, had not become a significant city. During this war, people came from the surrounding areas to work at two military installations, and the economy expanded. As soldiers returned home and settled, Charlotte began to evolve from a town into a regional city.

Growth was promoted by construction of Interstate Highway 85 along the same general path as the Great Philadelphia Wagon Road. Additional transportation investments, the absence of close competition, and the presence of a national textile export market strengthened the Charlotte area as a major population center (Dimensions, 1974). The pattern of decline reversed dramatically in the 1960s with a regional gain of 740,000 people, and this trend continued through the next decade with a net gain of 3.5 million people. For the first time, more African Americans moved in than out (Clay & Stuart, 1992), although the proportion of African Americans dropped from 28% in 1950 to 26% in 1990 (Bureau of the Census, 1991).

In the early 1960s, black and white leaders banded together to integrate private and public businesses, and by 1963 the city auditorium, coliseum, libraries, buses, parks, pools, hospitals, hotels and motels, restaurants, and community services were integrated.

Although civil unrest was expected, none emerged (Watters, 1964); however, change proceeded slowly.

The Supreme Court decision of 1954 in *Brown v. Board of Education* was followed locally by token desegregation in 1957. Rampant inequities and an agonizingly sluggish pace of change prompted the 1965 case of *Swann v. Charlotte-Mecklenburg Board of Education.* This lawsuit was not settled until the 1970–71 academic year, when a consolidated city-county school system instituted the nation's first court-ordered and court-supervised busing program designed to racially integrate schools. Desegregation was achieved by pairing predominantly black schools with predominantly white schools and then busing students among schools (Clay & Stewart, 1987).

Today, Charlotte-Mecklenburg Schools' basic desegregation plan is being revised by the addition of magnet, or specialty, schools designed to attract diverse students with similar interests and abilities. However, racial mix is still considered an important factor in the assignment of pupils to magnet schools. Charlotte-Mecklenburg Schools—the largest system in the Carolinas and the 25th largest in the nation—enrolls more than 78,000 pupils (Margaret Lynch, personal communication, December 21, 1992; O'Brien, 1992).

Writer H. L. Mencken coined the acerbic phrase "Bible Belt" around 1920 to describe the puritanical, conservative religious attitudes of the South. Presbyterians began to break the pejorative stereotype as Dr. Randolph Taylor, dynamic pastor of Myers Park Presbyterian Church, led a long quest for reunion of the Northern and Southern branches of the Presbyterian denomination. After ten years of active crusading, the two divisions united on June 10, 1983, and Dr. Taylor became the first Moderator of the combined church. Reunion healed the rift torn by the Civil War and brought together Northern, Southern, and Western factions of the denomination. For the first time, southern churches were required to adopt the Northern practice of electing women as well as men to the Session, or governing body, of each local church. Although individual churches in the south Piedmont remained almost completely segregated, black and white congregations merged into Mecklenburg Presbytery.

Religion continues to be a focal point "around which everything evolves" (Garfield, 1992, December 20, p. 8A). There are an estimated 600 churches in Mecklenburg County—one for every 852.4 people. (Compare this to sister city Atlanta, where there are 1500 religious facilities—one for every 1640 people.) More than 64% of Mecklenburg County's 511,433 residents belong to a house of worship, compared to a national average of 59%. According to local historian Mary Kratt, "the church is as essential as the post office" (Garfield, 1992, December 20, p. 8A). Although some feel stifled by, and others sneer at, the only national professional basketball team that begins each game with public prayer, most citizens treasure their religious affiliation and are proud of the services provided by churches. For example, churches provide 90% of the goods donated to the local food pantry, and they helped build 90% of 158 Habitat for Humanity homes for the working poor (Garfield, 1992, December 20). Nevertheless, eleven o'clock on Sunday morning probably remains the most segregated hour in the region (Garfield, 1992, May 4).

Charlotte-Mecklenburg has expanded to become a regional hub, which claimed more than half the population on 31% of the land area for North Carolina and South Carolina combined in 1990 (Clay & Stuart, 1990). Agriculture, once the primary occupation, has declined as a major source of employment. It has been replaced by banking, trade, distribution, and industry, including the manufacture of textiles, metals, machinery, and electrical equipment. One public and three well-known private institutions of higher education are located within the county. Recreational opportunities abound in twenty-one neighborhood parks, nineteen district parks, and six community parks and nature preserves. The cultural arts are thriving, as are auto racing and professional basketball; and the city was recently awarded a franchise for a professional football team. Known for "an unusual degree of fairness and equal opportunity," the city embodies the best of the New South (Kratt, 1992, p. 282).

THE NEIGHBORHOOD

Amid concern about slums in the shadow of the skyline, the Housing Authority of the City of Charlotte was organized and chartered in 1939. Its mission was to provide adequate housing, eliminate crime, and "stamp-out disease and epidemics" (Housing Authority, City of Charlotte, 1941, p. 21). Two segregated projects were begun. When the first completed buildings at Fairview Homes Negro Project were opened to the public on June 23, 1939, the African American churches in the city observed Housing Sunday. In its second annual report, the Authority stated,

> Many of the people living here left appalling housing conditions behind them. Critics of the housing program insisted that people accustomed to living amidst dirt and squalor could not adjust themselves to good housing conditions and would abuse them. The answer to this criticism is to be found at Fairview Homes, where this condition has been non-existent. (p. 17)

The Charlotte Housing Authority concurrently established Piedmont Courts to replace substandard housing and to provide affordable accommodations for whites, especially white families of military personnel returning from World War II.

Headlines from the *Charlotte Sunday Observer* read:

> Roosevelt Approves Additional Housing Funds
> Action means $309,000 here
> Grant recently earmarked by USHA made available
> EXPANDS WHITE PROJECT
> Will allow extra units, community house,
> and administration center (1b)

The twenty-two-acre site, located about a mile from the center of the city, was bounded on the north and east by small creeks, and on the south and west by city streets. Thirty-three substandard housing units were demolished and replaced with 368 one-, two-, and three-bedroom apartments configured in forty-one buildings. The completed project also included an administration building and a daycare center. The predominant land use of the surrounding neighborhood was by small businesses and light industries. The first families moved in on January 1, 1941. By the 1947, "The Courts," as the project was called, housed 1,417 adults and their 702 dependents in 368 units (Housing Authority, City of Charlotte, 1947).

Apartment design was basic but functional. Generally, two units shared a small rear porch, walkway, garbage can holder, and clothesline. Front yards and porches were slightly larger. The units were constructed without porch lights or lighting in stairwells.

Exterior, glass-paned doors lacked safety locks. Neither closets nor bedrooms had doors. Originally, apartments were heated individually by wood- or coal-burning stoves on the ground floor, and there were no flues or ducts to carry the heat to the second level. Floors and exterior walls were of thick concrete. Apartments were converted in 1953 to natural gas for heating, cooking, and water heating. Since it was anticipated that residents would use public transportation, there was minimal provision for automobile parking or vehicular traffic in the original plan.

All the first residents of Piedmont Courts were white. Adults were generally under age forty, and two-parent families were the norm. Most adults worked outside the home. When their financial circumstances improved, families were required to leave public housing. Consequently, there was continual turnover in the neighborhood (Gardner, 1992). Yet, residents were proud of their homes; they tended lawns and gardens and cleaned on Saturdays, and some even hired domestic workers (Morrill & Paddock, 1986).

As the population of the project aged, services were extended to senior citizens. The 1960 statistical report indicated that 48 families in Piedmont Courts were receiving Old Age Assistance, while only 35 families were receiving Aid to Dependent Children. Slightly more than half (54%) the families received some type of assistance, while the remainder were employed. The average family income at Piedmont Courts in 1960 was $2087.00, and monthly rent averaged $30.78. During this period, 119 families moved out of the Courts. The majority of these left because their annual income had grown beyond the limits for admission, $3,200 for a family of three or four (Housing Authority of the City of Charlotte, N. C., April 1, 1958–April 1, 1960).

The Civil Rights Act of 1964 had an immediate and dramatic impact on the community. Since Piedmont Courts had been built with federal funds, it was under immediate court order to desegregate, and racial integration began ten days after passage of the bill (Morrill & Paddock, 1986).

As black families moved into the Courts, white families left. In 1964, 567 whites and 852 blacks lived in four public housing projects in Charlotte. Two years later, at the same projects, blacks totaled 1,107 and whites 312 (Noblitt, 1966). An unidentified 'Negro leader' commented, "A lot of white families moved out of Piedmont Courts because Negroes moved in. And many of them were people who could have moved out before but just didn't because they had a good place to live cheaply. The result is that more units are becoming available for members of my race...and we're the ones who need them" (p. 9A). Sargent Shriver, director of the Office of Economic Opportunity, came to Charlotte on Thursday, June 23, 1966 to speak to the National Sunday School and Baptist Training Union conference, a branch of the National Baptist Convention which was then the largest black organization in the world (Lawrimore, 1966; Marsh, 1966). Shriver declared, "Poverty can be eliminated in this country by 1976—200 years after the Declaration of Independence—if the nation decides to make a large enough commitment." When questioned about the cost, Shriver responded, "A lot less than the war in Viet Nam" ("Shriver: No," 1966).

The war on poverty was supplemented with enthusiastic volunteerism. Citing a long history of altruism among wealthy Charlotte women, Reimler (1966) reported, "But suddenly for many of them it is not enough to raise money. They have found a need in themselves to become personally involved in filling the cultural, intellectual and economic needs in others. It's a heck of a way to fight a war" (p. 8A).

Not everyone shared this optimism. In August of 1966, North Carolina Governor Dan Moore held a press conference to denounce activities of the Ku Klux Klan (Shires, 1966). The Charlotte Area Fund, embroiled in controversy on several fronts, had difficulty raising the local share of its annual budget. Wallace Kuralt, director of the county welfare department, explained, "The Area Fund has failed here because it hasn't won the confidence of the people and because it has hired people who don't know anything about social work" (Freakley, 1967).

In the early 1970's, tenant representation was hotly debated (Martin, 1970). The first step was expansion of the Housing Authority from five to seven members (Arthur, 1971). This change was supported by a number of churches, which also pushed for open meetings (Martin, 1972) and mobilized public housing residents to press for tenant representation (Dembeck, 1972; "First Public," 1972). The first tenant representative, an African American woman, was elected to the Housing Authority on January 20, 1972. She was also the first female Authority member (Dembeck, 1972).

The full promise of tenant representation was never realized. Jablow (1966) cited lack of leadership as a problem. "The leader in a middle or upper class community is a man or woman with leisure time and connections, but the potential leader in a poverty area is likely to be a domestic who gets home late and has children to care for. There are no civic organizations and little time to attend meetings" (p. 4B).

In their 1973 study of the housing project, Savickas and Whisnant documented substantial problems. "The conditions in Piedmont Courts allow assault, robbery, and vandalism to exist as major threats and inhibit the security of residents" (p. 10–11). The authors found that residents were not taking advantage of services offered by the adjacent Neighborhood Center; and they noted the stigma associated with residence in the Courts. The architects concluded that modernization of the physical structure alone would not solve the problems of the community.

Neighborhood life continued to deteriorate. By 1984, unemployment had reached 80%; and three-fourths of the average family income came from government assistance programs. Women headed 90% of the families; and only 5% of adults were married (DeAdwyler, 1985; Smith, 1985). A typical newsletter from the Mothers Club asked, "Who is supposed to clean up the old mattress and litter behind the Learning Center? What can be done to re-activate the Residents Organization? When are they going to fix the drainage so water won't stand in yards?" ("Who, what," 1985).

Drug dealers openly plied their trade. Vacant buildings were boarded to keep out trespassers; and there was much fear and unrest among the residents. However, most crimes were not reported. Residents feared retribution and they believed police response would be inadequate (M. C. Michie, personal communication, Fall 1986). Margaret Bigger, a twenty-five-year veteran community organizer from Myers Park Presbyterian Church, testified before the Housing Authority Board, "Shootings are common occurrences. They occur most frequently on weekend nights but can, according to residents, be heard any night" (September 26, 1984). A year later, she again testified, "Still the shooting goes on night and day nearly every day" (October 25, 1985). Despite internal concern and a four-part newspaper series on crime in public housing, there was little public response (Wildman, 1982; Wildman & Schwartz, 1982; Schwartz & Wildman, 1982).

On November 30, 1985, Piedmont Courts again became the focus of intense local interest. A "shootout" among drug dealers left seven people injured. The incident occurred about three o'clock on a sunny Saturday afternoon when many families were visiting in their yards. In less than five minutes, more than 100 bullets were fired from an Uzi submachine gun (Mellnik, Minter, & Morell, 1985; Hidlay & DeAdwyler, 1985). One of the injured was a fourteen-year-old student, eight months pregnant (Webb, 1985). The city was shocked (Todd, 1986). A crackdown on crime ensued, and an assistant city manager pledged expanded assistance. However, residents remained skeptical (DeAdwyler & Minter, 1985).

The following Tuesday, a white police officer at the Courts shot and wounded a black man armed with a stolen gun (Morell, 1985). The district attorney ruled the action self-defense (O'Neill, 1985), but some residents complained that police were overreacting (Minter, 1985).

Following the shootout, an article in *The Charlotte Observer* spotlighted the disrepair and maintenance problems of the Courts. An assistant city manager, himself black, stated, "If you stock up any complex with people who have no hope, who have very little income, who don't have any skills, (and) then couple that with a management that's perceived to be unresponsive, you've got a mess on your hands" (Morrill, 1986, p. 8A). The article explained that the complex manager and work crews were afraid to walk across the site, "which had a rough reputation" (p. 8A).

The Housing Authority obtained a six-million-dollar grant from the Department of Housing and Urban Development for the renovation of the Courts ("Piedmont Courts," 1985; Martin, 1985), but a year after the shootout, construction had not begun and conditions had worsened. Trash accumulated between buildings; routine repairs were delayed; shot-out street lights were not replaced; and junkies and winos camped in abandoned buildings. Once again, the residents felt abandoned (Martin, 1986).

By 1986, more than 90% of the families in the Courts were headed by women, and more than half the residents were children (Vaughn, 1986). Unemployment soared to more than 80%, although the overall rate for the county was about 4%. Despite the crackdown on crime, about 200 robberies, assaults, and other crimes were reported annually in the area (McClain, 1986, p. 20A). In preliminary meetings, a special task force appointed by the mayor acknowledged "getting residents involved ranks even higher than crime as the project's top priority" (Conn, 1986).

Children faced difficulties in public school. "The children from Piedmont Courts are behind before they begin," their principal explained. "While other children start school armed with numbers, letters, and basic reading skills, those from Piedmont Courts walk into kindergarten never having opened a picture book. They can be very independent, but those are not necessarily the skills needed in learning to read" (Morell, 1986, 13A). After months of study, the Mayor's Task Force on Piedmont Courts identified the lack of effective parenting skills as a significant problem (Todd, 1986). The task force recommended that "A program to teach parent-infant education skills should be designed and implemented. Parents who enroll their children in programs designed for parent-child involvement must participate in these programs with their children, as opposed to using the program as an alternative baby-sitting service" (p. 33).

Renovations begun in 1987 took eighteen months to complete. Although the Housing Authority had a waiting list exceeding 1,600 applicants, ten of forty buildings were razed to reduce density (Maschal, 1986; Martin, 1987). The remaining 242 apartments were gutted and rebuilt from "floor to roof" (Martin, 1988, p. 1B), at a cost of $5,988,000, or $20,000 per unit ("Piedmont Courts," 1985). The police reinstated foot patrols to control drug peddling and use. The residents, united by two elders of Seigle Avenue Presbyterian Church, organized to "control their own destiny" (White, 1991), and they adopted the motto, "Working together works." One participant commented, "A lot of people believe that public housing residents are hopeless. We proved them wrong" (Valentine, 1991).

THE CHURCH

The histories of Piedmont Courts and Seigle Avenue Presbyterian Church are inextricably entwined (Bigger & Dunlap, 1995). Although the church was not officially constituted until November 1945, its ministry began in 1941 with recognition of the need to serve the residents of Piedmont Courts. That summer, 234 children attended Vacation Bible School in a tent across the street from the housing project. During the fall, Sunday School classes were organized in homes. It soon became evident that there was a need for a church building, which was subsequently established as a chapel outpost of Caldwell Memorial Presbyterian Church, a thriving, middle-class congregation ("History of Piedmont", circa 1946). Despite wartime shortages, a cinderblock building was constructed and dedicated on April 14, 1946 (Brockmann, 1962; "Dedicate New," 1946). For several years, this building served simultaneously as sanctuary, educational building, and manse (pastor's residence) (Trotter, 1947). The first minister was Rev. C. A. Harper.

A new sanctuary seating 300 people was built for about $30,000 ("Seigle Avenue," 1949; "Church plans," 1948) on land donated by local business leaders (McGill, circa 1948). The pastor, Dr. R. S. Snyder, solicited donations from friends across the country, prompting the sobriquet "Church of a Thousand Memories." Ground was broken on Armistice Day, a fitting tribute for a church serving veterans ("Ground Broken," 1948). A glossy photograph shows the cornerstone being laid by seven middle-aged and older, solemn, white men dressed in conservative business suits—no women were depicted ("Hold Service," 1949). The first worship service was celebrated on Christmas Day, 1949; and the new sanctuary was dedicated on January 1, 1950.

The Snyder Memorial Building for social and educational purposes was dedicated to the memory of Dr. Snyder in 1959 ("Church to Dedicate," 1958). The new sanctuary, the Snyder building, and the old education building comprise the current campus. In 1956, a three-bedroom manse was built about two miles away.

The transient nature of the neighborhood forced the church to depend on financial aid from the Presbytery and other local churches. This assistance supported a professional staff consisting of a minister and a director of religious activities. Regular events included Sunday School classes, morning and evening worship services on Sunday, choirs for children and youth, youth fellowship, a weekly prayer service, scouting for boys and girls, and a women's auxiliary which organized social groups called circles. In the 1953–54 annual report, an unidentified church historian noted, "We had tried having an afternoon circle for two years, but it was not successful, as most of our women work, so this was discontinued—the members joining evening circles." The building was also used to offer a well-baby clinic staffed by the Mecklenburg Department of Public Health, as well as the Sunshine Day Nursery, sponsored by the Charity League.

The church reached its peak in membership of about 350 in the early 1960s ("Myers Park's," 1974). Some members began to talk of the church's becoming self-supporting. Ray Gardner, Clerk of the Session for eighteen years, reports that this was an enticing idea because it meant no longer having to justify budget requests or to submit to annual evaluations by the local Presbytery (personal communication, November 6, 1992). However, after considerable discussion, the church officers decided that, because the community was impermanent, the church would always require more resources than membership alone could provide. During the period, church archives highlight events of middle-class life: children's choirs and activities, weddings, anniversaries, scouting accomplishments, scholarship awards, and family nights featuring fried fish dinners.

The slogan for the Snyder Building fund-raising campaign was "No man stands as straight as the one who has stooped to help a boy!" This maxim aptly captures the attitudes of the time. There was little stigma associated with residence in public housing, and residents and church workers were indistinguishable. Both were members of the dominant race; and, if residents were not yet middle-class, they were quickly working toward that goal.

In the year following integration of the Courts, church membership dropped to 255 (Lawrimore, 1966). Many white families who had retained allegiance after moving from the neighborhood opted to transfer their membership to other churches. This trend continued until only a small core of white members remained.

As a few black children began to trickle into the Sunday School and weekday programs, the remnant began to question how the church could minister to an integrated community. Church officers debated whether to move the church to the suburbs. After agonizing over honest differences of opinion, they ultimately elected to maintain an active ministry to black and white alike. Edith Gardner (1992), one of the first members of the church and the first woman elected Moderator of Mecklenburg Presbytery, remembers, "They reaffirmed the original purpose for which this church was founded—to minister to the Piedmont Courts community" (p. 2).

Myers Park Presbyterian Church began a tutoring program at Seigle Avenue in 1965, and within five years sixty-one adults were providing weekly sessions for children at the church. During this period, Margaret Bigger began to work nearly full-time as a volunteer liaison between Myers Park and Seigle Avenue churches. "When I came on the scene to tutor in 1965," she said, "white flight was rampant." By 1968, when she took over the tutoring project *Each One Reach One*, the flight was as obvious in the surrounding community as in the Courts. "Of the eight churches in the neighborhood when Piedmont Courts was all white, only two remained: the Salvation Army and Seigle Avenue Presbyterian. I was told that some of the remaining seventy members at Seigle Avenue vowed that until the Lord told them to close the doors, they would stay open." Unfortunately, most of those members were working full-time or were too elderly to be active except on Sundays (personal communication, July 15, 1993).

The primary strength of the pastor, Rev. Bill Stewart, was to prick the conscience of the white community. Bigger remembers this as "the frightening 'Burn, Baby, burn!' period of social unrest and violence, when 'integration' was a dirty word in southern, white communities" (personal communication, July 15, 1993). Bigger recalls that Stewart shamed complacent pew-sitters in the Presbytery into facing the problems of poverty and social injustice.

At Stewart's request, Bigger and Danny Verner, both members of Myers Park Presbyterian Church, organized a weekly coffee break for mothers of small children. A Baptist circle held a morning preschool program for two hours while the mothers socialized. From this small beginning, the Mothers Club evolved. (And many of the original members—now grandmothers and great-grandmothers—still meet monthly!)

Bigger recalled an early outing: "We planned to eat a meal at the airport restaurant, since we thought this facility would be accustomed to serving all races," she explained. "Two of the white mothers took me aside for a 'private word,' and my heart fell. Although we had agreed that Christian love could overcome racial barriers, I was afraid they were unwilling to appear in public with their black sisters. Instead, they said they were frightened because neither had ever eaten in a restaurant" (personal communication, November 13, 1992).

According to Bigger, the integrated group set an example for a city. "They showed people who were marching, shouting, and picketing that a calm, direct approach worked better." Members of the Mothers Club frequently wrote letters and sent delegations to the city and county officials, the Housing Authority, and the Model Cities program. The "Mothers Club Bridge," constructed across the creek between Piedmont Courts and Alexander Street Neighborhood Center, is one lasting result of their perseverance (personal communication, July 15, 1993).

In 1966, the church began the Hot Meals for the Elderly Program. Participants referred to themselves as the "Ever-Ready Club" because they were "ever ready to eat."

In 1969, the Mothers Club identified the lack of medical care as their primary concern and asked Model Cities to establish a medical clinic at nearby Alexander Street Neighborhood Center. The plan was rejected by the Department of Housing and Urban Development; however, civic leaders, led by volunteers from Myers Park Church, were not daunted. After two years of intensive effort, the Center was renovated and a clinic opened there with two physicians in July 1975 ("Neighborhood Medical," 1975).

Despite these efforts, the congregation of Seigle Avenue Presbyterian Church ultimately lost more than 200 members ("Seigle Church," 1970; Simpson, 1979). By 1974, membership had dropped to 64 ("Myers Park's," 1974). By 1979, visiting children and youth substantially outnumbered members. Average attendance on Sundays was thirty-five to fifty; and forty percent of the membership was black (Gaultney, 1979). Those providing funding questioned the viability of the church.

In order to maintain its mission of service to the Courts, Seigle Avenue Church renewed and strengthened its long-time partnership with the large, suburban congregation of Myers Park Presbyterian Church (Long Range Planning Committee, Seigle Avenue Presbyterian Church, 1983). Volunteers from Myers Park and other churches in the Presbytery continued to supplement outreach activities of the dwindling congregation. With this influx of additional energy and increased financial assistance, new programs were established to meet the current needs of the neighborhood (Gaultney, 1979). A leaflet from that period lists fourteen activities, including a breakfast program, boys' and girls' clubs, an after-school activities program, a tutoring program, and a summer program for youth.

Elder Edith Gardner calls the time from 1972 to 1985 "the period of community organization and trust building" (1992, p. 3). The church continued to offer a hot lunch program for forty to sixty elderly residents of the Courts. Charlotte Area Fund operated Eastside

Neighborhood Center at the church; and Central Piedmont Community College provided adult education in the Snyder Building. The Mothers Club delivered their monthly newsletter, *Mothers' Invention*, to every household in the Courts. They also held clothing exchanges four times a year. Apparel collected at Myers Park Church was available for exchange or was sold to residents for small sums that financed Mothers Club activities.

Rev. Robert Morgan assumed the pastorate in 1972. Morgan enjoyed community organizing and pastoral care. The church was constantly short of funds, and his repair skills kept the buildings standing and the van running.

Even the church was not immune to crime during this period. Although a burglar alarm system was installed, thieves repeatedly broke into the Snyder Building to steal food designated for the hot lunch program (Fischer, 1983; Williams, 1983).

The church continued its tradition of Christian Education with a full-time white female director, Mary Carol Michie, who provided programs for children ages five to thirteen. In 1979, a full-time male youth worker was hired to provide programs for teens. Richard Campbell, a former athletic coach with the public school system, was the first African American staff member. He organized tutoring, Bible study, recreation, and field trips, including a basketball league called "Full Court Press Against Crime." Later, after two trips to West Africa, Campbell established *The Akwaaba Drumming and Dancing Band* in 1991 ("Drumming and Dancing," 1992).

The second African American employee, Ann Cassells Bradley, began her involvement in 1974 as a volunteer in the children's afterschool program. A single mother and a resident of Piedmont Courts, Bradley obtained her Graduate Equivalency Degree and a two-year technical degree in early childhood education while she worked part-time for the church.

Despite the employment of two African American workers, this was a patronizing period. Membership continued to decline, reaching a low of 60 in 1985. Many of those enrolled rarely participated, and typical Sunday attendance ranged from five to twelve people. Of the six elders on the Session, only one, Bradley, was black and a tenant (Session Annual Statistical Report, 1985).

The black staff were indigenous workers who served as role models for the community; however, race, education, income, and class separated most of the church workers from the residents. Following the example of the War on Poverty, outreach activities were aimed at children, plucking them from their families for participation in middle-class experiences. Services were *given to* residents and the community, not *conducted with* them. Even the pastor succumbed to despair (Borden, 1985). After more than thirteen years in the pulpit, Morgan left in 1985, and the church embarked on a two-year search for a replacement.

The interim period between pastors was propitious. At a planning meeting on October 11, 1992, members of the congregation identified several events that changed the direction of the church and the neighborhood. First, the church proffered an African American female role model. The Rev. Brenda Tapia, an ordained Presbyterian minister and founder of the Love of Learning Program for African American Youth at nearby Davidson College, led Bible study on Wednesday evenings during the winter of 1986. Rev. Tapia often wore professional clothing; but even when casually dressed, she never entered the kitchen where most of the women gathered. If kitchen chores were not finished when she arrived, she read her Bible and waited patiently. Many residents had never seen a professional black woman outside of the welfare office, and they were inspired by her example.

The second significant event was the establishment of the Mothers Academy, by STEP (Strategies to Elevate People) and five local churches, in cooperation with Central Piedmont Community College and the Charlotte Housing Authority. The Mothers Academy offered comprehensive high school completion courses for women of the Courts.

Twenty-four women enrolled in the Mothers Academy the first year, and they met five mornings each week in the administration building. Some participants were able to obtain their high school diplomas by studying only four basic courses; those who were functionally illiterate had to take each course more than once. The director and teachers pushed and pulled, encouraged and challenged. When a student missed a session, the director went to her apartment to find out why. When someone experienced success, no matter how small, the director celebrated. Each student had a personal tutor and friendship team from a local church to help her identify and realize her goals; and annual graduation exercises were major community events (Bigger, 1988).

The Mothers Academy spawned literacy and self-confidence, and it also nurtured relationships. Prior to the Academy, women raised their children in isolation reinforced by turnover, arbitrary placement by the Housing Authority, and fear. They did not participate in the supportive kinship network identified by Stack (1974). The Mothers Academy brought women out of seclusion, introduced them to each other, and fostered friendships among them. Mothers were inspired to emulate Rev. Tapia by developing their own human capital. Ultimately, fourteen women obtained their high school diplomas during the two years of operation. When the program ended, all the women who wanted to earn diplomas had done so. Some went on to continue their education at the local community college.

The third significant event was the arrival of a new minister who derived meaning from the other events. Rev. Charles Summers had served as pastor of an urban congregation in Washington, DC, and more recently as chaplain of Davidson College (McClain, 1987). He came with the intent of empowering the neighborhood. When asked about problems faced by the church, he described the work of the congregation, "But we do not do it as outsiders who come into a neighborhood. We do it as a congregation who together are experiencing these problems. . . ." (Tarr, 1991, p. 34).

Summers motivated church members with a six-week study of the McKnight article, "Why servanthood is bad" (1989). For the first time, residents grasped the power available to them, and others began to comprehend the dangers inherent in helping. Residents who participated in this study applied its message by re-establishing the tenants' organization.

Under Rev. Summers' leadership, the congregation grew to 133 members—balanced by race, gender, and economic status—by June 1993. Of the eight elders elected to the Session in 1992, five were African American and three were Caucasian (Session Annual Statistical Report, 1992). Four were tenants. Youth work continued to be a major thrust, but families were incorporated into every program; and the needs of white youth were also considered.

THE PRESCHOOL COOPERATIVE

Seigle Avenue Preschool Cooperative was founded in 1987, while the church was in transition. Both staff and members recognized the need to provide more and better services to preschool children and their parents; however, they also realized that the church could not afford substantive new programming. The Director of Christian Education, in consultation with leaders at Myers Park Presbyterian Church, obtained a seed grant of $21,004 for the project from the Junior League of Charlotte (Matthews, 1987).

Weiss (1988) divides early intervention programs into two types: flagship and fleet projects. The flagships are characterized by a few dozen, university-supported, research demonstration projects, while the fleet consists of numerous small, fledgling, community-based operations. Seigle Avenue Preschool Cooperative is a ship of the fleet. Critical program variables as specified by Weiss (1987) are described below.

The first monies—$3,000—were spent to renovate the second floor of the original cinder block church building. This space had not been occupied since the Model Cities program was disbanded, and it still sported 1960s bright orange and neon green colors. Walls were moved to create two classrooms, a library, and a fourth area that doubled as an office and small storage area. During the second year the wall separating the classrooms was removed to create one larger space for team-teaching. All rooms open off a wide hall running the length of the building. The toilet occupies one end of the hallway, near the foyer leading up from the first floor. The entire area was painted soft beige. A mural featuring characters from the children's television program "Sesame Street" was added at children's eye level; and the worn linoleum floor was replaced with tough, brown carpet. The bathroom was cleaned and its walls papered in cheerful primary colors. New tables and child-sized chairs were purchased, and a Board member spent the summer collecting toys at attic sales. Members of Myers Park Presbyterian Church donated books and additional toys. When the preschool opened on September 21, 1986, the cabinets were replete with equipment and supplies, but there were no African American toys or books.

The preschool operates under the auspices of an eighteen-member volunteer Board of Directors, which includes two parent representatives and a member of the Junior League. Board members are recruited from a variety of fields, including law, social work, early childhood education, family relations, government, and finance. Board members are expected to work.

The Board maintains a symbiotic relationship with the church. The church pastor and the director of Christian education serve in an *ex-officio* capacity; and an elder is a voting member. At the time of this report, the lead teacher and the first parent coordinator are members of the church. Whenever possible, the preschool and the church cooperate on community activities.

A primary responsibility of the Board is fundraising. Since the building cannot meet state codes for licensing as a daycare center, no public monies are available; and operating expenses must be raised annually. Board members write grant applications, obtain financial support, and organize fundraising activities. The Board also supervises the director, approves major policies and procedures, disseminates information about the preschool, and supplements programming as requested.

The preschool developed a mission statement in the fall of 1991. It lists three objectives that the Board agreed to pursue vigorously:

1. To prepare the children for successful entry and performance in the public school system;
2. To provide a forum in which parents can receive the information, resources, and opportunities necessary to find solutions to common problems; and
3. To support the children and their families as they advance through the public school system.

The preschool began with two staff members, both classroom workers. For the first four years, substantial costs were underwritten by the Junior League (Boulware, 1990). United Way of Central Carolinas funded a position to monitor children's entry into public school in 1989, and a parents' initiative was established by the Foundation for the Carolinas in 1990.

Other major donors include Myers Park Presbyterian Church, the St. Francis Fund of Christ Episcopal Church, WBTV Children's Charities, The Blumenthal Foundation, Two Cents A Meal (Presbytery of Charlotte), the Good Samaritan Foundation, local churches, and individuals. These are well-respected local agencies, and their support lends credibility to the preschool (Halpern & Lerner, 1988).

The program is entirely dependent upon donations, since students pay no fees. The operating budget for 1992–1993 is $70,591, of which $59,498 covers salaries.

In 1992, there were five staff members; however, only the director was full-time. Part-time staff included a lead teacher, classroom aide, school liaison, and parent coordinator. The director and the lead teacher were white, middle-class, and college-educated, while the other staff were African American. The school liaison and parent coordinator spoke freely about their experiences as young mothers dependent on welfare, while the classroom aide came from a working-class background.

The paraprofessionals on the staff illustrate the strengths and weaknesses of lay workers as delineated by Halpern and Lerner (1988). They share a culture; and, because they are one step removed from a peer relationship, they serve as positive role models. They reach out to form "a trusting, relatively unbounded relationship with families," but their social distance inhibits exploitation and burnout (p. 196).

Maximum enrollment is eighteen children, ranging in age from three to five years. In the classroom, the staff/pupil ratio is 9:2, although this number is frequently supplemented by caregivers and volunteers.

Since the second year of operation, teachers have used the High/Scope curriculum, developed by the Perry Preschool Project in Ypsilanti, Michigan. Longitudinal research indicates this is an effective curriculum for low-income, disadvantaged children (Berreuta-Clement, Schweinhart, Barnett, Epstein, & Weikart, 1984). High/Scope focuses on language skills, self-control, following directions, planning and problem-solving, working independently and cooperatively, and completing assignments. The preschool complies with standards set by the National Association for the Education of Young Children (1986).

The preschool operates from 8:30 until noon, Monday through Friday, on days that the public schools are in session. At parents' request, children begin their morning with a simple breakfast. Originally, this was served in the Snyder Building; however, parents were concerned that instructional time was wasted while children donned coats and traveled to the preschool building. Consequently, folding tables were attached to the outside walls of the hallway. Breakfast is served here, and tables are folded flush when the area is needed for other activities.

After eating breakfast and brushing their teeth, the children join a circle on the floor while new materials and concepts are introduced. Together they plan their daily activities around centers or work stations. Each center is designed to foster specific skills. The corner with wooden blocks develops planning skills, fine and gross motor coordination, and cooperative play. Children who play "house" practice appropriate family roles, plan menus, develop language skills, and explore career options. Other centers feature puzzles, painting, crafts, and games. Centers are frequently rotated so children have new activities to explore and master. After a mid-morning snack, children engage in group games which develop gross motor skills. In pleasant weather, they play outdoors. In inclement weather, the hall becomes a racetrack for "big wheels," balls, and wagons. The program ends at noon. Because the building does not meet daycare codes, the schedule cannot be extended.

Caregivers are an integral part of the program. Most are mothers, although grandmothers, aunts, fathers, and even an uncle have sponsored children. Generally, mothers were teenagers when their children were born. All are African American and most have less than a high school education. Caregivers participate for one or two years, depending on whether their children enroll at age three or four.

Adult activities are scheduled every day, and a meeting room has been furnished especially for caregivers. Minimal conditions for participation include attendance at two meetings each month, working in the classroom twice per month, and participating in regularly scheduled home visits conducted by the preschool staff. In addition, caregivers must deliver and pick up their children on time, and they must assist their charges with daily homework assignments. This cooperative component precludes participation by employed parents.

Since the program began, official requirements have not changed, but the program has evolved as Halpern predicts (1990). Founders of the preschool misjudged parents' abilities. Because they did not consider parents capable of governance, they did not invite them to Board meetings. However, they assumed that parents possessed classroom skills. It took only a few sessions to realize the flaws in this reasoning: First, caregivers had definite ideas about program design. They needed an appropriate forum in which to communicate their concerns and wanted to attend Board meetings. Second, caregivers were reluctant—even fearful—of classroom participation, since most had only negative experiences in public school. Third, most caregivers were unfamiliar with requisite classroom skills such as appropriate use of praise, redirecting misbehavior, and rewarding small gains. Eager to help their children, they tended to "over-parent." The lead teacher explained, "Over-parenting is a corollary to pride. The mothers do not like to see their children fail, so they correct them constantly, often harshly. They give the child no room to learn on his (sic) own" (Dickens, 1989, p. 33).

During the second year of operation, caregivers were encouraged to attend Board meetings. A formal parents' program was initiated during the third year. Ann Bradley, working halftime for the church and halftime for the preschool, persuaded the Board to begin a daily program specifically for caregivers. The initial program was patterned after the parent training programs of the sixties and seventies.

Bradley began with Motheread, a literacy program initially developed to teach incarcerated mothers how to share time with visiting children. Motheread introduced books that spark parent-child interaction. Caregivers first read a book together. They anticipate questions children might pose; and they discuss their own responses. Many of the books feature African American characters.

Motheread quickly evolved into a weekly support group. "It helped me to understand this little boy better," said participant Madge McSwain, holding her son. "I understand myself better" (Minter, 1990).

Over the next two years, Motheread became ReadUp, and the entire caregivers' program evolved into a family support program. Currently, this component is considered as important as the children's program, and activities are offered every morning. Generally, programs are suggested by caregivers and arranged by the parent coordinator. Programs run the gamut from educational meetings to arts and crafts projects. Often community agencies such as the Charlotte Drug Education Center are invited to present workshops on topics of mutual interest; and often the mothers arrange field trips for themselves. Since the budget for the caregivers program is limited, participants occasionally organize fundraising events. Their favorite endeavor is the community fish fry, through which they raised more than $200.00 in 1991.

The preschool added daily homework assignments in 1991. Through this activity, teachers attempt to increase cultural continuity by involving caregivers in the homework process (Leichter, 1978). Since many caregivers do not have access to school supplies, the necessary equipment is assembled by parent volunteers, usually in brown paper bags.

One homework project may span several days. For example, on the first day, parents might be asked to help their children select pictures of favorite foods from magazine pages sent home that day; parents are also asked to talk with the youngsters about their choices. On the second day, parents receive safety scissors so children can cut out their favorite pictures. On the third day, parents get brightly colored paper and glue so the children can practice pasting. Finally, on the last day, crayons enable parents to label the cards as directed by the child. Teachers prominently display the completed assignments in the classroom, praising the children for effort and commending parents for successful oversight of the project. When necessary, usually at the beginning of the year, they carefully explain to parents that any attempt by the child is better than mastery by the parent. Homework becomes a valuable tool for shaping parental expectations and reinforcing parents as experts for their children.

A school liaison continues to work with families whose children "graduate" from the preschool and enter public school. She monitors each child's classroom performance, takes the caregiver to school for lunch with the child, and, if problems arise, serves as an advocate and intermediary.

The caregivers program has evolved because the philosophy of the program has evolved. Informed and fertilized by the same events which shaped the church, the preschool has moved from a "doing to" to a "doing with" philosophy.

CHAPTER 8

Participants

Each year in August, the family coordinator visits every eligible family in Piedmont Courts to invite caregivers and their children to attend Seigle Avenue Preschool Cooperative. The initial visit is followed by a colorful flyer. Finally, all interested families are invited to attend a reception and open house at the preschool during the annual Piedmont Courts Day festival. Through these efforts, every family with preschool-aged children is encouraged to participate.

Eighteen caregivers selected Seigle Avenue Preschool for the 1992–1993 academic year. According to agency records, this number is typical. No records indicate how many families have chosen other options such as Head Start or YMCA daycare; and there is no information about families who have declined preschool education for their children.

This chapter describes the fifteen participants active at the end of the 1992–1993 year. It describes nine caregivers selected for participation from earlier cohorts and recounts the method by which they were selected for participation. Finally, it addresses payment of participants.

FOCUS GROUPS

During the academic year, I refrained from asking probing questions, for fear of altering the process. At the end of the school year, focus groups were organized to elicit information about the preschool experience from the active members of the current cohort.

The focus group format was chosen for several reasons. First, caregivers were accustomed to meeting together each week, and this format was a natural extension of their required group sessions. Second, I was concerned that individual interviews might introduce a new, confounding experience. Third, caregivers had developed the level of trust and intimacy necessary for exploration of sensitive issues. Fourth, I expected group discussion to trigger synergy. Fifth, I determined that the more loquacious participants would serve as positive models for the more reserved.

This reasoning proved correct, and the focus groups yielded a rich, complete data base. The groups were also an efficient method of collecting large amounts of information on a variety of topics.

Fifteen caregivers were active during the last month of school. All were invited to participate in one of three focus groups, and all agreed. A copy of the letter soliciting participation and informed consent is included as Appendix C.

To facilitate discussion, I asked the staff to recommend groupings of compatible caregivers. Their recommendations were used to assign caregivers to particular groups. This was a fortuitous step, for it revealed interpersonal dynamics not previously apparent. These observations are discussed in the next chapter.

The focus group protocol is included as Appendix D. Groups met on the last three consecutive Wednesday mornings before the final day of school. No staff members were present. Beverages and breakfast sandwiches were provided, and the activity of eating seemed to help caregivers relax and converse freely. Several commented that they enjoyed the process. Each group was talkative and all sessions lasted the entire three hours allotted for discussion.

Sessions were recorded using a microcassette recorder. The presence of the recorder did not appear to distract the participants or inhibit their conversation.

DESCRIPTION OF THE CURRENT COHORT

At the end of the year, fifteen caregivers, all mothers, remained active. All were adolescents when their first child was born, although their current ages ranged from 22 to 33. Two mothers had only one child each; four had two children each; seven had three children each; one had four children; and one had five children.

Twelve caregivers had joined the program at the beginning of the academic year or early in the fall. Three did not become active until spring, although they had been eligible to participate in the fall. Six attended the preschool parents' program during the previous year, and one had attended in 1986. At the beginning of the academic year, none of these caregivers were attending school or employed outside the home.

INDIVIDUAL INTERVIEWS

The second phase of the study involved case studies of former participants. Information was gleaned through individual interviews. When the study began, the preschool had been in operation for seven years, with a stable staff and curriculum for the last six years. After the second year, there were few modifications or additions to the parent component of the program, and each cohort had similar experiences and opportunities.

One mother, Karen, had participated for the past three years, and she vouched for the constancy. "It's just a matter of getting used to different faces, different people." Lily, who had participated for two years under two different family coordinators, agreed.

The total population was limited to an annual enrollment of about eighteen people. For convenience, caregivers from previous cohorts were referred to as "graduates"; however, there was no official termination ritual for caregivers. Current and former staff were asked to review class rolls and identify individuals who made outstanding contributions to the preschool during its first six years of operation. The staff generated a list of ten names. These people were contacted by letter and invited to participate. A sample of the letter soliciting participation and informed consent is included as Appendix A.

Nine of these ten graduates agreed to participate. They were interviewed in random order over a three-week period. At the conclusion of each interview, I asked the respondents to recommend others whom they thought had done an outstanding job at the preschool. This technique produced exactly the same list of ten names, ensuring confidence that the sample represents the population of successful graduates.

DESCRIPTION OF THE GRADUATES

The nine graduates included eight women and one man. To ensure the confidentiality of all respondents, names have been changed and this paper refers to all as female. Other identifying information has also been deleted.

Originally, the research design specified that respondents would be residents of Piedmont Courts; it was felt that caregivers who had left the Courts could not substantially influence the community. As it turned out, two participants had never lived in Piedmont Courts. Because both were key players in their cohorts, they were retained in the sample.

Of the nine graduates, seven completed their work with the preschool in the spring of 1992, a year before they were interviewed; and two completed their involvement in the spring of 1990, three years before they were interviewed. Six graduates attended for two years, while one participated for only one year. The remaining two participated for three and four years, respectively.

Patton (1990b) states that "There are no rules for sample size in qualitative inquiry" (p. 184). However, Lincoln and Guba (1985) recommend sample selection to the "point of redundancy" (p. 202). This was achieved.

A sample of the protocol used for the individual interviews is included as Appendix B. As with the focus groups, each interview was taped with a microcassette recorder, but this did not seem to inhibit conversation. Caregivers in the first focus group eagerly told members of the community about the event, so that the others knew what to expect before I arrived. All nine welcomed me graciously, and they richly described their experiences.

PAYMENT

Although Jorgensen (1989) questions the exchange of money in research, for all subjects in this study the most valued reward was a tangible one that indicated their worth. Therefore, caregivers were paid $15.00 each for their participation. This figure was calculated from a base rate of $5.00 an hour, although in practice the individual sessions ran only about two hours. Participants agreed that this was an attractive and appropriate sum.

CHAPTER 9

Data Collection

Entry into the field involves two steps: negotiation with stakeholders for permission, as described in Chapter 6, and physical entry into the research setting. This chapter describes my physical entry into the field and the process of participant observation that followed. It also presents my personal background, discusses issues of difference, and explores my admission to the group.

ADMISSION INTO THE FIELD

The second phase of entry involved physical admission into the setting for collection of data. One way to gain entry is through sponsors. Sponsors must be known in the community as people who are legitimate and credible. They must be able to cross both worlds, at least to some extent; and they must engender trust.

Two sponsors were available and willing to assist in this investigation. They were Marsha Summers, lead teacher in the preschool, and Ann Cassells Bradley, family coordinator when the research began. Summers had been employed at the preschool for five years and she had earned the respect of caregivers through her interaction with their children. Bradley had worked with children and their parents in this community for more than fifteen years. A single mother who matured in this neighborhood, Bradley was a strong role model; and she too was highly respected by caregivers. Both Summers and Bradley supported the research and were willing and able to serve as sponsors.

ISSUES OF DIFFERENCE

Substantial efforts are required to achieve an understanding of the symbols, categories, and concepts that organize the everyday life of a family. "This is true both when the underlying assumptions of the family are different from those of the researcher and, in different ways, when the underlying assumptions are difficult to uncover because they are shared by the researcher and the family" (Leichter, 1984, p. 30).

To disregard the meaning of the situation for the subject is to risk invalid conclusions. "Significance of much of the behavior taking place in a given social setting *can* be understood, *provided* the observer has participated in the given setting in roles similar to those taken by the participants and is a member of or has had extensive experience in the subculture in which the setting occurs and from which the actors come" (Bronfenbrenner, 1979, p. 31).

Since I am a middle-class, well-educated white woman, and the program participants were disadvantaged African American women with limited formal education, issues of difference were present. They spanned values systems, patterns of behavior, linguistic styles, and "Weltanschauung" or world view, as Davidson and Jenkins predicted (1989). However, issues of difference did not impair the research effort. They provided the essence through which the culture of Piedmont Courts was understood and interpreted (Wolcott, 1980).

Because of my previous experience in the community, I was able to assume a social role which allowed me to function within the culture of the observed (Bruyn, 1963). Only in interactions involving humor or comedy did I have difficulty understanding meaning. (My husband affectionately points out that I would have this problem in any culture.)

PERSONAL BACKGROUND

One reason differences did not impede was because I was already a tangential member of the system. Although I did not know the individual caregivers in the study, my initial entry into the setting was facilitated by my long and active affiliation with Seigle Avenue Presbyterian Church and the Preschool Cooperative.

In 1984, I transferred my membership from Myers Park, a large, prosperous, suburban Presbyterian church to Seigle Avenue, where, for six years, I served as Clerk of the Session. As such, I was responsible for recording all the transactions of the governing body and for maintaining membership rolls. I participated in the founding of the preschool and was a charter member of the Board of Directors, serving as chair in 1989–1990 and as recording secretary in 1990–1992. My primary duties have included fundraising and planning. In the early years, I helped to develop policies and procedures as a member of the personnel committee.

Through these activities, I accrued both referent and expert power which contributed to the mutuality of the current research project (French & Raven, 1959). I was familiar with the stated goals and objectives of the preschool, and I was cognizant of the theoretical underpinnings that shaped these goals. As a member of the Board of Directors, I was acutely aware that there had been no formal evaluation to determine either the extent to which the goals were being implemented or the extent to which the implementation was successful in accomplishing the stated mission of the preschool. I did not need to develop a research persona, for I had already made the transition from stranger to friend prescribed by Everhart (1977).

Familiarity had both advantages and disadvantages that were opposite sides of the same coin. Patton discussed this in terms of unity and separation (1990b, p. 269). I was sufficiently a part of the situation to be able to understand what was happening; and, since I was a familiar person, my presence did not create undue disruption. However, I often ran the risk of over-involvement.

THE PROCESS OF PARTICIPANT OBSERVATION

Saleebey (1989) cautioned that even simple queries posed at a critical juncture can alter process. Since my overarching goal was to observe the natural unfolding of the caregivers' program in a grass-roots preschool, I asked few direct questions of staff or participants. Instead, I learned about the other participants they way they learned about each other—by listening, by watching, by socializing informally, and by working conjointly on assigned tasks and projects.

During the required meetings, I often wanted to make a suggestion, offer a comment, or draw on my experience to propose a solutior When the family coordinator asked the group for ideas about speakers, 1 wanted to suggest people I knew in the professional community who could contribute to the group. I refrained in order to avoid influencing the process.

The challenge was to maintain a fruitful tension between personal involvement and detachment, learning from experience and experiencing the learning. To this end, Peshkin (1988) recommended systematic analysis of subjectivity throughout the research process. Regular self-monitoring helped me develop a more complete understanding of the phenomenon and the process.

My ability to maintain a dynamic tension was established through prior professional training and experience. In addition to the master's degree in social work, I hold the master's degree in school psychology, and I am certified by the National Association of School Psychologists to administer, score, and interpret psychological tests; to conduct home and classroom observations using a variety of formal techniques; to evaluate adaptive behaviors and social skills; to counsel families; and to oversee behavior management programs. For six years I practiced these skills in elementary schools in the Charlotte-Mecklenburg school system.

This opportunity gave me a firm grounding in social work, education, and psychology; and consequently I was familiar with diverse educational programs, complex neighborhoods and community systems, and varied individual capacities. I developed a disciplined self-consciousness which emphasizes one's self as one's tool. The scientist's role as a research instrument seemed a natural extension of this canon, for through this experience I had acquired the skills that Borman, LeCompte, and Goetz (1986) identified as necessary to avoid subjectivity.

The resulting combination of skills, knowledge, and values enabled me to deploy both detachment and personal involvement in my role of participant-observer. Although I often discussed my experiences informally with colleagues, I did not need extensive de-briefing.

ADMISSION TO THE GROUP

Because I knew many of the key players and had been involved with the preschool since its inception, I expected to be welcomed as a member of the current cohort. Instead, I was initially treated as an outsider. I was acutely aware of the social distance between myself and the caregivers, especially when visitors deferred to me rather than to the family coordinator.

At first, I also assumed that all the participants knew each other. It was only after several weeks of introductory rituals that I realized others also felt isolated. Few caregivers could recite the names of the other participants.

By Christmas, I had attained a marginal position in the group. When caregivers planned surprise gifts for staff, I was excluded from the discussion; however, I did not receive a gift, either.

Immediately after the holidays, there were three deaths—one caregiver's companion, another's infant daughter, and my own best friend. All died suddenly and unexpectedly. I was included as group members rallied to console each other; and I knew I had gained acceptance soon after these events when members of the leadership group prepared a "plate lunch" for me.

A major test of my acceptance came in the spring when a caregiver attempted suicide. I was the only person present who was trained to deal with such a crisis, and the staff implored me to intervene. Since this was potentially a matter of life or death, I automatically moved into my role of social worker, called the mental health center and emergency room, and transported the caregiver to the hospital.

I worried that my transition from observer to professional might disrupt the reciprocity we had finally achieved, but it did not seem to affect my participation at all, either negatively or positively. The caregiver publicly thanked me for my efforts several times, but she also thanked other caregivers who had helped. Neither she nor the other caregivers changed their approach to me after this incident, so I concluded that it did not have a negative impact on the investigation. Perhaps the transition would have been more disruptive if it had occurred earlier in the year.

Affiliation with the group was reinforced by establishment of a reciprocity model through which caregivers also benefited from the research. Patton (1990b) stated that participants may acquire a sense of importance, useful feedback, or pleasure from the interactive process (p. 253). Since this project was designed to build on caregivers' strengths, it depended on willing cooperation and the honest exchange of information. It was crucial to establish and maintain rapport, mutual trust, respect, and an appreciation of individual and group differences. This approach enabled participants to know they were contributing to the research effort; and it engendered self-worth and a genuine desire to help. I knew I had successfully achieved reciprocity when, during one of the focus groups, a caregiver thoughtfully inquired, "And what has this group meant to you?"

The following chapters present my findings and conclusions after eighteen months in the field setting.

CHAPTER 10

Salient Program Features

If you want to move people, it has to be toward a vision that's positive for them, that taps important values, that gets them something they desire, and it has to be presented in a compelling way that they feel inspired to follow.

Attributed to Dr. Martin Luther King, Jr.

The parent program at Seigle Avenue Preschool Cooperative was the setting for action. The following sections describe the program and begin to identify salient features that appear to promote empowerment. The first section presents factors that attracted caregivers to this program rather than to another in the neighborhood. In the second section, the parent program is delineated in detail. The third section describes the subgroups that emerged among participants. Section four explores the roles and attitudes of staff who administered the program and the board, which oversaw it. The final section addresses programmatic barriers to empowerment.

ATTRACTING PARTICIPANTS

Both parent training programs and family support programs have been plagued by problems of attrition (Weiss & Jacobs, 1988). Since participation precedes change, the first questions in the study addressed caregivers' attendance at the preschool.

Residents of Piedmont Courts can send their children to any of three nearby preschool programs: Seigle Avenue Preschool Cooperative; an on-site daycare center operated by the YMCA; or

Double Oaks Head Start. Most of the participants had considered each of these options, and they clearly articulated the features that informed their decision to enroll their children at Seigle Avenue Cooperative. These fell into two categories. Programmatic factors prompted initial parental involvement; child-related and personal factors sustained the decision.

The Initial Decision to Participate

Caregivers recognized their children's needs for preschool education. Faye explained, "I knew she needed some sort of advance before she really started school." Ann agreed, "I felt it would help her out as she was growing."

The majority of those who chose Seigle Avenue Preschool cited convenience and location as their primary considerations. It was important to them that they could walk to the preschool if there were an emergency. Of the twenty-four participants in the study, six added that their children were too young for Head Start or that Head Start had a waiting list.

Word of mouth was an important source of information about the preschool. Half the participants noted that this program was recommended either by a neighbor or by Ann Bradley, the parent coordinator who lived in the Courts at the time. Bradley was well respected by the residents, and her suggestion carried substantial weight.

Dana reported:

> I thought I was not going to like that school because the teacher told me that she didn't work that closely with the kids as far as making them learn their ABC's. I felt I would give it a try anyway, and if my daughter doesn't like it, then I will take her out. When she came home the first day, she did not want to go to sleep. She was so anxious to get up and go to school the next day, and she loved it so much that she motivated me. She made me want to get up and take her.

Initially, most caregivers were reluctant participants. Maggie explained:

It took me a while to get adjusted because I was like petrified and terrified. I was like, 'Oh, God. Look at all these people. I don't want to come in here and start up a conversation and somebody be talked me down.' But you know, once I started coming over and got to know everybody. . .

Lily finished Maggie's sentence, ". . . It was A-OK! You felt you was home."

Sustaining Attendance

Given their initial discomfort, caregivers were asked what held their interest. They all said they continued to attend because they could see immediate benefits for their children. Their attention was held by interesting activities and, for some, by public recognition of their contributions to the program.

Benefits for children

Caregivers quickly noted that their children *enjoyed* the preschool. Most were amazed that the children responded so rapidly to the program. Hope, one of the most reserved mothers in the current cohort, described her son's reaction:

He done learn a lot! He opened up—he was real shy. He wouldn't talk to nobody. I mean nobody! So he opened up. He run a lot. And he likes books. He draws circles. It's a lot that he done learned here that I really didn't think he could do. And it didn't take but two days and he started opening up!

Dana described her daughter's response:

She really likes to go to school. She likes to learn and she likes the way she is being taught. If we wake up late and it is too late for her to go to school, she will cry. She wakes up on Saturday and Sunday and asks if school is out today. "I wanted to go to school, Ma."

Marlette echoed this sentiment. "Bobby liked school. He would wake me on Saturday and say, 'Mama, I'm going to school!' Andrea concurred, "Even when Dionne is sick, he be crying to go to school."

Shontay explained, "I didn't think Yolanda would take to it, 'cause by it just being me and her at home all the time, she don't be around a whole lot of other kids. When she came up here, it was just like she was at home with them."

Martha summarized the situation, "You know, if you place your children somewhere and they seem to be happy there, it will make you feel like being there too."

Benefits for adults

Personal factors also played an important role in early decisions to participate. Caregivers enjoyed the structure afforded by the preschool, and they liked being active. Further, they began to relate to each other through the required parent meetings. Ebony described her experience, "And when we have those meetings, everybody just be so comfortable and talk about everything. Like everybody just know everybody. It makes you feel good."

REQUIRED COOPERATIVE ACTIVITIES

In order for their children to participate, caregivers were required to attend two parent meetings each month, volunteer in the classroom at least one day each month, and transport their children on time. Parents remembered participating in a variety of different activities.

Judy's list is typical. She attended parent workshops and luncheons, and she chaperoned field trips, gymnastics classes, and music lessons. In the classroom, Judy recalls that she told stories, read, organized games, and supervised the housekeeping center. In addition, Judy helped with "fish frys," fund-raising events organized by parents to pay for their activities.

Most caregivers enjoyed the classroom activities. Kim recalled, "I loved that preschool. I was over there every day before I started going to school myself to get my GED [Graduate Equivalency Diploma]."

Maggie expressed similar sentiments. "Once you get inside that classroom with the children, the only thing they want is attention. Once they get your undivided attention, them the best children. It really gives you pride."

Three mothers in the 1993 cohort did not like the classroom requirement. Shontay was afraid she could not control her temper. "I'm the type of person I will not bite my tongue. I'll beat her butt right in front of the classroom. And then if someone say something, I'll be ready to jump on *them*."

Dana had similar comments. "I just cannot go into the classroom. I went one time and left. It is not because I am not interested in my daughter. I just don't have the patience for so many kids. I found myself wanting to scream at another person's child."

In general, the caregivers who avoided the classroom did not know how to manage small groups of children clamoring for adult attention. They were uncomfortable because they did not know how to redirect or discipline the children effectively. They would rather drop out of the program than face the challenge of the classroom.

Caregivers who expressed a strong aversion to the classroom were continually encouraged to attend, but the staff did not insist. To enable these caregivers to fulfill their classroom requirements, the lead teacher assigned projects they could complete at home. This usually involved assembling homework bags or preparing curriculum materials. Caregivers appreciated the alternative arrangements, and they did not appear to take advantage of this concession. None of the others complained about this special attention.

THE EMERGENCE OF SUBGROUPS

Staff groupings for the focus groups suggested that the cohort was actually an amalgam of three distinct subgroups, and the group interviews confirmed this hypothesis. (Since one parent was employed and did not attend required meetings, she was not included in this categorization.)

The Leadership Group

Five participants comprised the leadership group. They were Maggie, Lily, Karen, Marlette, and Andrea. These mothers consistently exceeded the minimum requirements for parent participation. They assisted in the classroom regularly, and they chaperoned most field trips. They consulted the family coordinator to discuss personal concerns, and they usually orchestrated special events and holiday celebrations.

The Followers

The second group, the followers, included Frances, Marline, Hope, Jessica, Joanne, and Ebony. These caregivers were more tenuously attached to the cohort. Although they fulfilled their minimum requirements each month, they attended less regularly, and they tended to be more critical of the preschool. Some of their charges were well taken, however, and their suggestions helped to improve the program.

The Uncommitted Group

Jean, Shontay, and Dana joined the program late in the year and they remained uncommitted to it. Each had participated for a portion of the previous year, so each understood the services available and the requirements entailed. Yet, their involvement was erratic. They fulfilled monthly obligations only because staff made allowances for them. They attended special events but did not help organize or prepare.

The uncommitted caregivers were preoccupied with the exigencies of daily living—food, rent, transportation, and their own moral development. Further, there was some suggestion of substance abuse. This group seems to support Bronfenbrenner's (1974) contention, "The conditions of life are such that the [disadvantaged] family cannot perform its child-rearing functions even though it may wish to do so"(p. 48).

THE ROLE OF RECOGNITION

The three subgroups demonstrated different levels of attachment to the program. The leaders were easy to identify. They enjoyed being with the children and they were active in the classroom. Andrea, a regular helper, found the experience rewarding, "I feel like when I go into the classroom, if I can just teach one child to do something that day, that boosts up my self-esteem." Jackie explained the role of the leaders in the classroom. "You have an opportunity to work with the kids as if you are part of the staff."

The leaders also took charge of the extra-curricular events such as parties and fund-raising activities. Planning was begun during business meetings, and all caregivers were invited to contribute; but the leaders orchestrated the festivities.

For the leaders, attachment was reciprocal, and they often offered support to the staff. Maggie frequently wrote notes of encouragement to Carrie, the parent coordinator. She remembered a morning when they were listening to singer Whitney Houston on the radio. Both began crying: "She in one end of the room and I in another—I don't know what we were crying for now. She said, 'Maggie, you mean so much.' And I was wondering why she was saying that. I guess whenever I was down I would come to talk to her."

Although the pacesetters turned to the staff for help with personal problems, they asked for little public recognition. In fact, they flourished on benign neglect, requesting only transportation to the grocery store and money for emergencies such as the two funeral meals they prepared.

The followers were tenuously attached to the cohort. Although they had strong bonds with each other, they did not coalesce as a unit or seek action as a group.

The individuals in this category needed and wanted public recognition—both from their peers and from the staff. Joanne spoke for Ebony and Marline when she explained, "Somebody has something to say if you are not here, but when you are there they don't have anything to say." These three realized that Carrie had been less involved herself immediately after Christmas, and they associated her attitude with the overall drop in attendance.

Occasionally followers were assertive, and their complaints and suggestions helped to refine the program. More often, however, they did not speak openly with staff or leaders; and their needs were often unmet. For example, members of the leadership group asked Frances to post signs advertising the event. The day was cold and rainy, and Frances was drenched as she walked the length of the complex. When she returned, one of the leaders accused her of doing nothing. Frances felt unappreciated, but she did not correct the leader. Instead, she withdrew from the group for a while; and the staff did not seem to notice her change in attitude.

The uncommitted participants were not attached to the cohort. They disliked the classroom and were suspicious of group events. Because they were concerned with activities of basic survival, they asked for practical assistance paying rent or obtaining services. Although they demanded large investments of staff energy and time, they eschewed public recognition.

Jackie described the uncommitted parents as "trifling." She said, "'Trifling' is a person who just won't do nothing. They won't even wash they own hand and face. They take from what the rest of them give." Jackie continued, "They are always complaining, but they don't never do nothing. They don't want to participate, but when something come up big, they get their money out of it." She concluded, "I feel like nobody can help them. They have to help themselves."

Martha agreed, "I just felt like some parents didn't care—they used it like a babysitter or to get rid of their children. It don't be the child's fault, it be the parent's. They just don't give a damn."

THE PROGRAM FOR CAREGIVERS

Once children were enrolled, caregivers were required to attend two meetings each month. In the fall, meetings were held every Wednesday, and parents could select two of the four. Since this system hindered group process, record keeping, and the exchange of information, it was later changed. Beginning in March, only two official, required meetings were held each month; however, the family coordinator still planned activities for every Wednesday, and caregivers were encouraged to participate regularly.

The Parlor

Parent meetings were usually held in the church "parlor," a charitable term for a much worn room with cast-off furnishings from several sources. The cinder block space measured 20'x 25'. Walls were a dingy cream color much the worse for wear and tear, and the wooden ceiling was stained a dark brown to camouflage exposed heating ducts. There were two windows, but they admitted little light and no air, being sealed against theft. In the winter, the room was cold; in the summer, it was very hot.

At one end of the room, two wooden tables were joined to form a long surface surrounded by straight chairs. At the other end sat two low sofas and an easy chair. Once considered "modern," they were tattered and oozed stuffing. The remaining chairs were wooden. There were two carpets on the floor: one was light gold and the other was dark gold. Both were obviously remnants cut in different shapes, so in some places one color was evident, and in some places, another. This parlor was the site for the required parent meetings.

The Curriculum

Each required meeting included a business session, a formal program, and discussion time. The Ruth Bowdoin curriculum for parent training was used erratically all year. In the spring, most meetings also included a ReadUp segment through which parents were introduced to new books they could share with their children. Twenty required meetings were held in 1992–1993.

Both family coordinators eschewed long-term plans. When I first began observing in the spring of 1992, I was astounded to learn that Ann rarely planned more than one week in advance; Carrie continued this pattern. Since I know few professionals who could speak to a group on less than a month's notice, I assumed that they would never be able to mount an effective program. I was wrong.

The family coordinators wisely used the content of one week to plan for the next. For example, when someone complained about the breakfast menu, Carrie asked a nutritionist to address the next session. When Lily decided she wanted to go to work, Carrie called in a job counselor. Over the course of the year, she scheduled the same topics I might have arranged; but I would have planned them far in advance. The difference was empowering; my schedule would have come out of my need for structure; hers evolved from the needs of the participants.

Rituals

Carrie used rituals to promote affiliation and teach new skills. She opened each meeting with an exercise called Positive Comments. Each caregiver was asked in turn to say something positive to the person on her right.

At first, Carrie modeled the initial statement with eye contact and a general comment such as "I'm glad you came. You make my day with your smile." Caregivers often had difficulty responding to each other, and this exercise gave them a much-needed opportunity to practice social skills in a non-threatening environment. In the spring, Carrie delegated responsibility for Positive Comments to the leaders in the group. This honor further empowered, encouraged, and rewarded participants.

Carrie often ended the required meeting with another ritual: Together, the group recited, "I am a little angel with one wing, but *together* we can fly." At first, caregivers seemed reluctant to speak out, but by the end of the year, they recited the adage enthusiastically.

Motivational Speeches

Through motivational speeches, Carrie addressed common problems. For example, in the second meeting, she presented a parable that captured the philosophy of the caregivers' program. Carrie explained:

> Geese fly in formation, led by a leader goose. Followers encourage the leader by honking. When the leader gets tired, she falls back a little way and other geese surround her. The followers flap more vigorously so the leader can rest on the air currents until she is ready to resume the lead.
>
> If a goose becomes sick or tired, other geese join the tired member to help and encourage her. They stay with her until she can rejoin the group or until she dies. No one is left alone in the formation.

The caregivers listened to this story with rapt attention. They referred to it throughout the year, especially when they felt close to one another or when they felt threatened or disturbed.

Guest Lectures

Most of the speakers were African Americans. Some were members of the professional community, and they came with prepared remarks on such topics as personal safety or drug abuse prevention. Others speakers were middle-class citizens who told of their struggle to escape poverty.

The final guest, Board member and former Charlotte Mayor Harvey Gantt, was well known as the first African American to attend Clemson University. However, most speakers were average people who wanted to contribute to the community. Denise Rowan, a computer consultant, captured the spirit of their mission. "When King was assassinated, I remember seeing people who turned their backs. I vowed not to be one of those people, but I was. You have given me a chance to come back," Denise said as she thanked the group.

Gray and Wandersman (1980) stated:

Hopes for one's children may be universal, but in many ethnic groups there are distinctive values their members would be reluctant to abandon. The problem for the program planner is how to enable parents and children to move into the cultural mainstream if and when they desire, but at the same time be able to hold on to the valued aspects of their cultural group. (p. 996)

The African American speakers were especially important as role models. They also brought concrete evidence that caregivers could escape welfare dependency, and they demonstrated how caregivers could accomplish their goals without violating their African American culture.

Physical therapist Pam Mullis illustrated this process. After discussing the need for personal responsibility, mutual aid, and community action, Mullis stressed the strong heritage of African American women:

In the Fellowship Hall, I was looking at pictures of black leaders who have gone before and paved the way: Sojourner Truth, Harriet Tubman, Martin Luther King, Jr., Malcolm X. . . . And the leaders of the future are here: Andrea, Jessica, Lily, Karen, Joanne, Dana, Hope, Maggie, and Ebony.

When the mothers realized Pam was calling their names, they became excited. "That's me! That's me!" they buzzed as they exchanged glances. They seemed inspired by Pam's public recognition and her confidence in their abilities.

Caregivers listened carefully to speakers. Many had never seen middle-class African American women other than those working in the welfare office. Jean and Hope were touched by women who understood their plight in life. They took their advice and found that it worked, "If you really try." Jessica acknowledged the didactic and emotional content of the presentations saying, "The speakers give good advice, telling you how to cope with your kids and life and building you up so you can do better."

Business Sessions

The business portions of the meetings were designed to empower. Marsha Summers, lead teacher for six years, observed that their format paralleled the High/Scope curriculum used with children. Both children and adults are taught to plan, act, and reflect. The business meeting provided the opportunity for formal planning and reflection by the group, as when they selected discussion topics or organized a party.

Business meetings also offered an opportunity for caregivers to influence the program, as the following incident illustrates.

At the conclusion of each session, a door prize was given to someone in attendance. Door prizes were chosen from donations to the preschool, and the supply of items for adults was limited.

In March, Joanne received a child's toy as a door prize. Disappointed, she confronted the staff at the next business session. She had practiced her speech all week, and she delivered it calmly and assertively:

> I want to talk about what happened last week. You know, all the other times when we be getting a door prize, they be for the parent. I been waiting and waiting for my name to be pulled, and it never was. And then last week, someone finally pulled my name, and I was so excited! I was jumping up and down. I wanted to get something for *me*.
>
> But Carrie said I had to choose between two *toys*! And they was *nothing*. The children been playing with them while we was meeting, and I never thought they were for parents. They was just little things you pick up for the chaps when you are out shopping.
>
> The parent gift should be for the *parent*, not for the kids. My child gets toys. This should be my turn!

This was the longest speech I had ever heard a caregiver utter, and it was followed by stunned silence from the group. When the director responded, she seemed defensive at first as she explained that toys helped children learn. Other parents agreed with Joanne, and the director began to negotiate. Joanne maintained her position.

After discussion by the group, the director conceded without making promises she could not keep and without confusing their roles. "We might not always have prizes for adults, but we do have enough to award an adult door prize for the rest of this year. Is that acceptable?" By giving participants the final say, her response was again empowering.

Other Activities for Caregivers

In addition to the required meetings, the preschool celebrated five holidays: Halloween, Thanksgiving, Christmas, Valentine's Day, and Graduation. Each special occasion included a meal prepared by caregivers and a program, usually of games and awards. Caregivers were also encouraged to participate in the fish fry and attic sale held in the fall to raise money for parents' activities.

Field Trips

Carrie organized regular field trips. The favorite destination was a shopping center. Bus service from the Courts is extremely difficult because it always involves a transfer downtown. Field trips provided transportation and an opportunity to shop without having to tend to several children at the same time.

Faye particularly enjoyed the field trip to the African American Cultural Center. Although this facility is located less than a mile from Piedmont Courts and charges no admission fee, Faye and many other caregivers had never been there. Faye recalled the event. "We learned about ourselves and our history. We had a good time. We really had a good time. Them memories will always be there."

Arts and Crafts

Arts and crafts days were also regularly scheduled. Although participants enjoyed these sessions, the finished products rarely looked finished to my middle-class eyes. I realized that most caregivers had never examined samples of the items they were creating, and they had no internal models to emulate. For example, no one knew how to cut a valentine with an inner heart that could be lifted to reveal a special message. No one had seen a Christmas door wreath made of fresh greenery.

The arts and crafts times were special because they allowed participants to explore topics of general interest. During the Valentine session, Marline described her decision to have a child at age nineteen, and the group discussed birth control methods, toilet training of boys, discipline, and church attendance.

Spontaneous Activities

Caregivers were empowered by the staff in less formal ways as well. Caregivers were encouraged to contribute ideas, which staff then helped them implement. The lending library provides the most striking example of this approach. Terry wanted to start the library, so the staff solicited books from the Junior League and Myers Park Presbyterian Church. Then Terry and others organized the books and developed a checkout system still in use three years later.

Staff offered opportunity and assistance when asked, but they did not direct an activity or even offer specific suggestions. For example, when one caregiver's daughter died, the director, Cynthia Bailey, suggested that the group comfort the family in any way they could. When caregivers asked, she agreed to take them shopping for food for the family, but she left entirely to parents the responsibility for grocery lists and all details. It was this facilitating without directing, encouraging without controlling, that seemed to give mothers confidence, for it allowed them to practice new behaviors in a safe environment.

STAFF ROLES AND ATTITUDES

The success of a family support program often depends not on program content but on the staff's ability to deliver that content. Staff can make or break a program. According to Weissbourd (1987), community workers can be particularly effective staff members because they share the culture of the participants. They serve as models of people who have successfully mastered the system—often against great odds. Since they are familiar with the community, they can extend networks, broker services, and identify families in stress.

Halpern and Larner (1988) found that the qualities which made lay helpers successful include flexibility, sensitivity, and the worker's sense of herself as a woman (p. 123). These authors stress that the goal is to establish a comfortable relationship marked by intimacy and reciprocity, but not necessarily by peer relations.

Slaughter (1988) adds that staff attitudes must include self-respect, enthusiasm, the belief that people can and do change in positive ways, and a desire to be part of that change. Finally, staff members must demonstrate camaraderie and a shared commitment to the program.

These qualities and attributes accurately depict the staff of Seigle Avenue Preschool Cooperative.

Role of Staff

To determine the role of the staff in the process of empowerment, participants were asked, "Who helped you?" Then they were asked to describe how that person helped. Jennifer responded:

> The staff. There is nothing they don't care about. They pay attention to everything. They can be talking to five people, but they pay attention. There is nothing they won't do for no one. They will help you in any way they can.

Several caregivers commended the breakfast cook, Wilma Petty, a resident of Piedmont Courts who also serves as a role model for the mothers. Joanne said, "I like the way she talks to the kids, and I like the closeness they have gotten with her." Marline expanded, "She know who don't like eggs and who don't like grits." Joanne concluded, "That is important. When the person that is feeding your child cares, she cares!"

The entire staff assumed a variety of roles as needs arose. They were available to talk both formally and informally. Sometimes they provided advice and practical assistance; and they often counseled. When necessary, they were not afraid to act on behalf of a caregiver. Jean explained her relationship with Connie, the school liaison, "I could talk to her about anything and she'll listen to me, and then she helps me."

Staff recognized their own limitations and the limitations inherent in the preschool. When appropriate, they referred caregivers to other agencies for needed services. For example, when a caregiver's infant died, the director immediately called KinderMourn, a local agency that provides bereavement counseling for parents. KinderMourn provided counseling for the family, staff, and participants, and the director made certain that messages were delivered, transportation was arranged, and written materials were copied and distributed.

Although staff developed strong bonds with caregivers, they did not appear to be possessive of these relationships. Rather, they encouraged participants to connect with other agencies within the community and across town. When caregivers formed friendships with their teachers at the local community college, for example, staff did not display jealousy. They rejoiced at the extended networks that were established.

Role of the Family Coordinator

Bronfenbrenner (1979) and Edelman (1986) maintain that children need to have a stable caregiver. The same principle appears to be true for parents. Like their children, caregivers in this study needed a stable, dependable mentor or guide. They needed someone with whom they could try new behaviors with impunity, a person with whom they could laugh, cry, tease, fight, rebel, reconcile, and love. In this setting, the family coordinator was that person, and it was not surprising that she was most often identified as the helper.

From the inception of the position until 1992, Ann Bradley worked in this capacity. Ann was a resident of Piedmont Courts. She began her career in human services as a volunteer at the church. When the preschool was established, she accepted a job as a classroom aide. Ann knew firsthand the barriers that families face, and she convinced the board that children could be best served by strengthening their families.

In 1992, Ann resigned to accept longer hours in a similar position sponsored by the YMCA. However, she continued to direct the after-school program at Seigle Avenue Presbyterian Church, and she was available to consult with Carrie Shropeshire, who assumed the position of family coordinator at the beginning of the 1992–1993 academic year.

Ann Bradley had served as family coordinator for all the program "graduates" in this study, and Carrie fulfilled this function for caregivers in the current cohort.

Shontay explained the need for a family coordinator:

> There's a lot of pressure and tension in the neighborhood. The things that we are going through, the problems that we got, we don't really know how to go about solving. So we go to somebody that's older and that's been there. And they can sit us down and just be square whether we want to hear it or not. Them's the best ones to talk to 'cause people, when you go to them, tell you what you want to hear—tell you what you want to hear, but you don't need to hear. I already know that. Tell me something I don't want to know. Tell me the truth.

Caregivers knew Ann would listen to their concerns. Faye described Ann's approach. "Well, if you had a problem, you could go to her and talk to her about it, and she would sit down and say, 'Faye, you should do this.'" Whether or not she agreed with the caregiver, Ann would respond honestly. According to Nancy, Ann always told people both the positive and negative aspects of a situation.

Ann often refereed spats among the participants. Again, Faye described her experience:

> If she see that we were mad, she would talk to us. She could tell when we were mad or had tension on us. She would say, "Y'all come in here and let's talk now. I feel the tension on y'all. I can see it in your face."
> She would talk us out of being mad, and we would sit there and laugh. She made us feel happy and welcome and stuff. She didn't make us feel like we were wasting our time there.

Ann did not show anger herself. Faye continued, "Ann wouldn't blow up at you. She was there for us." Jackie agreed, "Ann don't get angry or blow off. She is still calm like ain't nothing ever happened."

When needed, Ann provided practical assistance, especially transportation. She learned to drive and even purchased a car so she could take caregivers to important appointments. But Ann's primary emphasis was on education, and she was persistent. Kim described the role Ann played in her return to school:

> Miss Ann kept saying, "Kim, go back to school!" I said, "I'm *not* going back to school!" She said, "Yes, you is. Just watch and see. I am going to see that you go back to school."

Everyday, Miss Annie would come to my door and say, "Kim, I know you are in there. Come out." She will come in and look at me until I say, "Okay." So I didn't have no other choice but to go to school.

Both Ann and Carrie believed in the cause they were representing, and neither was afraid of rejection. Often they had to approach a caregiver many times before an offer was accepted. Carol was the beneficiary of Ann's determination, and her story is typical:

I could be asleep and she would come get me up. "I thought you were going to do this!" "I thought you were going to do that!" She really pushed me. It made me feel confidence in myself because she told me I could do it.

According to Carol, Ann would not stop pushing her until she tried to help herself:

She would say, "Carol, you are a go-getter. You can go be *doing* something right now." She put the pressure on me everyday. So one day we were in a parent meeting and some parents asked for somebody to come do the GED. I know I needed the help and I accepted it.

Nancy shared a similar experience:

Ann stuck by me from thick to thin. She said, "If you don't come, I am going to come and get you. I am going to wake you up. You are going to get over here [to class]." If it hadn't been for her, I would still be home sleeping, and that's the truth!

Ann provided information, but more importantly, she encouraged. Through her example, caregivers learned to believe in themselves and have confidence they could succeed. Nancy discussed her personal epiphany:

Before you were ready, Ann was there. She pushed you and told you what was available. She say, "Nancy, you got the potential. You got it! Won't you use it 'cause I know you got it? Don't let nobody try to bring you down saying you ain't got this and ain't got that. You got it!"

So I thought about it about a week and I told her I was ready to go to school.

Above all, Ann was dependable. Nancy explained, "When you ask her to do something for you, she will be there. If *you* ain't there, she will come looking for you."

Ann served as a role model for everyone. Terry called her an "inspiration." Jackie explained her influence. "I used to be by myself all the time." Then she started associating with Ann. "She is an active, talkative person, always talking to people and trying to get them in programs and stuff. It was a gradual change for me. You be around something, and you eventually start doing it too."

Though Carrie had been with the preschool only a short time and was just beginning to learn the neighborhood, she had a profound effect on caregivers in the current cohort. The mother of a retarded adult daughter, she had previously worked as a house parent in the group home where her daughter lived.

Like Ann, Carrie was a good listener, a role model, and a mentor. Ebony elaborated on Carrie's approach:

> She knows where you at, where you been, and what you going through, 'cause she says she has been through the same things. She know how it is in Piedmont Courts, how the income is, how the situation might feel. You have the feeling she has been there. It is one word that describes it all: care.

Often, Carrie responded discreetly and nonverbally to concerns. Joanne says, "She know when I am feeling bad. She won't just come up and say, 'Joanne, I know you feeling bad.' She will just give me a hug and I know that feedback was for my needs."

For several caregivers, it was important that Miss Carrie never criticized anyone in public. Marline noted that Carrie maintained her confidentiality: She takes you out and talks to you privately. She don't discuss your business all out. If you got a problem, she will discuss it in the parent meeting, but she will say it in a different way. She won't bring your name straight out.

Sometimes caregivers railed at preschool rules. Maggie commented, "If it's something making you mad or upset, and it has made you want to flip, Miss Carrie always got a way to turn that flip around." Andrea expounded, "She can be playing with you and be serious at the same time. She might say, 'Andy, what's wrong with you?' and laugh. When that happens, I say, 'I don't know.' I want to know, but I don't know."

The current cohort agreed that Carrie provided information, comfort in times of trouble, and honest feedback. Further, she never appeared to get angry either. Maggie described her attitude toward work and life, "She takes her job serious, and she wants parents to do their responsibility, but she's got a 'joy pocket.' She is always happy, always smiling."

Perhaps because she was more removed from the neighborhood and had more work experience, Carrie was better than Ann at interpreting preschool policy. Caregivers knew when Ann disagreed with a decision, although she counseled them to accept the decree. In discussing the staff decision against allowing non-graduating children to wear caps and gowns in the graduation ceremony, Dana explained, "And then, Ann said for us just not to worry about it since it isn't going to be their last year anyway. So we didn't."

Carrie's position was more difficult to determine as she responded to a similar question the following year:

> You don't get to wear a gown and march when you finish eleventh grade. That's a special event for seniors. It means you have completed this part of your education. It's the same way with preschool. You can't wear a cap unless you are *graduating*. You don't get to march just because you are leaving.

Marline pleaded, "But my child is going to Head Start and they don't have caps and gowns. I want him to march. He'd be so *cute!*"

Carrie did not back down an inch as she reported the staff decision. "All the more reason to keep him here!"

It is clear from these excerpts that the family coordinators empowered caregivers at all stages in the process. They inspired confidence, pushed reluctant learners, opened opportunities, welcomed feedback, encouraged practice, preserved dignity, and affirmed success.

The family coordinators had more difficulty when they were asked to present prepared curricula materials such as the Ruth Bowdoin series on parent-child interaction. Carrie dutifully handed out books and encouraged parents to read them, but she rarely prepared an interesting lesson using these materials.

THE ROLE OF THE BOARD

The Board of Directors was ultimately responsible for the operation of the preschool. Each year, two parents were selected to serve as parent representatives to the board. These caregivers were usually elected by their peers. Once appointed, they were assigned to board committees and encouraged to present regular reports on parent activities at the monthly board meeting.

Each cohort found fault with some element of the preschool program. The current group objected to the breakfast menu and they were concerned about contaminated sand in the sandbox. A former group had disliked plans for a year-end celebration. Another had felt that the director was withholding money that rightfully belonged to the parent program. Several groups had objected to the graduation policies that decreed that only those children going on to kindergarten could wear caps and gowns. Each cohort used parent representatives to take its concerns to the Board of Directors.

The board would not budge on the graduation rules; however, it handled all other concerns in ways that empowered the complainants. Ebony reported on her experience, "You know the school is good, but we had to go against it to meet our needs and do what we think is right for our kids." Joanne summarized her efforts, "And it wasn't like, 'Because you all don't pay no money, you can't have no say-so.' It wasn't like that at all. It worked out ever since then."

The "Applesauce Incident" is the most famous example of board involvement. In 1992, after serving a snack, a Junior League volunteer stored the remaining applesauce in the original can. Several days later, another volunteer scooped out the now-discolored applesauce and served the remainder to the children. A mother saw the discolored applesauce, and she thought the children were being given spoiled food. She told other caregivers, and together they responded by calling the local television station. As Dana said, "I had to do what was right for my kids. Any mother would have done the same thing."

When board members arrived later that morning for their regularly scheduled monthly meeting, they were met by the media. The board chair and the executive director responded calmly. They publicly apologized for the incident and promised to remedy the situation by purchasing storage containers and instructing volunteers in their use. Then, before the rolling cameras, they praised the caregivers for doing what they thought was right for their children.

The segment was aired on the local television news twice that day, and caregivers were astonished, for they had expected reprimands and perhaps expulsion. Like others before and after them, they learned that the board is a benevolent authority established for their benefit. They were proud that they stood up for their principles, and, through the process, they learned to negotiate with the establishment on its own terms.

BARRIERS TO EMPOWERMENT

The staff and program of the preschool were not perfect, and a number of barriers to empowerment were observed. Generally, these were defined by missed opportunity rather than by obstacles intentionally erected to deter.

Despite their good intentions, the staff overlooked a number of occasions to empower. The breakdown usually occurred when staff ran out of time for group process or when money was involved. For example, parents were not included in planning the graduation exercises, a learning experience to which they could have made a valuable contribution.

Lily felt caregivers should have had more say in the field trips that were selected, particularly after the staff canceled a trip that would have cost $3.75 per person. Lily had taken this trip the previous year, and she felt it was well worth the expense. "I'm pretty sure that the parents would have come out of their pockets with $3.75 if they had known," she observed.

Since the preschool building could not meet building codes for a state license as a daycare facility, it could remain open for only three hours a day. A number of caregivers mentioned limited hours of operation as a barrier to empowerment. As Dana said, "By the time you walk down there to Central Piedmont [the community college], you wouldn't even have a chance to write your name on the paper before you be walking back up here to come and get your chaps."

Ebony echoed these sentiments, "Five minutes would help me. It would. Sometimes I need to be at the library. If I had that time, I could go to the library, do what I have to do, type what I have to type, and you know I won't have to worry about who is going to keep her." Although they did not want to take them out of the preschool, several caregivers were considering placing their children at other daycare facilities so they would have adequate time to pursue personal goals.

Finally, members of the leadership group expressed concern about the curriculum. Andrea explained, "I wish they could have taught them to write their ABC's a little earlier than they did." Lily understood the rationale behind the curriculum. "I think they was preparing them," she responded. The group nodded, but they did not appear satisfied.

An important opportunity to empower was missed by a failure to communicate. The entire year, no board or staff member explained the children's curriculum or the philosophy driving the parents' program. Parents could have been more enthusiastic supporters of the preschool if they had understood it better. This information would have helped caregivers who were trying to decide whether to place their children in other programs. By failing to explain the goals of the program, staff missed an opportunity to affirm parents as the first teachers of their children.

CHAPTER 11

Changes in Family Life

I would tell them that you *need* to participate even if you don't enjoy it at first. Do it for your children, and then if you do it for them, you will probably start enjoying it. It will stop you from doing a lot of things that were wasting your time.

Geneva Williams, 1993
Resident of Piedmont Courts

All the participants were asked what difference the preschool had made in their lives, and they responded quickly and enthusiastically. Their answers generally addressed the transition from isolation to affiliation, increased parenting skills, and improved relationships with family members and partners. Their reports are the subject of this chapter.

FROM ISOLATION TO AFFILIATION

Membership is an important aspect of empowerment, for people who are alienated are extraordinarily vulnerable (Bronfenbrenner, 1974, 1986; Saleebey, 1992). One of the most dramatic changes involved the transition from isolation to affiliation. Without exception, the fifteen caregivers in the current cohort reported that they had been sequestered in their apartments, fearful of crime and disorder, before they joined the preschool.

Isolation: The Common Condition

Ebony and Andrea shared typical experiences. Ebony moved to the Courts eighteen months ago, and she said she still did not know anybody. Andrea had been in the Courts for two years. When asked to provide the names of two emergency contacts, she could not give even one. Maggie and Andrea lived two doors from each other but had never met. Andrea explained, "I was scared to come outside. I didn't want people to see me, and I didn't want to see people. I was afraid."

Marline had developed a strategy of superficial politeness. She spoke to everybody but knew no one:

> I mind my business, but I just speak to everybody. You know, these days people will hurt you over little old stuff, so I just speak to everybody. If they don't wave back, they just don't wave back and I walk on.

Ebony did not pretend to be friendly. "I don't bother with it. I just keep on walking." Shontay adopted the same tactic, "When I first moved over here, I wouldn't say nothing. I walked right by like I didn't see nobody." Hope's comments were similar, "I can walk past. I mean, somebody can be standing right here, and I won't say nothing."

Shontay joined the program in early spring, and she demonstrated this attitude of aloofness during her first required parent meeting. She sat in a chair in the corner, almost behind the door, avoiding eye contact. She kept her hand to her brow as she stared down into her lap. Miss Carrie welcomed Shontay and asked her to contribute a positive statement, but Shontay refused. She spat, "I don't want to be here. I don't like people. I am not a sociable person."

Later, Shontay elaborated on her approach to life:

> "That is why I think I stay depressed and have an attitude like this. I don't go nowhere. I stay in the house all the time. I don't have no friends. I'm not working. I'm bored. I'm tired of looking at TV. I done seen everything on Cinemax and HBO."

The Transition to Affiliation

The Leaders

When people are brought together, they create new and unexpected patterns and resources for solving problems (Gutierrez, 1992). The caregivers in the leadership group quickly learned to work together.

They all liked to cook, and the kitchen became a focal point for their activities. I was allowed to peel and chop, so I had a firsthand view of their development. The pattern was established at the first holiday celebration, a Halloween party.

The menu was planned by the entire group at the second required parent meeting. Miss Carrie indicated that volunteers were needed for cooking and decorating, but she did not compile an official list of helpers. By common consent, caregivers self-selected for the work groups. Although no formal schedule was established for cooking, a crew assembled in the kitchen as soon as the preschool opened on the day of the party. When I arrived at around 10:30 expecting to assist, I learned that preparations were complete and the bonds of the leadership group had been forged.

By Thanksgiving, this group had taken over meal preparations. Plans were made at the required parent meeting. Each caregiver agreed to contribute food stamps or cash. A couple of participants offered to supplement the menu with favorite family dishes prepared at home. However, there was no further discussion about who would cook, for the group had been established. Maggie remembered the flurry of activity around that meal. "Now I enjoyed the Thanksgiving holiday! Those old people say, 'Too many cooks in the kitchen spoil the broth,' but you know that broth wasn't spoiled!"

By Christmas, group solidarity was apparent. A large party was held for children and adults. As usual, the staff distributed presents to each family. Then, in a surprise move, the leaders presented gifts to the staff. The gifts had been purchased secretly using funds donated by participants, and several staff members were so touched that they wept. Maggie discussed the significance of this event:

> When it comes to older adults, you gets nothing [for Christmas]. But I am growing to get out of that because this Christmas, I really enjoyed it. It was a heart-filling thing when we were all in there. Tears just came down my eyes. I was trying to hide it, but Miss Carrie caught me. She said, "What are you crying for?" I said, "I don't know." But it was the warmth. You could feel the warmth of all of us in there.

In January, one caregiver's infant daughter died when she choked on a piece of wiener her three-year-old brother tried to "share" with her. A week later, another's common-law husband passed away suddenly in his sleep. The preschool rallied around both families with comfort, support, and practical assistance.

The pain of these losses was so deep that no one knew what to say. Marlette explained, "When that [the husband's death] happened to her, I was wanting to say something to her so bad, but she had the look like, 'Don't say nothing to me!' And I really didn't know what to say." Instead of talking, the leadership group provided food. They cooked several meals together to take to the homes, and they fed the extended families after the funerals.

Before they joined the preschool, these caregivers tended to avoid trouble by walking away from disagreements. This tactic prevented trouble, but it also precluded intimacy. Lily explained, "If we weren't in the kitchen and cooking, I would say, 'Child, I like your nerve.' And you would be upstairs saying, 'Who she think she is, talking to me like that!'

In the spring, the leaders learned that they could disagree and still be friends. Although she had graduated the previous year, Jackie began to assist with the cooking, and she and Maggie got on each other's nerves at first. One morning, Jackie quibbled with Maggie's method of frying chicken. Since frying chicken is a point of honor in the South, such criticism constitutes "fighting words." Maggie laughed as she remembered the incident:

> We were all in the kitchen and I was studying fussing at Jackie. She said, 'You know something? You keep on and this chicken is going to burn up.' And a couple of pieces of it did.
>
> I continued fussing with her and then I forgot all about that chicken. It didn't burn up, but it was sure enough done. It was crisp, too!

Before the morning was over, however, Maggie and Jackie apologized and chuckled over their differences.

Because they took their cooking so seriously, the leaders would not leave the kitchen when they were miffed. Instead, they learned to talk out their differences and settle arguments among themselves.

Andrea exclaimed, "We were like a family in the kitchen, wasn't we?" Lily agreed, "It's like we were in a family reunion."

Andrea and Lily found they could be friends outside the preschool when Lily took some craft materials home to make valentines. Andrea saw the materials and asked if she could make a valentine too. Lily agreed to share, and their friendship blossomed. Andrea exclaimed, "I really had a good time!"

In the spring, Andrea felt overwhelmed. One evening, she took an overdose of medication that had been prescribed for seizures. The next day, she followed a different route to preschool. "I didn't want to be seen, but Maggie saw me and we talked and I told her everything." Maggie supported Andrea as she told the parent coordinator what she had done. Maggie continued to care after Andrea returned from the hospital. Maggie explained, "Every time I seen her walk to her door, I say, 'Hey, what you doing in there?' And then I said, 'You come over here. I'm going to keep an eye on you.'"

By the end of the school year, the leadership group had become concerned with the injustice created by the inconsistent participation of a few caregivers. Karen explained, "See, when you have the graduation, you can invite anybody you want. That is why we all chip in and buy food so it will be enough for everyone."

Lily elaborated on the problem, "Then they pack up plates to go out. We don't mind that, because we don't want no extra food. But the thing of it is, they ain't giving nothing. So they don't have no business taking nothing away."

The group handled this problem without staff assistance. Before the graduation party, Karen sent a letter to all caregivers specifying individual responsibilities. Karen defended her action, "If they don't bring anything or give anything, they will not eat none of our food, and I mean that! They will be marching right back out that door."

Apparently the letter was effective, for there was no grumbling in the kitchen on graduation day. Everyone contributed, and fewer plates were packed to go.

Members of this informal group saw their new-found intimacy extending to their children. Andrea commented, "They are closer together. They go off playing with each other. Dionne has left me plenty of times coming from the store just to be with Justen and John. And when we go the other way, it's TJ." The group hopes this closeness will continue. As Maggie said, "They could become best buddies—from childhood up! 'Man, I knowed you when you were going to preschool!' That will give them something to put up in their senior high school scrapbook.'"

The Followers

In general, the followers appeared to operate at a different developmental stage. For example, before the Valentine party, the leaders were cooking in the kitchen, as usual. The followers spent the morning sorting bags for cards, writing cards for their children, and counting cards to be sure that each child received an equal number. The leaders noticed that the followers offered no assistance and declined to decorate; and they called the followers "selfish." The followers, on the other hand, did not appear to notice that others made the party possible. They seemed oblivious to the actions that enabled them and their children to enjoy the event. The uncommitted did not assist in any way—they arrived just in time to eat.

The followers did not attend as regularly and did not form as intimate an association as the leaders, but they became friends through the program. They proudly report that they now converse when they meet in the neighborhood. Perhaps this group will become the leaders of a future cohort.

The Uncommitted

For caregivers in the uncommitted group, the first epiphany emerged during the focus group at the end of the year. Just before the morning break, Shontay volunteered her impressions of the session. She seemed surprised, "You know, I'm glad I did come to this meeting. I'm glad I came. Gives us all a chance to really get to know each other. We don't sit down and talk like this."

Hope described the group's reluctance to participate, and she agreed with Shontay, "Everybody was saying the same thing. We all glad we came 'cause, I don't know, this group here is just getting to know each other."

Shontay still mistrusts people in the Courts and refuses to refer to neighbors as friends, but she is beginning to trust people associated with the preschool:

> Because we see we all got something in common and we see each other everyday. But it's something about the people that are up here that we can sit down and talk to them. If we had to sit down

with the people in Piedmont Courts, ain't no way in the world we could have this conversation. Nice as we be talking now, somebody would be arguing or fighting or something would be said before the day was over."

Shontay suggested that her behavior outside of the group was also changing slightly. She and her neighbor Hope have become friends. "Now if I see her, I speak and hold a conversation. My attitude has changed a little bit—just a little bit." She seems to understand the reciprocal nature of friendship. "A lot of them say I'm mean—which sometimes I am mean. But once you get to know me, I'm not really mean. You just have to take time to know me, and I got to take time to know you!"

By the end of the meeting, this group had also formed bonds that may extend to their children. Before the group disbanded, Shontay lamented her daughter's isolation, "Once she gets home, she really don't have nobody to play with. I wish she could stay up here all day." Then Shontay turned to Hope, "Now I know where you stay, I might let her come up there."

The Graduates

Caregivers from earlier years also found friendship at the preschool. Kim's comments were representative:

> I learned that you can trust other people when you have a problem that is too big for one person to solve. Before preschool, I didn't know anybody over here except for one lady and her child. I stayed in the house, and when I did go out, it was just to hang out my clothes or go to the grocery store or the doctor. Preschool got me to get out and meet people."

Martha spoke poignantly about her transition from isolation to affiliation:

> Before, I was just comfortable just sitting home and being left alone. I really didn't want to be bothered with nobody. Then I started going down there, and I started enjoying myself so good. And I found out that I wanted to be around other people. I found out

I could enjoy life a lot better just being around people. I found out I could say what I felt like saying. I found out that I didn't have to worry about it as long as I was clean and didn't stink—that it didn't make no difference what I wore. These people were still going to love me anyway."

PARENTING SKILLS

Attendance at the preschool also helped parents become more aware of their responsibilities toward their children. Jennifer's comments were typical. She explained that, before she began attending the preschool, "There would be some mornings we would just lay in bed all day." Now Jennifer works full-time, but she still arranges quality time with her daughter:

> I spend more time with my child. I try to do the things she likes besides the things I like all the time. We try to go places together—we didn't used to go anywhere. Whatever she does at school, I try to push her a little further so when she goes back the next day or whenever they have the lesson, she will know more. I used to didn't play with her.

Terry expressed similar views:

> I learned a lot of parenting skills. Everybody knows how to have a child, but nobody knows how to go about being a real good parent. I learned how to discipline without hollering. I learned how to relax, take time out before I say things I do not mean. I learned how to develop a close bond with my children. I always say, "The only people you will always have forever is your children." So I make sure I keep a close bond with my daughter and son.

Shontay says she never had a childhood, and that affects her relationships with her daughter today. The oldest of seven children, Shontay was responsible for the care of her siblings, and she resents her mother for imposing this burden. She explained, "There were six up under my wings. That is another reason I am distant with children, too, because I didn't have a childhood. I was grown at four years old." Without an adequate role model, Shontay learned few parenting skills in her family of origin.

Shontay is succinct about the difference the preschool has made in her life, "I used to tell Yolanda to leave me alone. But now she'll come to me and I'll take time to listen and talk to her, so that's a start." She continued, "Now I have to read more often, write more often, and talk more often. I'm beginning to open up to my child." Later Shontay described her own response to these changes. "I'm talking, I'm smiling, and I'm laughing!" she exclaimed.

Jackie described a typical day before she became involved with the preschool:

> When I first moved here, I used to sleep all day long 'cause I didn't have to get up and go to work. I didn't have to do nothing but sleep. Get up when I wanted. If I didn't want to get up at all, I just stayed in bed. I wouldn't even leave my yard.

The preschool strengthened Jackie's ties with the neighborhood and gave her a purpose in life. Other caregivers have nicknamed her "Guardian of the Courts" in recognition of her new role in the community. Jackie elaborates on the changes she has made and shares her philosophy:

> It brought me to do more with the kids. There are a lot of kids out there that have parents, but they parents don't take time to work with them and do things with them and share with them. The children are very attached to me. They need as much attention as they can get, and they can't get it from themselves. They have to get it from somebody. If their parents are not there to give it to them, I can give it to them. And I am willing to give it to them!

Caregivers claim the required group meetings helped them learn responsibility. For them, the concept of "responsibility" includes controlling tempers and learning more effective methods of discipline. Since preschool policy forbids any form of corporal punishment, this was quite a challenge for a group accustomed to "beating butt." As Maggie said, "I learned to be able to cope with my children a little better—to be able to take the nagging two inches more." Jennifer's comments are characteristic:

> It helped me be more responsible and have a better attitude toward my children. You know, we were all talking about how not to get so angry with your child. That had helped me a lot and the conversations that they be having really helped me out. Talking back and forth with the parents, it seemed like we all had the same problems and we were all trying to accomplish them.

Several caregivers are teaching their children to be responsible by asking them to help with chores. Joanne reported, "Dionne is washing dishes. I'm not going to say how clean they are, but at least he's washing them."

One of the primary benefits of participation came from the addition of structure to family life. Because they had to be at preschool on time, caregivers learned to establish an evening routine. Maggie says, "By 8:00 everybody is out of the tub, and by 8:30, my child is in bed." Mornings also required discipline. Terry noted without complaining, "There used to be a time when I would turn over. And there are some times now that I don't *want* to get up. But you have to realize that it is something you have to do."

Ebony rises at six o'clock to get her older daughter ready for a seven o'clock bus. Then she attends to the younger children. "I will have their clothes and stuff all ready at night so I just put them on."

Andrea is still working on organization. She notes how much time it takes to be disorganized. "I don't like looking for socks—looking for the other mate. I think once I get organized it will be easier."

Most caregivers enjoyed the homework assignments. As Kim said, "I learned how to teach my children at home. I was so excited when I learned my daughter how to read!" Regarding homework, Dana said "It showed me things Mary was smart about—things I thought she could never do!"

With patient reassurance by the staff, caregivers learned that any effort by a child is better than a perfect performance by a parent. Caregivers reported that they and their children read books to each other. They also said that they talk to each other more. Frances described a typical interaction with her son. "He say, 'First, you draw a house.' Then I draw things and he will draw what I draw."

Shontay was the only caregiver who expressed a dislike for homework, and she set strict limits on her own participation. For example, when asked to walk around the neighborhood with her daughter, she refused. "I do not go to the park because it is too hot and there are too many people there. And I am not going to walk around Piedmont Courts picking this flower and that flower because I ain't got the patience!" Shontay's daughter also likes to draw. She goes to the bedroom to produce her masterpiece. Shontay responds, "I say, 'Yeah, Baby. This is pretty.' I don't even know what it is." Shontay has not yet learned the art of asking.

Relationships with Extended Families

Most participants reported they became closer to their children. Several, like Maggie, reported that they also became close to their mothers. When she first had children, Maggie lived with her mother. As she began to assert her independence, their relationship deteriorated. Recently, they have become close again. "I go to her house every weekend, and we don't be arguing anymore," Maggie explained. She talked to the preschool staff confidentially about her conflicts with her mother. "We communicate more. I say, 'Now look, Mama. There are a lot of things I need to do, but what I need for you to do is just give me a little bit of time to get this thing together." Maggie even asked her mother not to pay her rent. "I had to tell her," she exclaimed. "In order for me to learn responsibility, I had to tell my mom not to pay my rent."

Andrea also worked on relationships with her family of origin:

> I learned to release the past. I hated my family for years, especially my mother. If I didn't release the past, I wouldn't have gotten up there to see them. It took me five years to go back and visit. When I went back, I realized how much I missed my family. When I opened the door, tears fell, and I said, 'I'm home!' If it wasn't for the preschool, I would have never made it back to New York.

Relationships with Men

Caregivers were uniformly reluctant to talk about the men in their lives since this information could be used against them by welfare agencies.

The word "friend" was used to refer to a male companion. It was not clear which women were living with a friend and which had dating relationships. It was clear, however, that men are important in the lives of these women and their children. It was not unusual for a man to attend a required parent meeting with his partner or in her place, and friends frequently came to the parties.

Ebony's comments captured feelings of most of the caregivers. Her friend, Dave, spent as much time at the preschool as she did and she depended on his willingness to parent the children:

> If it weren't for Dave, Lord, Lord! Some days I can't take it. I say, 'You better take them somewhere!' He will take them out and they will ride around in the car for hours until I get—until I go to sleep or cook or whatever.

Frequently, caregivers had stable relationships with men who were not the fathers of their offspring, and this caused conflict at times. Maggie speaks for the common condition. "In reality he is not their father. They know who their father is." When the children see their biological father, they run to him and he spoils them. Maggie continues:

> That is something I cannot control. He offered me $150.00 for each of them—$300.00. I told him, "I don't need your money!" He hasn't done anything all these many years and now he wants to offer me money for them. I told him, "I don't *even* need your money."

Friends helped caregivers in a number of ways, from contributing money to the household to assisting with chores. In order to hear Lily's first choir performance, her steady friend violated his religious principles and entered a Presbyterian church. Josh, a decade older than Marline, helped her son with his ABC's. "His daddy is not around because he is somewhere he shouldn't be at." Joanne's friend took time off from work to attend a father/child celebration. She says, "If it weren't for him, I don't know where I'd be."

Maggie was impressed when a speaker told the caregivers they each needed a "BMW"—Black Male Working! She relayed this mandate to her friend. She reports, "And my financial situation, it's a little bit better now." Maggie said she knew he should be helping, and hearing the speaker gave her the courage to insist.

Members of the leadership group acknowledge the important role of men in their families. Maggie says, "A man parent needs to be involved with the children. I cannot do the man activities and be the mama too." This group would like to see the Preschool sponsor more events for the men in their children's lives. "They need to have more activities not only for the mothers, but for the fathers, too. The ones that is in the home, not just their (biological) fathers."

Both Marline and Joanne hope to marry someday in traditional celebrations. Joanne discussed her concern:

> I could have gotten married before, but I have always said that when I get married, I want it to be right. I mean with a capital RIGHT! I don't want to have to worry about no divorce, and I don't want to have to think about no separation. I want things to be *right*!

It was not surprising that women in the uncommitted group had fewer ties with men. Shontay claimed her relationships with the opposite sex have changed since she became active at the preschool.

> You may talk, but you will not get. I tell them, "You ain't going to get no [sex]! If you want to talk to me after I say that, then you will sit down and talk to me." Most of them go on about their own business.

Hope echoes these sentiments. "A relationship is not based on sex. Friendship is not based on sex." Recently a man told Hope she needed a man in the house. The father of her oldest child is in prison in another state and the father of another is married to someone else and doesn't accept his child. Hope responded vehemently, "Let me tell you something: All this stuff I got in this house, didn't no man put this in here. It came out of my pocket. So I don't need no man!"

Jean has also renounced men. Her daughter's father went to prison before he began to contribute to her support. He tells the child he is coming to get her, but Jean knows this is not possible. She states, "The only men I want in my life now are my sons."

CHAPTER 12

Changes in Occupation

The key to all the problems in Piedmont Courts is the people. If we could start motivating the people, then everything would change. A lot of people think they are doomed and there's no way out. They are wrong.

Ann Cassells Bradley, 1986
Resident of Piedmont Courts

The concepts of cultural capital and human capital are inexorably entwined with the concept of empowerment. Caregivers gain cultural capital which they translate into human capital, or economic self-sufficiency. This sequence constitutes empowerment. This first section of this chapter describes the cultural capital acquired by caregivers. The second section explores the occupational changes made as caregivers translate cultural capital into human capital. Each is illustrated by a case summary.

ACQUISITION OF CULTURAL CAPITAL

The term cultural capital refers to linguistic styles, manners, patterns of behavior, recreation and leisure activities, knowledge, and titles such as degrees (Shirley, 1986). It also involves verbal facility and general cultural awareness (Swartz, 1990). In other words, cultural capital is an individual's bank of abilities and capacities. It encompasses *Weltanschauung*, the person's total outlook on life.

The concept of cultural capital is consistent with the strengths approach. Both are based on the assumption that adult development is not completely instinctive. Both theories assume that all parents can benefit from support and reinforcement, since parenting and managing a household are demanding responsibilities (Weiss, 1987).

Caregivers in this study shared a desire for middle-class consumer goods and a better life for themselves and their children. They did not lack cultural capital. Rather, they lacked a specific type of cultural capital—the type required to obtain self-sufficiency. Outlays of time and energy enabled them to begin to acquire the type of cultural capital they needed and desired.

Acquisition of Skills

Attitudes and abilities are the currency of cultural capital. Changes in attitude were explored in earlier chapters, and they are illustrated in the case study of Jennifer which concludes this section.

There was considerable variety in the types of skills needed and acquired by caregivers in the process of reaching their goals. Chapter 11 explored gains in parenting skills and elaborated on interpersonal skills gained through friendships, preschool task groups, and improved relationships with family members and male friends. This section presents other types of skills identified by caregivers.

At the most basic level, caregivers acquired language skills. The conversations quoted verbatim in this report illustrate the language abilities of the caregivers. The need for language stimulation was vividly underscored by a cooking lesson.

As caregivers watched warily from across the kitchen, a Junior League volunteer—a white, upper-middle-class woman—showed them how to make lollipops. The volunteer tried to involve mothers by asking them to read the recipe and mix ingredients. No one offered to participate; a less dedicated teacher might have been daunted by the stony silence. But this volunteer held up a measuring spoon, as a television chef might. In a kind voice, she announced, "Add one teaspoon of flavoring." From across the room, a murmur of interest arose. "What's that?" the group inquired. The volunteer displayed a ring of measuring spoons and described their use. Someone proudly asserted, "Oh yeah, I think my aunt had one of them one time."

Through exposure, caregivers learned to label concrete items, concepts, and emotions. They learned to express themselves, even in difficult situations; and they learned to negotiate for what they wanted.

As Faye discussed some of the interpersonal skills she acquired, the role of language was clear. Faye learned to identify her feelings as part of the process of communicating with others:

> I was sort of shy, but when we all got into it, Ann, she taught us how to talk up for ourselves and stuff. And she told us, she said, "You all not going to get nothing done by just sitting around and letting one person think of everything to do." So she taught us to talk up and stuff. To share our feelings.

Frances learned to respond more assertively in parent meetings. "Miss Carrie always picked on me, and I just bent down and wouldn't say nothing much. But now, I talk back," she explained.

Hope used the language skills she learned at the preschool to negotiate with a public school teacher when she thought her older son was being mistreated. Hope said she told the teacher that her son was being singled out for punishment. According to Hope, her words helped the teacher realize she had made "a big mistake."

Sometimes the search for new parenting skills leads to other gains. Maggie and Frances reached a significant milestone when they realized they could learn from, and depend on, each other. Frances's son was whining, and Frances was frustrated. "I was fixing to choke the living daylights out of him," she exclaimed. Frances asked Maggie to intervene, and Maggie effectively disciplined the toddler. Frances marveled, "Oh, Girl, how did you do that?"

Often caregivers gained practical skills necessary for daily living in a working-class environment. Hope was most impressed by information about saving money. She was almost speechless when she realized that if she saved ten dollars a month she could accumulate $120.00 in a year. Carol learned to make a long-distance telephone call when the board chair asked her to obtain information about a field trip to a zoo in a neighboring state. At first, Carol was reluctant to tackle this new task. A volunteer demonstrated the procedure, but the line was busy, and the volunteer left without telling Carol what number she had dialed. For several weeks, Carol worried about her assignment. Finally, she decided to act. Carol said, "I told Ann, 'I am just going to get on that phone.' And I did what I had to do!"

As attendance at preschool became a habit, caregivers gained other working-class skills, including the ability to develop a schedule and adhere to it, the ability to accept supervision, the ability to follow directions, and the capacity to work on a team. Many caregivers gained skills associated with the concept of personal responsibility. Ebony explained she learned "to take control—over myself, mostly. When I know I need to do something, do it then. Don't let nobody come in and tell you it can wait."

Most caregivers made the connection between the acquisition of skills and employment opportunities. Faye described this link: "Going into the classrooms gave me skills in how to deal with kids in case I wanted to get a daycare job or other work with kids."

Not all these skills were acquired at the preschool. Classes at the community college and the YMCA provided formal education, including basic literacy and high school completion courses. As caregivers increased their repertoire of abilities, their confidence in themselves also increased.

A Case Study in Cultural Capital

Jennifer's experiences were typical of caregivers who had graduated from this program. Jennifer was about twenty years old, with one child, age four. She attended the preschool for two years. By the end of the second year, she had gained a domicile, transportation, and full-time employment with a janitorial service. Jennifer described her accomplishments:

> My life has turned all the way 'round now, 'cause I was staying with my aunt. And now, I have my own place, a car, and a job. I am going back to school in July or August. I have accomplished all my goals that I had written down on that piece of paper last year.

In order to attain these goals, Jennifer had to change her attitude and gain many skills, including the ability to set goals for herself. Jennifer said she was "nervous and scared" at first. "I didn't know how the parents was going to react to a new parent."

Jennifer knew she had a bad attitude. "I used to not be too friendly," she explained. "Sometimes I just be too scared to say something to people." She rarely ventured from her aunt's house.

"But I was tired of sitting at home, tired of doing nothing when I wasn't at preschool. And I needed money," she continued. Although she disliked her circumstances, Jennifer did realize she had the capacity to change them. Her first—and perhaps most important—acquisition was the conviction that life could be different.

Jennifer attended parent meetings, spent time in the classroom, accompanied the children on field trips, and occasionally helped cook for special events. Her favorite activity was to help the teacher prepare for class, and she proudly explained that she learned how to operate the copy machine. "I took time and did all the alphabets and ran seventeen copies of each alphabet!"

Through group meetings, Jennifer learned that she was not alone. She stressed, "The conversations that they be having really helped me out—talking back and forth with the parents. It seemed like we all had the same problems and we were all trying to accomplish them." Role models were also important, for they provided practical advice and gave Jennifer hope that she too could succeed.

Slowly Jennifer gained confidence in herself and her abilities. "I have learned that I wasn't such a bad person. I used to think that. Don't seem like I could never move towards anything," she reflected. "I'm not as bad as I thought I was. I really think I'm a nice person."

Jennifer also learned to work with others to bring about change. She joined a band of mothers who agitated for improvement of the breakfast menus.

First she signed a petition. Then, she explained, "We talked to the Board and the vice president and everybody! And now it is all right."

The staff helped Jennifer establish realistic goals and work towards them. Sometimes staff made concrete suggestions, but more often their aid was in the form of emotional support. Jennifer said the staff helped, "By being there for us, talking to us, being there when we needed them. Whatever we needed help with, they were there."

Jennifer declared that the preschool made a difference in her life because it helped her become more responsible and more dependable. She gained job skills and information about the community. Her interpersonal skills improved and she learned to "get along with people." The preschool also helped Jennifer change her attitude and become friendlier. She observed, "But I guess the more I went to the meetings, the shyness got out. I just started opening up and talking. I can go anywhere and talk to anybody. If you are standing there, I am going to talk to you."

It was this willingness to talk to others that got Jennifer her job.
She explained:

> One day last year we was just somewhere across town and I saw this
> girl with a uniform and I asked her about it and she told me. And I
> went in the next day and got hired that day and I been there ever
> since. It has been almost a year now.

Jennifer was proud of her work and the goods and services she could
purchase with her income. She planned to move from a high-crime area
to a stable, working-class neighborhood; and she hoped to attend the
local community college in order to obtain an even better job with
more money and security.

TRANSLATING CULTURAL CAPITAL INTO HUMAN CAPITAL

Cultural capital is a collection of attitudes and abilities that can be
wielded to obtain money, or human capital. According to Bourdieu
(Robbins, 1991), the very rich generally obtain their human capital
through wise investments of inherited wealth. For most middle-class
citizens, human capital is obtained through wages. The underclass often
depends on government assistance for a modicum of human capital,
which secures for them a marginal existence.

This study presumed that the underclass can have direct access to
human capital by first obtaining cultural capital. It further presumed
that the empowerment process is compete when cultural capital is
translated to human capital and caregivers become self-sufficient
members of functional communities.

The Current Cohort

By the end of the 1992–1993 academic year, twelve of fifteen caregivers
in the current cohort were clearly engaged in the process of obtaining
cultural capital. Three remained uncommitted to change.

Of the twelve, only one, Jennifer, had begun to convert cultural
capital into human capital. Jennifer had obtained steady employment,
purchased a car, and established a residence for herself and her daughter.

It is not surprising that only one caregiver in the current cohort had
achieved self-sufficiency. The preschool was founded to empower

caregivers beginning the process of empowerment. It was not established to serve working parents already earning human capital.

One aspect of this study looked at how caregivers might use an unexpected influx of money. A week after each focus group ended, participants were asked how they spent the $15.00 they were paid for the interview. The list of purchases included food or household supplies (4), school pictures for a child (3), personal items (3), transportation (2), fees for the church's annual Women's Retreat (2), toys (2), a special trip for the family (2), children's clothing (1), and household furnishings (1). Since caregivers spent money in more than one category, the total exceeds 15.

Participants reported they spent their unexpected windfall carefully. Most used the money on items they could not have afforded otherwise. The leadership group and the followers supplemented household budgets, paid for pictures or the church retreat, or took their families on outings. Members designated as uncommitted typically spent money on themselves—two had their hair styled.

In all cases where money was spent on ephemeral items such as toys or ice cream, caregivers indicated that they wanted to provide something special for their families. Like Marline, caregivers wanted their children "to have things like everybody else have."

Graduates

Of the nine graduates, seven completed their work with the preschool in the spring of 1992, a year before they were interviewed; and two completed their preschool involvement in the spring of 1990, three years before they were interviewed. Six graduates attended two years, while only one participated for one year. Two attended three and four years, respectively.

Of the nine interviewed, four had attained self-sufficiency—three in only one year. Martha and Terry were employed in the public sector, and Jackie and Minnie were earning money through their own entrepreneurial endeavors. Jackie appeared to be doing well styling hair. She was very talented, and she reported a good income "when they [subsistence] checks come in."

Minnie's means of existence were less obvious, and her route to empowerment was atypical. Since her children had been removed from the home, she no longer qualified for public assistance. She suggested that she received support from her friend and from odd jobs. At any rate, Minnie was self-sufficient, although perhaps not by choice.

Three of the 1992 graduates were still in school. Kim and Carol were working on Graduate Equivalency Diplomas, while Nancy was enrolled at the technical college to become a licensed practical nurse.

Only Judy and Faye were neither employed nor enrolled in school. Both stated that they wanted to remain at home about two years, until their youngest children entered public school—a very middle-class ambition. Faye then planned to complete her high school education and obtain a part-time job. Her goal was to make money "to afford things for the children." Faye did not mention career aspirations. Judy, on the other hand, had already completed three years of college, and she planned to return to school and pursue a career in human services.

A Case Study in Human Capital

Martha has attained self-sufficiency, and her story is instructive. At forty-nine, she was older than most of the caregivers at the preschool. She attended for three years with her granddaughter. Like Terry, she was invited by the family coordinator, and she relished the experience:

> I got some self-esteem from them. I enjoyed being around all of those other kids and looking at the difference between the children. I got to talk to Marsha [lead teacher] and Ann [family coordinator]. I got to meet new people and it made me feel good about myself.

Miss Ann pushed Martha to do more than Martha thought she was capable of doing. Martha explained, "I didn't know I could cook as good as I could. I knew I could cook well enough for my family to enjoy it, but half the things I cook they don't like—like string beans and stuff." Martha joined the cooking crew of her cohort and gained confidence and pride in her abilities. "It made me feel so good when people said, 'Oh Martha, this is *good*!' It makes you feel so good to know that you did something that some other people appreciate."

Participation in the classroom helped Martha examine career options. At first, she too thought she wanted to be a preschool teacher:

I always thought I wanted to teach children because that was what I had been doing all this time. Sitting around all those children, I saw the differences between them and I realized they didn't all act the same way. I changed my mind about them!

I looked at the difference between the other children and my granddaughter, and then I realized that some of them weren't as fortunate as we were, even though we didn't have no more than they did.

Martha decided to send her granddaughter to her father so she could obtain employment. She explains, "I just got tired of being on welfare, and I needed something to do after I stopped going to the preschool."

She obtained a position in a textile manufacturing operation. "I was so glad to go to work. I enjoy it," she exclaims. "I haven't missed a day since I been there!"

Nevertheless, Martha's legs swelled from standing all day on the production line, and it took determination for her to continue. "I had to force myself to walk on them." Her oldest sister advised her to take her mind off her troubles. Martha responded, "How can you take you mind off something when it's killing you?" She could not bend her knees, but she tried not to think about the pain. Martha continues her story, "I just said, 'Well, Lord, I got into this and I can't back down now. You will just have to help me.'"

In the past two years, Martha has been elected treasurer of the Residents' Organization and Elder of Seigle Avenue Presbyterian Church, where she also teaches Sunday School and cooks for special events. She has completed her GED and obtained employment. As a volunteer in the Community Service Center, she helped organize a city-wide celebration of the fiftieth anniversary of the founding of Piedmont Courts. Each month she edits a community newsletter.

Martha believes that the preschool is successful for many people:

Probably somewhere in their subconscious, they was wanting to do something anyway, but they didn't know how to go about doing it. They don't have nobody to talk to or trust—especially in a neighborhood like this. The preschool helps them uncover goals that were there, but hidden.

Summary of Outcomes

It is too early to draw final conclusions, but it appears that graduates identified by staff and peers as "successful" were able to acquire cultural capital while participating in the preschool. Even when active involvement with the preschool ended, most caregivers continued to pursue cultural capital through either education or employment. Caregivers who chose to focus on parenting did so with intention, not by default. All those who had not obtained employment expected to do so within two years. Finally, several caregivers had translated cultural capital into human capital, thus breaking the cycle of welfare dependency.

CHAPTER 13

The Process of Empowerment

Empowerment is an ecological theory which considers the person and the environment, including roles, relationships, resources, costs, and benefits. As defined in Chapter 3, empowerment is one of the hallmarks of a strengths perspective. Proponents of empowerment maintain that the cycle of poverty can be broken by empowering adults to change their social milieu, thereby creating a matrix in which poverty cannot survive.

Researchers have generally defined empowerment as a process, not a state. This process includes a number of non-linear, epigenetic stages. Jennifer's story, in Chapter 12, illustrates the sequence of events observed in the process of empowerment observed in this setting. Six stages emerged:

1. Caregivers gained a personal awareness that their lives could be different.
2. They came to believe in themselves and their ability to promote this change.
3. Caregivers established parameters for success. This step involved collecting information about opportunities and setting realistic short- and long-term goals for themselves.
4. They acquired the skills needed to reach their goals.
5. Caregivers encountered opportunity.
6. Finally, caregivers attained their goals. Caregivers felt they had succeeded when they had obtained employment, established stable families, and become active members of the community.

Throughout the process, caregivers worked to improve family relationships and to nurture a supportive network that included family, neighbors, and preschool personnel.

These stages were similar to those reported by other authors and summarized in Chapter 3. As Vanderslice (1984) suggested, the process was neither sequential nor linear. Caregivers tried many new behaviors before they found their personal styles, and they often investigated several jobs before deciding on a career. Sometimes they became discouraged. Often, only courage and determination kept them going. But most persevered.

Although the transition was not linear, it was continuous. Looking back, none of the caregivers was able to identify a "turning point" which propelled her to action; and no one could distinguish a discrete event similar to the "mobilizing moment" reported by Kieffer (1984). As Terry said, "One thing started and then the next thing. It wasn't just one thing, all of a sudden. It was more: Annie give you courage. You got motivated. You had some success. And you realized you could do it." Nevertheless, in the future, participants may well view the entire preschool experience as a turning point.

The following sections describe the six stages observed at Seigle Avenue Preschool Cooperative.

THE PROCESS

Awareness

The first stage involved awareness. Before their association with the preschool, many caregivers had no idea that their lives could be different. They assumed that isolation, powerlessness, and dependency were normal. As Jennifer said, "I just stayed cooped up in the house all the time. I didn't know no different."

Once they began to participate, caregivers began to realize that a different life was possible. Joanne described her recognition that she had options. For her, those options involved education.

> My personal thing that I discovered is I can go to school, because, like I say, it is your *choice.* I like going. I like my teacher. I am going because I want to go. I want to make a change in my life. It makes me feel better on the inside.

Judy explained, "I think I am more aware of the things around me."
Karen summarized her experience succinctly, "It makes you think
differently."

Change was often difficult, as Marlette explained,

> It took me a while to get used to the parents. I was kind of reluctant
> to come to the meetings, 'cause I was kind of shy. She [the family
> coordinator] didn't really put you on the spot, but you had to tell
> about yourself and it was like, "I don't want to do that!" It took me
> a while to start coming to those meetings.

Confidence

Those who persevered were rewarded. During the second stage,
caregivers began to acquire confidence in their capacities and abilities.
Kim summarized her accomplishments in this arena: "I learned that I
have good self- esteem, a good sense of humor, a nice personality, and
I'm smart in things I didn't think I was smart in. I got some confidence
in myself!"

Nancy spoke forcefully about her gains, "For me, I learned that I
have more to give. I learned I can put my daughter in school, and I can
go to school myself. And that is what I am doing now!"

Goals

In the third stage, caregivers first set realistic goals. Then they began to
identify the skills they would need to acquire in order to attain their
goals. Judy was the only caregiver living in an intact, two-parent
family. Like the others, however, she was inspired by her children and
the responsibility she felt for them. "That was first priority," she
explained. "What will be the best for the children? We will work around
that." Judy planned to return to the work force when her youngest son
entered school.

For all the graduates and twelve of the current cohort, goals
involved either education or employment. For most, education was seen
as the route to employment. For example, Marline and Nancy wanted to
attend the community college to become nurses, and Marlette wanted to
obtain training so she could work as a dental hygienist. Joanne, Andrea,
and Maggie planned to attend a technical college. Joanne wanted to

teach preschool, while Andrea and Maggie intended to become social workers.

Only two caregivers, Martha and Lily, identified employment as their sole goal. Martha had already obtained her GED through community programs while she attended the preschool. Considerably older than the others, Martha was determined to become independent as soon as possible. Lily appeared to be illiterate, and she avoided discussions of further education.

Skills

Chapter 12 explored the wide variety of skills obtained by caregivers. Some of these skills were acquired naturally as a by-product of participation. Others were acquired only through hard work expended over a long period of time. Role models and staff linkages to community resources were described in Chapter 10; these were especially helpful to participants. As caregivers gained new skills, their confidence soared.

Opportunity

Opportunity constituted the fifth step in the process of empowerment demonstrated at the preschool. At the most basic level, opportunity began with the freedom to participate as a contributing member of a team. The staff members did not do *to* or *for* caregivers, they did *with* them. Felisha alluded to this reciprocity when she described the response of the classroom aide, Miss Brenda. "She acts like she really needs the help I give her, and she appreciates my help! She do!"

Opportunity extended to relationships with other community agencies. Caregivers were encouraged to enroll in community college classes, visit the public schools, and attend community events. Despite initial hesitation, caregivers responded enthusiastically. For example, Felisha offered a prayer for more than two thousand people at a community breakfast; and Lily appeared on a national poster for world hunger.

Opportunity also included access to resources of the middle class. When the two deaths occurred, members of the Board provided financial assistance and even clothing for the funeral services. They helped the families negotiate with county agencies, the funeral home, and other family members. Other caregivers watched the negotiations closely, fascinated by the Board's success in opening resources. This process demonstrated the wealth of opportunities open to the middle class and the value of knowing the right people in the community.

Opportunity was not equally distributed. Dana and Marline did not live in Piedmont Courts, and they felt the lack of opportunity acutely. As others described their community involvement, Marline looked sad. She explained that she had no community—her neighborhood was just a collection of houses.

Determination

Over the course of just one year, the fifteen caregivers in the current cohort experienced the death of a child, the death of a husband, an attempted suicide, several threats of eviction, and numerous months when families lacked money for food and basic goods. Given their marginal existence, this is probably not an unusual number of crises.

There were chronic pressures as well. It was not easy to get up and get going when every one else seemed to be taking it easy. Lily explained that she used to work on an assembly line. She quit when the company relocated. It was just too much trouble to get to the new site using public transportation.

The ability to weather crises and overcome adverse circumstances was enhanced by a number of qualities. First, the caregivers demonstrated profound inner strength. Many, like Maggie, relied on faith:

> When I have a problem, I get on my knees and pray, and I put my hand on that Bible and go to sleep. It may take me two or three days to figure out what I am doing, but it will be the right thing. I don't sit there and hold it in no more.

Minnie prayed every morning. She said, "I thank God for getting me up clothed in my right mind." Hope concurred. "I kneel down beside my bed and pray," she explained. "Then I am OK."

Some caregivers relied on their extended families, especially their mothers. Additional stress was removed when their preschool experiences helped them improve relationships with family members.

Caregivers were pleased when they overcame obstacles themselves. When asked about her ability to make so many changes in such a short time, Nancy proudly described her inner resources. She exclaimed, "I didn't know I had that much in me—really, I didn't!"

Finally, many caregivers sought companionship when they were troubled or discouraged. Although they depended on the staff for counseling, not all of the help they received was formal. Frances explained, "I come up here. The kids—you know—they make you feel better."

ANALYSIS OF THE EMPOWERMENT PROCESS

The process recorded here is similar to that reported by Cochran (1987, 1988) and Saleebey (1992). For those who were making changes, the sequence of stages appeared stable, although it was not rigid or invariant. In particular, the acquisition of skills was often intertwined through several steps; and, as caregivers progressed through the sequence, their confidence in their own abilities steadily increased.

Caregivers appeared to move through the continuum at different rates. Some, like Jennifer, took less than a year to complete the process, while others, like Martha, worked toward goals for more than five years. The amount of time required appeared to depend on a complex constellation of factors, including ability level, opportunity, ambition, motivation, inner resources, and availability of social support.

Dunst and Trivette (1988, 1990) found that by working together, individuals increase self-esteem, create positive peer pressure, ward off harm, contribute to family well-being, and encourage change. This statement was certainly true for this sample. The process of empowerment was enhanced by the networks of affiliation formed by caregivers. As Weiss (1990) reported, part of the attraction of the process was the opportunity to give as well as to receive.

Empowerment in the Current Cohort

At the time of this study, caregivers in the current cohort were at a number of different points along the empowerment continuum. For example, members of the uncommitted group were just beginning the process, and they were often consumed by the exigencies of daily living. Shontay says she is frequently overwhelmed, but she rarely reaches out to the resources around her. "I get in the house. Lock my doors. Take the phone off the hook. And sometimes I will just cry to myself. After I cry, sometimes I feel a whole lot better." Note that Shontay said she *sometimes* feels better; her strategy is not always effective.

Dana operates from a similar position. She missed a required meeting and did not hear about the Mothers' Day Luncheon. Further, her daughter did not bring an invitation home—or if she did, Dana did not see it. Dana does not blame the preschool, but she does not take responsibility either. She just complains that she missed a party.

Given her limited contacts and lack of training, Dana's goal to become a famous recording star is probably unrealistic. The other members of this group have no immediate goals.

Although caregivers in the uncommitted group demonstrated some awareness of their condition, it was unclear whether they would pursue empowerment. Dana concluded, "I can't say I have learned that much more about myself through this program."

The other caregivers in the cohort were well on their way toward empowerment. With confidence in their abilities, they were determined to change their lives. All had established networks of support and were actively pursuing goals set during the year. Three vignettes illustrate the tremendous growth experienced by the current cohort.

Hope was the silent member of the group. During an introductory exercise at a required meeting, Frances told her that she was nice but very quiet. Hope observed, "And I didn't really know I was that quiet! It opened me up a lot." Hope regrets her extreme shyness as she explains, "I just can't up and carry on a conversation." Her goals are to improve her social skills and make more friends. She is beginning by talking to the preschool staff about her difficulties.

Changes in attitude did not come easy for most. Marlette describes her first impressions of the cohort:

> When I first came, I assumed that everybody didn't like me. I looked at Lily and I say, "I don't think me and her are going to get along." I looked at Joanne and I said, "She look like she got an attitude." I was looking at everybody picking out the negative things.

Marlette was also looking at negative attributes in herself. In the required meetings, she learned more effective ways to communicate with friends and family, and she realized she had valuable strengths and abilities. Currently she is pursuing a career as a dental hygienist. Marlette summarizes her progress by saying, "I became a whole person."

Maggie, the sensitive member of the leadership group, has set her sights on a career in social work. Though she is beginning with a part-time job at the YMCA, Maggie has already mastered a basic tenet of the profession. "I am used to listening," she explains. "I can't solve a problem for you, but I will try to give you pointers so you know what steps to take."

Empowerment of Graduates

Of the nine graduates interviewed, seven were making substantial progress along the empowerment continuum. For two, progress was less obvious. Faye never lived in Piedmont Courts, although her sister resided there. She was retained in the sample because of her key role in the "applesauce incident," mentioned earlier. Last year when her friend was working nearby, Faye came to the Courts everyday and visited with her sister while her daughter attended preschool. This year, transportation was not available, so Faye remained in her community and sent her child to a program there. Faye said she knew few people around her, and she claimed she had no opportunity for community involvement or further education. She hoped to obtain part-time employment when her youngest child entered school.

Minnie has experienced recurring bouts of mental illness. This condition seriously impaired her ability to parent; and at the time of the interview, all her children had been removed from the home and placed in custody of the Department of Social Services.

Although she is unable to care for or manage her children, Minnie goes to GED classes every day. On Wednesday evenings and Sunday mornings, she attends a church "more holy" than Seigle Avenue Presbyterian. Minnie describes the service. "They clap and he preach. He don't *talk*." Further, Minnie has a new friend who "sticks with" her; and she adds, "If it wasn't for that man, I don't know if I could keep my mind straight."

Minnie remembers her experience in the preschool fondly. "I didn't know I could do all them things," she explains. "I just got out there and tried."

Although she is not able to follow the traditional path towards empowerment, she has not been idle. Minnie is able to engage in praxis, or reflective thinking; and she demonstrates a wisdom that transcends mental illness. Referring to her eleven-year old daughter accused of being sexually active, Minnie poignantly explains, "We studied on it at the preschool, and I done told her time and time again. Ain't but three things can happen when a young girl goes with an older man—she gets pregnant; she gets disease; or she gets knocked about."

A CASE STUDY OF EMPOWERMENT

Terry's experience is representative of the seven caregivers who are clearly and successfully traveling along the empowerment continuum. Terry is currently in the fourth phase of the process, skills acquisition. Having gained substantial social skills during her stay at the preschool, she is currently enrolled in a work-study program at the local technical school. Although the income she earns supports her family, Terry's primary focus is on her education.

Terry moved to the Courts from the Battered Women's Shelter. She described her first impressions of her new home. Like many of the other caregivers, she was frightened of her surroundings. "Once I got up here and got my apartment, I was feeling kind of scared here. I wanted to stay to myself. Finally it could be just us, and I could be safe." Ann Bradley invited Terry to attend the preschool, and Terry describes her response to this visit:

> I let her know what was going on. I felt I wasn't by myself. I am not the only one. I just can't sit home and mope about it. "Go out there and do something about it!" she told me. I decided if she could do it, I could do it.

Terry accepted Ann's invitation and placed her daughter in the program. She began attending regularly herself and she was elected president of the parents' group. Terry used the opportunity to increase her parenting skills and deepen her friendships. "Having little kids, you are going to meet people if you want to," she explained.

> At preschool, I met parents on a different perspective. The meetings were great. It was like a close bond. You became close

friends. Before, you would just speak to people. Up there, you became like a close family. We all worked together. It was great!

It was important to Terry that her children be exposed to people of other races. "To have a black child just grow up around black children, they don't know anything else when they get in regular school." She felt they would have a hard time adjusting to white teachers. Terry also believed it was important for black and white adults to mingle. "You have your separate identity, they have theirs. But it is all right. You can still do as much as anyone else."

Terry gained leadership skills during her presidency. She found she had a cooperative style:

> I had to get involved and work with the committees, but not be the boss, you know. I never felt like, 'I'm the leader.' I shared all the things with everybody. You have your own job, but the president still needs to work with everybody else.

As she gained self-confidence, Terry also gained resolve:

> My determination is that I want the best for my children. If the best is getting up every morning and going to school—going to work to a job that I hate at the same time I am going to school—hey, that is what I have to do.
>
> I don't want to be under the Housing Authority at all. It is not just Piedmont Courts and the people here. It is just my determination that I can be better. I can work for what I want. And living over here for sixteen or seventeen years is something I definitely *don't* want. I want to take my children and put them somewhere they can feel freedom, go outside and don't have to worry about gunshots or anything.

For Terry, the preschool "was an inspiration. That is why I went to school for my diploma—because I wanted to teach there. Then once I got to school, I learned that there were so many things I can do."

Terry obtained her high school equivalency degree, and she is currently enrolled in a work-study program. In the past year, she has held four different jobs. She works twenty hours a week, attends school full-time, manages her family, and maintains a high grade-point average. Terry has already received a certificate in early childhood development. Next quarter, she will attain a technical degree in correctional and juvenile services. Her goal is to acquire a position as a corrections counselor.

For two years, Terry has been involved in a serious relationship with a man she has known since high school. At times, Terry says she becomes frightened. "I think if he get too close, this is going to happen. . . . He may be too obsessive, or—you know—then the beatings will start."

Together, Terry and her friend are working on communication skills. Her friend admires her strength. He says, "She set her goals and she is really going for them." It is clear that he is a source of support and help.

Terry acknowledges the path she has chosen is hard. She explains, "I don't want to take the easy way out no more." At times, Terry feels overwhelmed and discouraged. Yet, when she feels like saying, "Forget it!" Terry remembers how far she has come and proudly admits, "I would be crazy to stop now."

CHAPTER 14
Community Impact

Caregivers not only acquired cultural and human capital, they also transferred these assets to their neighborhood. Caregivers who attended the preschool had a significant impact on Piedmont Courts through their involvement with two major institutions: the Residents' Organization—sponsored by the Charlotte Housing Authority—and Seigle Avenue Presbyterian Church. Both these institutions receive external support; however, their success depends on neighborhood leadership and active participation by residents. This chapter describes the ways in which caregivers were able to transfer their gains into community improvement.

Caregivers had less impact on public schools, and they had no apparent impact on agencies located outside the community. Their efforts with these groups are also chronicled in this chapter.

For many caregivers, the transition from preschool to community was difficult. The following section examines the movement toward community involvement by relating the experiences of two caregivers.

TRANSFERRING LOYALTIES

Martha was aware of the loneliness that ensued after her granddaughter graduated from the preschool. After three years of intense involvement, her life seemed suddenly empty. She explained, "I had gotten used to talking to all those grownups and doing things with them." Although she has since filled her life with a full-time job, she reminisces, "I still miss them."

Carol did not verbalize this feeling, but it showed in her behavior. Her four children attended the preschool, and she was intensely involved

175

for four consecutive years. In 1990, Carol was president of the parents' group. When her youngest child graduated from preschool in May 1992, Carol began work on her GED, but she continued her pattern of "hanging out" at the preschool in the fall. The leadership group resented Carol's presence. She tried to tell them what to do. She ate their food without contributing, and she showed up although not invited. After impassioned discussion, current caregivers decided to inform Carol that she could attend only when specifically bidden. Carol subsequently turned her energies to the Residents' Organization. She explained, "Them skills I learned there helped me run the Residents' Organization."

LEADING THE RESIDENTS' ORGANIZATION

Piedmont Courts is only one of at least forty-four public housing projects under the aegis of the Charlotte Housing Authority. According to William (Butch) Simmons, Assistant Director of Residential Services, Residents' Organizations were begun twenty years ago to give a voice to tenants (personal communication, July 26, 1993). At each site, the Residents' Organization is responsible for advising the Housing Authority on the physical condition of the property. Members of the Residents' Organization also apprise the Housing Authority of programming needs such as talks on substance abuse or available services. The Residents' Organization may also implement community programs.

The Housing Authority provides a funding allotment of $3.00 per unit per year to support the activities of the Residents' Organization. Of this amount, $1.00 is diverted into a scholarship fund for high school graduates. At Piedmont Courts, that leaves $484.00 for annual programming. The Residents' Organization supplements its allotment with grants, donations, and fundraising events.

Residents' Organization Secretary Mary Frances Streater has been active in the group for more than three years. She said that the Residents' Organization at Piedmont Courts typically sponsors an annual Christmas celebration, an outdoor beautification project called Clean Sweep, holiday parties for children and the elderly, and a Halloween Carnival. In August, a week of activities is capped by Piedmont Courts Day, a neighborhood festival involving choirs and musical groups, food, games, and outdoor demonstrations by community agencies (personal communication, July 26, 1993).

By statute, each tenant in public housing is required to attend four of twelve monthly meetings. At Piedmont Courts, average attendance varies from fifteen to twenty people, although more than fifty residents attended the July meeting (Mary Frances Streater, personal communication, July 26, 1993).

The caregivers in the uncommitted group did not fulfill even these minimum obligations. Dana says she does not attend meetings because she does not like "phony people." Jean avoids them because she dislikes the apartment manager. Although she too shuns meetings, Shontay further charges that the Block Captains do not keep her informed. Her attitude is one of hopelessness and angry resignation as she complains about Clean Sweep, "Piedmont Courts is full of people dropping trash. You cannot keep them yards clean."

Two caregivers were unaffected by the Residents' Organization because they did not live in the Courts. Of the remaining ten caregivers, three attended monthly meetings voluntarily because they wanted to be involved in the community. Three more served as Block Captains, a position of somewhat greater responsibility.

In addition, three of the five officers of the Residents' Organization were graduates of the preschool. Carol is the vice president. Since May, she and Streater have substituted for the president, who was hospitalized with cancer. Carol maintained that the skills she learned at the preschool prepared her for this challenge. "I was on the preschool Board for two years straight," she noted, "That is what really gave me the courage to be able to talk out in front of people."

Martha edited a monthly newsletter produced by the Residents' Organization. Simmons observed, "Many of our projects try to put out a newsletter. None have been as reliable or consistent as Piedmont Courts. They get their publication out almost every month" (personal communication, July 26, 1993).

Mary Frances Streater has seen the influence of preschool graduates firsthand. She says they have had a major, positive impact on the Residents' Organization. She explains, "By putting themselves into it with their kids, they learn things. They start attending meetings. When you ask them to help, they are more likely to agree, and they have more skills."

Simmons concludes that the Residents' Organization at Piedmont Courts is different from the many other groups he observes:

> For one thing, they work together despite their petty differences. Then, too, they stay focused on their goals and ignore diversions. The president delegated authority, and each person has learned to contribute to the whole. This group is always seeking knowledge, not for power or prestige, but to put it to work in the community.

Simmons maintains that Piedmont Courts Residents' Organization has surpassed all others in effectiveness, and he credits the preschool with this success. "By their working together," he said, "they learned to do the job."

SUPPORTING SEIGLE AVENUE PRESBYTERIAN CHURCH

A number of caregivers attend churches outside the neighborhood. Ebony and Maggie are typical. They worship with their mothers, siblings, and extended family every Sunday in the churches in which the family grew up.

Hope represents another, less common, pattern. She does not attend a church, but she sends her children, on a van that stops at her house each Sunday. She is not sure which church it represents, but she thinks they go to a nearby town for worship.

Three caregivers have joined the neighborhood church, Seigle Avenue Presbyterian. Four mothers attend regularly and they have expressed an interest in joining. A number of other caregivers attend on special occasions. Lily described her decision to make a commitment to the church, "If you are going to be involved in something, you ought to do it in style!"

Caregivers have been very active in the life of the congregation. Two sing in the choir. When school is in session, Carol and her children attend the weekly "Wonderful Wednesdays" program which the Church offers in lieu of Sunday School. Jackie and Martha both cook for Wonderful Wednesdays, and Jackie often assists family coordinator Ann Bradley with the after-school program. In addition, Jackie was elected to the Usher Board in the spring of 1993.

In 1992, Lily and Jackie joined a committee trying to send a work team to the country of Honduras. After a year of intensive study and preparation, the organizing committee asked them to join the six-member adult team actually traveling abroad. They represented the church, worked on building projects, and supervised nine teenagers for a week in an impoverished foreign country. In a personal communication on July 22, 1993, Jim Curtis, committee chair, commented on their selection for this working honor:

> They were chosen not only for their capacity to work effectively under adverse conditions, but also for their ability to establish meaningful relationships with the people of Honduras. They know what it is like to survive on limited resources, and they are willing to use their knowledge to help people who have even less.

Jackie and Lily have stayed with the process all year. Their compassion for others is unequaled.

Martha has also assumed a leadership role in the church. After serving on the Usher Board for two years, she was elected Elder in the spring of 1992. The Session, which includes eight Elders, oversees all operations of the church. For three years, Martha helped organize a summer Bible study program in homes in Piedmont Courts. She also took her cooking skills to church, where she managed covered dish dinners and other festivities.

Caregivers have not been shy about encouraging their friends to join them at church. In 1985, the year before the preschool was established, church membership reached a new low of 56 (Borden, 1985). By June 1993, church rolls had swelled to a new high of 133. Pastor Summers reports that about half this number are residents of Piedmont Courts. Martha explained, "If you believe something is right for you and your family, you got to believe it is right for others."

The pastor, Charlie Summers, described the impact of caregivers on the church:

> Preschool graduates [caregivers] have gotten to know the church not only as a corporate body, but also as a collection of individual people. New members tell their neighbors about their experiences with the church, and this increases our personal presence in the community. As a result of this communication, the church

becomes more approachable, and it is more able to offer appropriate help. (Personal communication, July 22, 1993)

CONNECTIONS WITHIN THE COMMUNITY

As Dr. Summers suggested, there is a great deal of cross-fertilization in Piedmont Courts. Like the process of individual empowerment, community impact is not a one-way street. In a neighborhood of almost a thousand people, there is overlap and interplay. Many of the leaders play important roles in more than one institution. For example, Clarence Westbrook, the president of the Residents' Organization, is also an Elder of Seigle Avenue Church and he serves on the preschool Board of Directors. He was prompted to re- activate the Residents' Organization after participating in a church study group evaluating the philosophy of McKnight (1989). Westbrook has helped to teach the preschool directors what it means to empower a community.

This interplay is significant because it means that caregivers who develop leadership skills with one group can transfer those skills to another group sharing the same philosophy. Strong community networks support and encourage new efforts. In times of crisis, these networks can be rapidly mobilized to provide additional services and care. Westbrook has captured the spirit of this community with the slogan he coined for the Residents' Organization: "Working Together Works!"

SCHOOL CONNECTIONS

There are no neighborhood elementary schools near Piedmont Courts. Children from this housing project are bused to achieve racial integration, and some ride as long as ninety minutes each way. With neither private automobiles nor reliable public transportation, caregivers have an equally difficult time getting to their children's schools.

Despite these obstacles, all the caregivers in the sample who had a child in public school attended either a PTA meeting or a parent/teacher conference during the academic year. Many also ate lunch with a child at school or attended a special school event such as a Book Fair or a Halloween Carnival.

Though they made token appearances, caregivers' relationships with the public school system were tenuous at best. Caregivers reported they had little involvement with or impact on their children's education. There was no indication that schools were unfriendly, unresponsive, or intimidating; rather, caregivers in this group simply could not attend often enough to form opinions. As Kim said, "I just don't have bus fare. When parent conference comes, I call her father on his job and tell him to bring me bus fare so I can get there. Sometimes he will bring it to me." More often, he did not.

CONNECTIONS TO OTHER RESOURCES

In addition to the institutions located within the neighborhood, a number of agencies and groups provided assistance from without. Caregivers received instruction through a variety of courses at the local community college, located about two miles away. This instruction included high school completion courses, courses in self-esteem, and technical training. One of the instructors, Debbie Anshel, was a particularly talented teacher of adults. She worked from a framework of empowerment, encouraging and inspiring several of the caregivers in the study.

Motheread, which evolved into ReadUp, sent a family literacy coordinator to provide reading instruction at required parent meetings. The coordinator, Dionne Greenlee, empowered caregivers by teaching them to read simple books to their children. As a group, caregivers read a story and then discussed its meaning. They learned appropriate techniques for reading to children; and they developed questions to help children grasp meaning. The lending library was an important feature of this program. Caregivers were able to borrow books, which often featured African American characters. Although ReadUp was popular, it was an established program with a predetermined curriculum. Caregivers had little opportunity to influence ReadUp.

Finally, Foundation for the Carolinas, Inc., a regional philanthropic organization, funded the Strengthening Families Initiative. Three agencies were linked through this endeavor: Project Uplift, a home instruction program for young mothers with children from birth to age two; Seigle Avenue Preschool Cooperative; and Success by Six, a family-oriented project designed to prepare five-year-old children for public school. Located at the Johnston YMCA, Project Uplift and Success by Six also sent workers into the neighborhood to prepare children for preschool and to ensure their continued development. Although the staffs cooperated with each other, these programs had little direct impact on caregivers; and caregivers had no apparent impact on these programs.

In summary, caregivers made a difference in the community programs that were open to influence: the Residents' Organization and the church. They benefited from the community resources designed to help them, but they did not impact these systems. Caregivers had no affect on established programs that were not open to change, even though these programs could have benefited from their input.

CHAPTER 15

Summary, Conclusions, and Recommendations

This final chapter summarizes the findings of this research project by retracing the changes reported by caregivers; by reviewing the salient program features essential to these changes; and by analyzing barriers to empowerment encountered in this setting. The chapter then examines the theoretical constructs undergirding the investigation, analyzes the role of the researcher, presents limitations, and explores ways in which findings can be generalized to other settings.

RECAPITULATION OF FINDINGS

How did Caregivers Change?

Prior to their preschool experience, the twenty-four caregivers in this study were involved in virtually no activities outside their apartments. They espoused no goals, for they believed they were incapable of changing their plight in life. Surrounded by a neighborhood of a thousand people, they felt isolated and alienated. By their own report, despair ruled their lives.

After participating in the parents' program of Seigle Avenue Cooperative Preschool, these same people were attending school, seeking jobs, managing their community, and participating in neighborhood churches. They displayed new and improved parenting skills, and they had established networks that reached beyond the physical boundaries of the neighborhood. They espoused realistic goals towards which they were striving. They believed in their own capacities, and they expressed hope for a better future.

To what extent did Seigle Avenue Preschool promote this change?

Definitive cause-and-effect answers are elusive in a qualitative study. Clearly, maturation can be a potent force in adult development; and maturation may unite with history to produce unanticipated, powerful results.

Yet, the people being studied believed that their involvement in the preschool was the one factor that made a difference for them; and they were convinced that none of their changes would have taken place without the influence of the preschool. This study chronicled their stories and presented empowerment as perceived by the newly-empowered.

What personal characteristics were linked to empowerment?

Individuals who benefited from this program were free from major personal and environmental stressors. Although most lived in public housing and subsisted on marginal incomes, they were able to provide food, shelter, and clothing for themselves and their families. Among those who were clearly engaged in the process of becoming empowered, there was no evidence of substance abuse or other destructive behaviors.

A number of personal characteristics seemed to be linked to empowerment. First, caregivers demonstrated self-awareness and a willingness to engage in personal reflection, or praxis. Second, they were willing to embrace change. Third, individuals were not reluctant to work hard and take emotional risks in order to accomplish their goals.

Differential responses were noted among the members of the current cohort. A leadership group emerged early in the academic year. The leaders consistently exceeded minimum requirements for participation, consulted the family coordinator in times of trouble, orchestrated special events, and bonded as a group.

The followers were more tenuously connected to the preschool. Although they fulfilled minimum requirements, followers attended less regularly; and, as a group, they were less cohesive. The followers tended to be more critical of the program. Although staff sometimes resented their charges, the followers' suggestions helped to improve the program.

A third, smaller group remained uncommitted to the program. Their attendance was erratic, and they fulfilled monthly obligations only because staff made allowances for them. The uncommitted caregivers were preoccupied with exigencies of daily living. They required vast amounts of staff time and energy, and they returned little to the program.

What cultural capital was acquired?

Caregivers gained skills as diverse as their own personalities. Common gains began with language and extended to affiliation. Caregivers learned to set and work towards realistic goals, often under adverse conditions. They increased their parenting skills, and found new ways to accomplish the activities of daily living. They returned to school to pursue career goals, and they developed schedules and work habits that prepared them for employment outside the neighborhood.

To what extent was cultural capital translated into human capital?

During the 1992–1993 academic year, members of the current cohort had little opportunity to translate their newly acquired cultural capital into human capital. However, graduates were beginning to achieve self-sufficiency. Even when active involvement in the preschool ended, graduates continued to pursue their goals. At the conclusion of the study, it appeared that the majority of graduates would accomplish their goals within two years.

What process of empowerment was observed?

As previously noted, empirical research suggests that adolescent child-bearing often disrupts normal adult development by truncating the number of years the mother spends in school. Although this study supports those conclusions, it also suggests that caregivers need not remain stuck in a quagmire of arrested development. Participation in this family support program fostered empowerment and helped caregivers resume the process of adult development.

The process observed in this study consisted of six steps similar to those reported by other researchers. The first step involved a change in perception as individuals gained awareness that their lives could be different. Second, caregivers began to believe in themselves, and they gained confidence that they could bring about desired changes. Third, caregivers set realistic goals for themselves. In the fourth stage, caregivers began to acquire the skills they needed to attain their goals. In the fifth stage, they encountered opportunity. Sixth, caregivers demonstrated the capacity to persevere under difficult and adverse circumstance. Throughout the process, they worked to improve family relationships, establish friendships, and develop community networks.

Although the process appeared stable, it was neither linear nor invariant. In particular, the acquisition of skills was intertwined with several steps; and confidence increased throughout the sequence.

Caregivers began the process at different points on the continuum, and they progressed at different rates. Timing appeared to depend on a complex constellation of factors, including ability, opportunity, and motivation. The process was enhanced by social support.

What Program Features Promoted Empowerment?

A number of programmatic elements were essential to the empowerment process. The preschool was convenient and easily accessible. This fact encouraged caregivers to try the preschool, for they knew they could walk across the street and remove a child if the experience was not positive. Later, proximity promoted a sense of ownership.

The introductory invitation was extended by neighbors and community workers the caregivers knew and trusted. Caregivers initially joined for the sake of their children, but they continued to participate because they also found substantial benefits for themselves.

How did the curriculum foster change?

Weekly or biweekly meetings for caregivers provided information on practical topics such as school choice, nutrition, and reading with children; however, the content was not nearly as important as the process. The meetings introduced caregivers to like-minded neighbors and provided a safe environment in which they could practice new behaviors such as assertive negotiation, planning, and evaluation. Through rituals and group discussions, caregivers learned that they were not alone. They began to make friends, develop confidence in their own abilities, and nourish hope that they could find a better life for themselves and their children.

What staff qualities empowered?

Staff built on strengths by encouraging, inspiring, and inciting. Staff were always available for consultation and counseling. Working together, they modeled appropriate behaviors in individual and group settings. They were not afraid to show their own feelings, and they continued to offer encouragement even in the face of rejection. When necessary, staff stepped outside traditional roles and brokered concrete services or advocated for clients within the wider community. They forged linkages with other agencies. Most important, they used every teachable moment as an opportunity to empower, rarely doing for caregivers what caregivers could be enabled to do for themselves.

How did role models contribute?

African American speakers served as role models for caregivers. They demonstrated new ways of behaving which did not violate ethnic and cultural norms. Like staff, they encouraged and offered hope that the caregivers could also achieve their goals of self-sufficiency. This was the first time many caregivers had seen successful African American women outside the welfare office, and the caregivers were inspired by their stories. Role models offered tangible proof that caregivers could escape poverty and could find a more rewarding way of life.

What was the Impact on the Community?

The quality and quantity of observed difference was enhanced by the propensity of agencies in the neighborhood to work together. Caregivers found fertile ground on which to pour their new talents; and they were encouraged—not discouraged—by existing networks. Graduates had significant impact on the community through their involvement with the Residents' Organization and the neighborhood church. They were less able to effect change in public schools and other established agencies serving the neighborhood.

What were the Barriers to Empowerment?

Despite their best intentions, staff missed a number of opportunities to promote empowerment. This occurred most often when staff was pressed for time or when decisions involved money. The staff consistently demonstrated difficulty sharing responsibility for monetary decisions with caregivers, even those elected to the board.

As is probably true with many grassroots programs, the curriculum was not connected to any consistent theory. This created a supermarket approach to programming, as the family coordinator designed sessions based on random availability rather than systematic doctrine. When topics arose from the participants' interests, this flexibility was empowering. When topics were chosen at the last minute based on convenience, they were less helpful.

Program goals for caregivers were not consistently pursued. Grassroots programs should be as specific in setting goals for parent programs as they are in establishing goals for children's activities. It is important for caregivers to understand those goals and the philosophy that drives the programs. A number of different goals are possible and appropriate, including acquisition of knowledge about child care and child development, an increase in positive parent-child interactions, and parental governance of the preschool itself.

It is not surprising that there was attrition during the year among caregivers who did not understand the program. Caregivers need to "buy into" goals set by staff and boards. Only in this way can preschool education become a true cooperative effort.

Since staff turnover is often high in grassroots programs, new staff members also need to go through the process of "buying into" program goals and philosophy. Executive staff cannot hand a new employee a list of objectives and say, "This is what you must do this year." Staff must believe in those goals; and to be successful, they must also live them. As in a therapeutic community, every interaction then becomes an interaction with a purpose—that is, attaining mutually-agreed-upon goals.

CONCLUSIONS

This study indicated that self-sufficiency was a realistic and attainable goal for caregivers who participated in the parents' program of a cooperative preschool. Self-sufficiency was achieved through small steps taken over several years. It was predicated on skills training and further education. Consequently, employment became a long-range goal, often achieved years after preschool involvement ended. Empowerment strengthened families by promoting new patterns of affiliation, increased parenting skills, and improved family relationships. Caregivers gained occupational skills, including education, which they translated into financial resources. The empowerment of individuals also bolstered major institutions in this neighborhood and strengthened the fabric of a fragile society.

ANALYSIS OF THEORETICAL CONSTRUCTS

The process of empowerment demonstrated by this project confirms the general sequence identified by other researchers. As others have suggested, the process was not linear and the stages were successive rather than consecutive. In this study, empowerment was a helpful construct that facilitated an evaluation of the direction, magnitude, and duration of individual change.

The theoretical constructs of cultural and human capital delineated by Bourdieu provided a helpful framework for analyzing caregiver changes, essential program elements, and encumbrances. These theoretical constructs dovetailed smoothly with the concept of empowerment and a strengths perspective. Further, Bourdieu's material provided a practical framework from which lasting community impact could be assessed. Overall, the theories of cultural and human capital provided a unifying theme that spanned multiple systems and united diverse research streams.

One recurring criticism of these constructs, however, is their abstract nature. This is complicated by Bourdieu's abstract writing style. In the field, conceptual ambiguity becomes both an asset and a limitation. The vague exposition of the constructs permits wide application, while the lack of precision precludes rigorous evaluation of specific elements. In this study, the vagueness of the Bourdieu concepts was supplemented by the specificity of the empowerment material.

The fact that the constructs of cultural and human capital are not well known in the United States also limits their usefulness. In order to explain my results to colleagues, I find I must first teach the constructs. This would be true for any new theory, and this limitation will be lessened as more professionals become familiar with these theories and a shared language is developed. In fact, colleagues who know Bourdieu's work immediately grasp the significant of this project and quickly generalize the findings to other situations.

In and of itself, this theory does not favor one class over another. As presented by Bourdieu, the constructs of cultural and human capital are values-free. They simply propose that, in order to move from one class to another, people must learn the ways and mores of the new class. According to Bourdieu, this movement can be toward wealth or poverty. Each class requires specific knowledge, values, and skills, and a way of looking at the world which newcomers must absorb.

Nevertheless, Bourdieu's theory could be construed to advocate a bias toward upward mobility. For example, although he does not extol the virtues of the upper classes, Bourdieu assumes that others want to share the wealth and privilege of the upper classes. Likewise, many Americans may assume that self-sufficiency is a better condition than welfare dependency. The imposition of values such as these onto the theory could produce a "classist" interpretation that favors middle-class ethics. To avoid bias, researchers must rigorously specify their values and expectations at the outset, as this study has done.

This research touched on, but did not investigate, a number of related concepts, including moral development; normal development of women; creation of social networks as a means to empowerment; roles of fathers and male friends in matriarchal families; and development of intimacy, self-efficacy, and social competence. These theoretical constructs are not mutually exclusive, although some appear to have broader utility than others. Each of these topics deserves further consideration through quantitative and qualitative studies.

Columnist William Raspberry maintains that spirituality is "the one thing successful social programs have in common" (1992). Though spirituality permeated the program and the setting, this study did not evaluate the spiritual or religious dimensions of change. This also is an area which merits further investigation.

ROLE OF THE RESEARCHER

In a qualitative study, the ability to gain entry is critical. Skewed access or lack of acceptance can affect the amount and quality of data obtained in the field; and access problems can bias the interpretation of data.

The significant differences in cultural and human capital and social distance reported earlier required that I grasp the habitus of these participants without intruding on their process. I was reluctant to ask direct questions for fear of disrupting the course of events. Instead, I recorded my queries and asked them after the official observation period ended. By talking with colleagues and friends familiar with this or similar communities but who were not involved in the study, I clarified my general impressions of life in this community.

Throughout the eighteen months I spent in the field, I tried to maintain my stance as an observer. Nevertheless, my presence as a Caucasian woman in a group of African American women presented some difficulties. For example, although she appeared to accept me fully from the outset, the family coordinator later told me that she did not lose her skepticism about my motives until January—fully four months after the school year began.

This skepticism may have been reinforced by the behaviors of the speakers—both black and white—who came to address the group. No matter how casually I dressed, no matter how insignificant I tried to appear, each speaker looked to me for an introduction and permission to begin. I assume I received this "honor" simply because I am white, and—in their experience—whites are usually in charge. I consistently ignored these cues and waited for the family coordinator to take the lead, which she invariably did with grace and dignity.

In some ways, issues of difference were a benefit. Caregivers were quick to share their successes with me, for they soon learned that they would find a sympathetic and encouraging ear. Caregivers were more guarded when the issues were less pleasant or more personal. At first, they avoided talking about intimate topics when I was present. After about six weeks, they continued their conversations as long as I remained unobtrusive. By January, I found I was occasionally invited to join the discussions. It is probably no coincidence that my acceptance by the group coincided with my acceptance by the group leader.

I did not have equal access to all the subgroups that emerged during the year. The leaders welcomed me into their cohesive band, although I never graduated from the kitchen duties of peeling and chopping. They appeared to talk freely when I was present. Occasionally the leaders asked for my opinion, although they never allowed me to turn a piece of frying chicken!

I had more difficulty accessing the followers, for they did not appear to form a cohesive group and they tended to participate only when required. Because they were more tenuous in their affiliation with the preschool, I was unable to capitalize on referent power with these caregivers. I tried to gain acceptance by unobtrusive measures, but I was only moderately successful during the year. The leaders were clearly scornful of the followers, and it is possible that my affiliation with the former group precluded access to the latter. I learned the most about this second crew through their vocal contributions to the focus group.

The uncommitted caregivers were neither guarded nor reserved, but their lack of regular attendance made them even less available than the followers. After a brief period of adjustment, however, the uncommitted poured out their troubles to me. When they found I was not going to do anything to solve their problems, they desisted. Despite an aura of outward hostility, this was a loquacious group, and I learned a lot about them just by sitting near the smoking corner and listening. My presence was generally ignored, and it did not appear to change the direction of the conversation.

The focus groups gave me an official opportunity to clarify my impressions and to ask the questions I had withheld during the year. We all enjoyed this process. I was pleased that my tentative assumptions were confirmed; and the caregivers said they were amazed at how much they learned about themselves through the process.

It seemed that the focus groups solidified the gains caregivers had made by making their accomplishments both public and explicit. If this is the case, exit interviews each year may be an important addition to the program.

Graduates were interviewed individually in their homes after the focus groups were concluded. They responded richly and fully, perhaps because they had already heard of the study from their neighbors. Clearly, the promise of payment encouraged participation, but the depth of their responses exceeded my expectations. Though the details differed, the stories followed a consistent pattern supported by the literature and other research in the area. I did not hesitate to probe, inquire, and delve; and caregivers appeared to answer openly and honestly.

Overall, the role of participant observer was an effective strategy in this investigation. Frequency and duration were critical issues, and I do not think I could have obtained reliable results with less frequent observations or a shorter period in the field. The fact that I attended for two academic years helped me establish which elements were idiosyncratic to a particular group or leader and which were enduring program characteristics. I did not obtain equal access to all groups during the observation period, but the addition of focus groups ensured equal representation. Triangulation of data with colleagues and others in the neighborhood assured me that I obtained adequate data. My interpretations were confirmed by the participants themselves during the focus groups and in interviews with graduates.

LIMITATIONS OF THE STUDY

This study examined one ethnic group participating in an empowerment program at one preschool. Extensive reflection on outcomes with caregivers and staff strengthen generalizability; however, as with all exploratory studies, this work leaves ample room for further research. While the outcomes reported were positive, the exploratory nature of the investigation precludes definitive conclusions regarding, for example, essential program elements, necessary staff qualifications, or critical caregiver attributes. The study suggests that this particular configuration of people and programs was effective, but it does not indicate which elements were critical to that success, what features could be modified with no loss, or what adjustments could magnify success.

As previously mentioned, this study confirmed several theoretical propositions, and it also raised a number of practical considerations critical for replication of a grassroots program. These include, among other things, self-selection of participants, staff selection and training, issues of dosage, and development and implementation of clear objectives.

Self-selection

Self-selection of participants was of particular concern. There are two components to self-selection. First, the concept refers to those who initially enrolled in the program. Through extensive recruitment efforts, all caregivers in the neighborhood were invited to participate at the beginning of the academic year, and eighteen accepted this invitation. However, other caregivers—especially those who were employed—enrolled their children in Head Start or the YMCA daycare program, both of which offered longer hours of operation. Further, some caregivers did not take advantage of any of these opportunities. This study did not examine inherent differences in these groups or the impact of self-selection on a particular preschool. The emergence of three distinct subgroups and the author's previous experience suggest that the sample was representative of the non-working caregivers in the neighborhood; however, this fact cannot be assumed.

Second, self-selection refers to the process of remaining involved in a program. Fourteen of the original eighteen completed the 1992–1993 year; however, caregivers who terminated early were not interviewed, and this study did not specify the conditions under which some parents became attached while others remained aloof and uncommitted. Clearly, self-selection is an area that demands further research; for knowledge of moderating variables could enable program planners and staff to reduce barriers to participation and deploy resources more wisely.

Staff training

Staff selection and training are also critical components of lay helping. Graduates were especially clear about staff qualities that contributed to their success, yet this study did not examine these macro-practice issues. It did not determine, for example, whether desirable staff qualities were inherent personality traits or whether they were skills that could be learned by any dedicated employee. Although differential staff responses were noted, the study did not decide which reactions would be most effective in promoting empowerment among different groupings of caregivers, nor did it determine how to teach diagnostic and intervention skills to lay helpers.

Issues of dosage

Although caregivers were welcome in the parents' room every day the preschool was in session, minimum time commitments were established at the beginning of the year. These were changed in the spring to accommodate staff needs. There was no evaluation of the impact of this modification. Some caregivers were present almost every day; while others attended only when their presence was absolutely necessary.

This investigation did not examine issues of dosage; in other words, it did not determine how much association was necessary to produce change. Questions of dosage are critical in human service, as contact is costly; and this is another area which requires further study.

Program objectives

There was no clear mission statement or specific elaboration of goals and objectives for the caregivers' program; therefore, it was not possible to compare staff actions with program intent or to compare the services delivered with those proposed. This study could only evaluate what actually occurred in this setting.

As mentioned previously, the lack of clear objectives negatively affected a few participants who did not understand the novel philosophy. Occasionally, staff had difficulty implementing a program not clearly articulated, and their actions were not always in keeping with the intent of the Board. The absence of clear objectives is apparently common in grassroots endeavors that pioneer new programs, but it hindered research efforts. This is a practical issue which also needs attention by this and similar programs.

Other limitations

This study began to demonstrate one approach through the evaluation of outcomes. Another approach would be to evaluate competence in everyday activities and interactions. Additional information about history and personality can help planners and managers determine whether leadership is inherent or whether it can be taught to all participants through grassroots programs such as this.

There are still no good measures of competence for adult caregivers. If programs are to continue to improve and learn from each other, it will be important for fleet and flagship programs to work together to improve the evaluation technology.

It is difficult to establish an experimental design in a naturalistic setting; however, before these results can be generalized, they must be replicated, and other populations in other settings must also be studied. Grassroots programs can advance research technology by banding together to compare efforts across similar programs.

RECOMMENDATIONS

This study suggests that parent participation in a cooperative preschool can have substantial benefits for families and communities. Further research is needed to determine exactly which program elements are most effective, what staff qualifications are essential, and who can best benefit from participation. Greater definition of the caregivers' program is essential to maximize the benefits of required participation. Minor additions such as entrance and exit interviews, greater participation in matters involving money, and planning functions would also benefit this particular preschool.

Despite the limitations already specified, the results of this investigation should be widely disseminated, for they suggest that grassroots programs can have an enormous impact on families and communities. Social workers would do well to examine the qualities of lay workers who make such programs successful. This study highlights the potential benefits of community organization, a field currently receiving little attention in social work or social work education.

Since it is difficult to establish an experimental design in a naturalistic setting, grassroots preschool programs should band together to compare and contrast programs, staff, participants, and outcomes. Through collaboration and consultation, grassroots programs can determine what works, as well as how, when, for whom, and under what conditions. This information is vital, for we cannot "fix" children without first giving their families the tools they need to obtain the goods and services they want.

Partnerships between religious groups and private facilities are often overlooked in the professional literature, yet they may be powerful sources of change within a community. Social researchers would do well to investigate collaborations between churches and civic agencies.

Like the concept of family support, the notion of family empowerment should be extended to other populations, other problems or life transitions, and other settings. Replication will increase our understanding of the process and permit planners to specify the salient conditions which foster empowerment and allow individuals to develop self-sufficiency.

Early intervention is a blossoming area of study with few formal ties to established social work. Consequently, many early intervention programs are just now learning lessons which social work absorbed decades ago. Social workers need to become involved in this field, sharing their expertise and allowing newer vocations to benefit from the accumulated knowledge of an established profession.

Information Letter for Individual Participants

Case Western Reserve University
10900 Euclid Avenue
Cleveland, OH 44106–7164

March 26, 1993

Dear _____:

This year I have been studying the caregivers' program of Seigle Avenue Preschool Cooperative. I would like to permission to enroll you as a participant in this research project.

The purpose of my study is to find out what happens to parents after their children leave the preschool. Few studies have asked preschool parents about their experiences. I am interested in learning what kinds of things you have been doing. I also want to know what you think about the preschool. This information can help the preschool develop better programs for adults.

To participate in this study, you must attend one interview, which will last about three hours. You will be paid $15.00 for this session.

The interview can be scheduled in your home, at Seigle Avenue Presbyterian Church, or a place of your choice. I will provide refreshments.

If you have questions about this study, they will be answered. I can be reached at 533–8092. Dr. Wallace Gingerich, my advisor, is available at 216/368–2270. You may call him collect.

You do not have to answer any questions which make you feel uncomfortable. You may withdraw from the study at any time. The information you share will be held in confidence; and your privacy will be protected. Your name will not be used. No one will know what you have said.

Thank you for considering this important project. Your ideas are important!

Attached is a consent form for you to sign before our interview. I will call next week to see if you have any questions. If you would like to participate, I will schedule an appointment then.

Sincerely,

Katherine M. Dunlap, MSW, ACSW
Enclosure

CONSENT FORM FOR INDIVIDUAL INTERVIEWS

     I, _____, consent to participate in a research study conducted by Katherine M. Dunlap, MSW, ACSW, of Case Western Reserve University. I understand that this study is exploring the experiences of caregivers who have participated in Seigle Avenue Preschool Cooperative. I understand that the potential benefit of the study is to propose better programs and services for caregivers in the preschool.

     I also understand that my privacy will be protected and the information used in this study will preserve my confidentiality. I know that I do not have to answer any questions that make me uncomfortable. I understand that all my questions will be answered.

     I am aware that I may withdraw my consent and discontinue participation at any time. I understand that I will be paid $5.00 an hour for my participation in this interview.

Date: _____

Signature: _____

Date: _____

Signature: _____

     Katherine M. Dunlap, MSW, ACSW

Protocol for Individual Interviews

Introduction

Thank you for agreeing to talk about your experience in the parents' program of Seigle Avenue Preschool Cooperative. As you know, I am studying the effects of this program. Today, I want to hear about your experiences. Your comments will help the preschool improve its services. You can also help other preschool programs develop better programs for parents and caregivers.

Informed Consent

Before we start, I want to be sure that you understand your rights. As we discussed, your confidentiality will be protected. When I share my results, I will not use your name or any information that could identify you. No one will ever know what you have said to me.

You do not have to answer any question that makes you feel uncomfortable. You may stop or withdraw at any time. If you have questions at any time, your questions will be answered. You will be paid $10.00 at the end of this interview.

Do you have any questions now about this study or the interview?

Questions

1. You and _____ attended Seigle Avenue Preschool in _____. First, would you each tell me a little about your experience in the parents' program? How long did you attend?

    a. There are several daycare centers in this neighborhood. Why did you decide to participate in *this* program?

    b. In order for children to participate here, mothers or caregivers must volunteer their time. What kind of things did you do?

    c. How did the preschool make a difference in your life?

    d. What did you accomplish by participating?

    e. What did you learn about yourself?

    f. Tell me about your life since you "graduated" from the preschool.

2. Let's talk about the changes you have made for yourself.

    a. How do you see yourself differently now?

    b. In what ways did your participation in this preschool change you? Please give me specific examples?

    c. Was there a turning point for you?

    d. Who really made a difference for you or helped you?

    e. What kinds of preschool activities or experiences made you feel powerless?

  3. We have been talking specifically about the parents' program. Let's look at the whole preschool program.

    a. What other aspects of the program were helpful to you?

    b. What kinds of things were not helpful?

    c. If you were designing an ideal program for mothers and caregivers, what would your program be like?

  4. You "graduated" from the preschool ____ years ago. Your child, _____ , is now in the _____ grade. Is that right?

    a. What kinds of things have you done since you left the preschool?

    b. Many people become interested in community activities when they feel empowered. In what ways have you been involved in the neighborhood since you left the preschool?

- Have you been involved in a church? Which one?
- Wonderful Wednesdays or Sunday School
- Sunday Morning Worship
- Usher or Elder
- Other
- Have you pursued your education?
- GED
- Central Piedmont Community College
- Other
- Tell me about your employment since you left the preschool.
- How have you participated in your children's education?
- PTA
- School visits
- Parent/Teacher conferences
- Other
- What influence did the preschool have on your friendships—with mothers, volunteers, men?
- Tell me about your personal talents (crafts, hairdressing, listening to friends).
- How has your family life changed?

- In what ways are you involved in this neighborhood?
  - Residents' Organization
  - Special events
  - Other organizations
5. What personal qualities or inner resources helped you get where you are today?
6. What other people or agencies have helped you? (For example: family, friends, agencies) Please tell me about these.
7. What other experiences helped you feel empowered?
8. What people or experiences have made you feel powerless?

Conclusion

Our time is up! Do you have any final thoughts you would like to share?

For this project, I am interviewing adults who benefited from the preschool. Who would you recommend for an interview?

Thank you for letting me talk with you. Your comments have been helpful, and I appreciate your help.

If you have any more questions or think of something you want to share with me later, please call me. My telephone number is in the envelope with your money.

Research Consent for Focus Group

Case Western Reserve University
10900 Euclid Avenue
Cleveland, OH 44106–7164

March 26, 1993

Dear _____ :

As you know, I have been studying the caregivers' program of Seigle Avenue Preschool Cooperative. I would like to permission to enroll you as a participant in this research project.

The purpose of my study is to find out more about parent programs. Few studies have asked preschool parents about their experiences. I am interested in learning what kinds of things were helpful for you this year. I also want to know about things which did not work for you. This information can help preschools develop better programs for adults.

To participate in this study, you must attend one focus group. You will be paid $15.00 for this session.

The focus group will meet from 9:00 a.m. until 12:00 noon on Wednesday, May 12, 1993. The other participants will be the parents who had children in the preschool this year. We will meet in the parlor of Seigle Avenue Presbyterian Church. I will provide ham biscuits and beverages at 8:30.

If you have questions about this study, they will be answered. I can be reached at 533–8092. Dr. Wallace Gingerich, my advisor, is available at 216/368–2270. You may call him collect.

You do not have to answer any questions which make you feel uncomfortable. You may withdraw from the study at any time. The information you share will be held in confidence; and your privacy will be protected. Your name will not be used. No one outside of the focus group will know what you have said.

Thank you for considering this important project. Attached is a consent form. I will call next week to see if you have any questions. If you would like to participate, please sign it and bring it to our session.

Sincerely,

Katherine M. Dunlap, MSW, ACSW

Enclosure

CONSENT FORM FOR FOCUS GROUP

I, _____, consent to participate in a research study conducted by Katherine M. Dunlap, MSW, ACSW, of Case Western Reserve University. I understand that this study is exploring the experiences of caregivers who participate in Seigle Avenue Preschool Cooperative. I understand that the potential benefit of the study is to propose better programs and services for caregivers in the preschool.

I also understand that my privacy will be protected and the information used in this study will preserve my confidentiality. I know that I do not have to answer any questions that make me uncomfortable. I understand that all my questions will be answered.

I am aware that I may withdraw my consent and discontinue participation at any time. I understand that I will be paid $15.00 if I participate in the focus group interview from 9:00 a.m. until 12:00 noon.

Date: _____

Signature: _____

Date: _____

Signature: _____

Katherine M. Dunlap, MSW, ACSW

Focus Group Protocol

Introduction

Thank you for coming here today to talk about your experience in the parents' program. We have been through a lot together—birth, death, and almost everything in between.

As you know, I have been attending the caregivers' group with you all year. Today, I want to hear about the changes you've made in this program. Your comments will help the preschool improve its services. You can also help other preschool projects develop similar programs for caregivers.

Let me be clear about one thing: I am not evaluating staff. I am only interested learning about your experiences this year.

Informed Consent

You all received a letter describing the goals for today. Before we start, I want to be sure that you understand your rights. As the letter said, your confidentiality will be protected. When I share the results of the study, I will not use your names or any information that could identify you. No one will ever know who said what in this meeting.

You do not have to answer any question that makes you uncomfortable, and you may stop or withdraw at any time. If you have any questions at any time, your questions will be answered. This session will end at noon, and you will be paid $15.00 for your participation.

Do you have any questions about this study or this group?

If you have not already given me your signed letter, I will take that now. Thank you.

Questions

1. First, please tell me a little about your experience in this program.

    a. There are several daycare centers in this neighborhood. Why did you decide to participate in *this* preschool?

    b. In order for children to participate in this preschool, mothers or caregivers must also volunteer their time. What kind of things did you do?

    c. How has the preschool made a difference in your life?

    d. What have you accomplished this year?

    e. What have you learned about yourself?

2. Let's talk about the changes you have made.

    a. How do you see yourself differently now?

    b. In what ways has your participation in the preschool changed you? Please give me specific examples.

    c. Was there a "turning point" for you?

    d. Who really made a difference for you or helped you?

    e. What events or situations made you feel power*less*?

    f. The preschool program ends soon. How will you continue to develop?

3. We have been talking specifically about the parents' program. Let's look at the whole program now.

    a. What other aspects of the program were helpful to you?

    b. What kinds of things were not helpful?

    c. If you were designing an ideal program for mothers and caregivers, what would your program be like?

4. Many people become interested in community activities when they feel empowered. In what ways have you been involved in the neighborhood since you joined the preschool? (The following list can prompt responses.)

- Have you become involved in a church? Which one?
- What do you do at this church?
- Wonderful Wednesdays or Sunday School
- Sunday Morning Worship
- Usher or Elder
- Other
- Have you pursued your education?
- GED
- Central Piedmont Community College
- Other
- How have you participated in your children's education?
- PTA
- School visits
- Parent/Teacher conferences
- Other (Halloween Carnivals, Book Fairs, etc.)

- Tell me about your personal talents (listening to friends, crafts, hairdressing).
- How has your family life changed?
- What influence did the preschool have on your friendships—with other mothers, volunteers, neighbors, men?
- In what ways are you involved in your neighborhood?
- Residents' Organization
- Special events
- Other organizations

5. What personal qualities or inner resources helped this year?

6. What other people or agencies have helped? (For example: family, friends, agencies) Please tell me about these.

7. We have talked about many good changes. Are there other benefits we have not discussed?

8. Outside of the preschool, what other experiences helped you feel empowered?

9. Outside of the preschool, what types of things that make you feel power*less*?

Conclusion

Our time is up! Do you have any final thoughts or comments you want to share? Thank you for coming. Your ideas have been very helpful, and I appreciate each of your contributions.

If you have any more questions, I will be at the church until one o'clock. We can talk individually or in a group. If you think of something you want to share with me later, please call me. My telephone number is in the envelope with your money.

Thank you.

Field Notes

Date:

Place:

Activity:

Time:

Participants

    Caregivers:

    Staff:

    Others:

 Narrative:

Comments:

Bibliography

Adams, D. (1976). *Parent involvement: Parent development*. Berkeley, CA: Center for the Study of Parent Involvement. (ERIC Document Reproduction Service No. ED 186 511)

Allen-Meares, P., & Lane, B. A. (1990). Social work practice: Integrating qualitative and quantitative data collection techniques. *Social Work, 35*(5), 452–458.

Alter, C., Deutelbaum, W., Dodd, T. E., Else, J., & Raheim, S. (1992, March 1). *Integrating three strategies of family empowerment: Family, community, and economic development*. Paper presented at the annual program meeting of the Council on Social Work Education, Kansas City, MO.

Anglin, J. P. (1988). The Parent Networks Project: Toward a collaborative methodology of ecological research. In Pence, A. R. (Ed.), *Ecological research with children and families: From concepts to methodology*. New York: Teachers College Press, 35–48.

Anyon, J. (1990). Social class and the hidden curriculum of work. *Journal of Education, 162*(1), 67–92.

Argyris, C., & Schon, D. A. (1989). Participatory action research and action science compared. *American Behavioral Scientist, 32*(5), 612–623.

Arnstein, S. R. (1971). Eight rungs on the ladder of citizen participation. In E. S. Cahn & B. A. Passett (Eds.), *Citizen participation: Effecting community change*. NY: Praeger.

Arthur, B. (1971, December 28). Housing unit to add 2 members. *The Charlotte Observer*, p. 1B.

Baker-Miller, J. (1984). The development of women's sense of self. *Work in Progress, No. 12*, Wellesley, MA: Stone Center Working Papers Series.

Baratz, S. S., & Baratz, J. C. (1970). Early childhood intervention: The social science base of institutional racism. *Harvard Educational Review, 40*(1), 29–50.

Barr, D., Cochran, M., Riley, D., & Whitham, M. (1984). Family empowerment. *Human Ecology Forum, 14*, 4–13, 34–35.

Bateson, G. (1978). The pattern which connects. *The CoEvolution Quarterly, 18*, 4–15.

Baumrind, D. (1972). An exploratory study of socialization effects on black children: Some black-white comparisons. *Child Development, 43*, 261–267.

Becher, R. M. (1986). Parent involvement: a review of research and principles of successful practice. In L. G. Katz (Ed.), *Current topics in early childhood education* (Vol. 6, pp. 85–122). Norwood, NJ: Ablex Publishing.

Becker, G. S. (1962). Investment in human capital: A theoretical analysis. *The Journal of Political Economy (Supplement), 70*(5, part 2), 9–49.

Becker, G. S. (1975). *Human capital: A theoretical and empirical analysis, with special reference to education* (2nd ed.). New York: National Bureau of Economic Research, Columbia University Press.

Bee, H. L., Van Egeren, L. F., Streissguth, A. P., Nyman, B. A., & Leckie, M. S. (1969). Social class differences in maternal teaching strategies and speech patterns. *Developmental Psychology, 1*, 726–734.

Berger, P. L., & Neuhaus, R. J. (1977). *To empower people: The role of mediating structures in public policy.* Washington, DC: American Enterprise Institute for Public Policy Research.

Bernstein, B. (1960). Language and social class. *The British Journal of Sociology, 11*, 271–276.

Berrueta-Clement, J. R., Schweinhart, L. J., Barnett, W. S., Epstein, A. S., & Weikart, D. P. (1984). *Changed lives: The effects of the Perry Preschool Program on youths through age 19.* Monographs of the High/Scope Educational Research Foundation No. Eight. Ypsilanti, MI: The High/Scope Press.

Berrueta-Clement, J. R., Schweinhart, L. J., & Weikart, D. P. (1983). Lasting effects of preschool education on children from low-income families in the United States. In *Preventing school failure: The relationship between preschool and primary education: Proceedings of a workshop on preschool research held in Bogota, Colombia, 26–29 May 1981.* Ottawa, Canada: International Development Research Centre, pp. 42–51.

Bigger, M. (1988, September 25). Graduation is sweet for former dropouts. *Mecklenburg Neighbors*, pp. 15, 17.

Borden, P. (1985, July 7). Era coming to end at Seigle Avenue Church. *Mecklenburg Neighbors*, p. 14.

Borman, K. M., LeCompte, M. D., & Goetz, J. P. (1986). Ethnographic and qualitative research design and why it doesn't work. *American Behavioral Scientist, 30*(1), 42–57.

Boulware, S. (1990, Holiday). Seigle Avenue Preschool Cooperative: Providing a head start. *The Crier*, pp. 40–41.

Bourdieu, P. (1971a). Intellectual field and creative project (S. France, Trans.). In Young, M. F. (Ed.), *Knowledge and control: New directions for the sociology of education*. London: Collier MacMillan.

Bourdieu, P. (1971b). Systems of education and systems of thought. In Young, M. F. (Ed.), *Knowledge and control: New directions for the sociology of education*. London: Collier MacMillan.

Bourdieu, P. (1977a). Cultural reproduction and social reproduction. In Karabel, J., & Halsey, A. H. (Eds.), *Power and ideology in education*. New York: Oxford, 487–511.

Bourdieu, P. (1977b). Symbolic power. In Gleeson, D. (Ed.), *Identity and structure: Issues in the sociology of education*. Driffield, England: Nafferton Books, 112–119.

Bourdieu, P., & Passeron, J-C. (1977). *Reproduction in education, society, and culture* (R. Nice, Trans.). London: Sage. (Original work published in 1970.)

Bowles, S., & Gintis, H. (1976). *Schooling in capitalist America: Educational reform and the contradictions of economic life*. New York: Basic Books.

Braun, S. J., & Edwards, E. P. (1972). *History and theory of early childhood education*. Worthington, OH: Charles A. Jones Publishing Company.

Brim, O. G. (1959). *Education for child rearing*. NY: Sage.

Brockmann, C. R. (1962). *Mecklenburg Presbytery: A history*. Charlotte, NC: Heritage Printers.

Bromley, K. C. (Ed.). (1972). *Investigation of the Effects of Parent Participation in Head Start*. (Midco Educational Associates). Washington, DC: Office of Child Development (DHEW). (ERIC Document Reproduction Service Nos. ED080 215 through ED080 218)

Bronfenbrenner, U. (1969). Motivational and social components in compensatory education programs: Suggested principles, practices, and research designs. In Grotberg, E. (Ed.), *Critical issues in research related to disadvantaged children*. Princeton, NJ: Educational Testing Service.

Bronfenbrenner, U. (1974a). *A report on longitudinal evaluations of preschool programs. Volume II: Is early intervention effective?* DHEW Publication Number (OHD) 76–30024.

Bronfenbrenner, U. (1974b). Is early intervention effective? *Teachers College Record, 76*(2), 279–303.

Bronfenbrenner, U. (1974c). The origins of alienation. *Scientific American, 231*(2), 53–61.

Bronfenbrenner, U. (1975). Is 80% of intelligence genetically determined? In Bronfenbrenner, U., & Mahoney, M. A. (Eds.), *Influences on human development* (2nd ed.). Hinsdale, IL: Dryden Press.

Bronfenbrenner, U. (1978). Who needs parent education? *Teachers College Record, 79*(4), 7667–787.

Bronfenbrenner, U. (1979). *The ecology of human development: Experiments by nature and design*. Cambridge, MA: Harvard University Press.

Bronfenbrenner, U. (1988). Foreword. In Pence, A. R. (Ed.), *Ecological research with children and families: From concepts to methodology*. New York: Teachers College Press, ix–xix.

Bronfenbrenner, U. (1986). Alienation and the four worlds of childhood. *Phi Delta Kappan, 67*(6), 430–436.

Bronfenbrenner, U., & Mahoney, M. A. (Eds.). (1975). *Influences on human development* (2nd ed.). Hinsdale, IL: Dryden Press.

Brophy, J. E. (1970). Mothers as teachers of their own preschool children: The influence of socioeconomic status and task structure on teaching specificity. *Child Development, 41*(1), 79–94.

Brown v. Board of Ed. of Topeka, Kan., 75 SCT 753; 349 US 294.

Bruyn, S. (1963). The methodology of participant observation. *Human Organization, 22*(2), 224–235.

Bureau of the Census (1991). *1990 Census of population and housing: Summary population and housing characteristics—North Carolina*. Washington, DC: U.S. Government Printing Office.

Burgess, J. C. (1982). The effects of a training program for parents of preschoolers on the children's school readiness. *Reading Improvement, 19*(4), 313–318.

Calabrese, R. L. (1988). The structure of schooling and minority dropout rates. *The Clearing House for the Contemporary Educator in Middle and Secondary Schools, 61*(7), 325–328.

Caldwell, B. M., & Smith, L. E. (1970). Day care for the very young—Prime opportunity for primary prevention. *American Journal of Public Health, 60*(4), 690–697.

Caliguri, J. P. (1970). Will parents take over Head Start programs? *Urban Education, V*(1), 53–64.

Campbell, D. T., & Stanley, J. C. (1963). *Experimental and quasi-experimental designs for research.* Chicago: Rand NcNally.

Card, J. J., & Wise, L. L. (1981). Teenage mothers and teenage fathers: The impact of early childbearing on the parents' personal and professional lives. In Furstenberg, F. F., Lincoln, R., & Menken, J. (Eds.). *Teenage sexuality, pregnancy, and childbearing.* Philadelphia, PA: University of Pennsylvania Press.

Cassels, J. (1976). The contribution of the social environment to host resistance. *American Journal of Epidemiology, 104*(2), 107–123.

Church plans new building. (1948, August 14). *The Charlotte Observer,* p. 10A.

Church to dedicate memorial building to late Dr. Snyder. (1958, November 14). *The Charlotte News,* p. 3A.

Cicirelli, V. G. (1972). The effect of sibling relationship on concept learning of young children taught by child-teachers. *Child Development, 43,* 282–287.

Cicirelli, V. G. (1975). Effects of mother and older siblings on the problem-solving behavior of the younger child. *Developmental Psychology, 11*(9), 749–756.

Clarizio, H. F. (1968). Maternal attitude change associated with involvement in Project Head Start. *The Journal of Negro Education, 37*(2), 106–113.

Clark, R. (1983). *Family life and school achievement: Why poor black children succeed or fail.* Chicago: University of Chicago Press.

Clarke-Stewart, K. A. with Apfel, N. (1978). Evaluating parental effects on child development. In Shulman, L. S. (Ed.), *Review of research in education.* Itasca, IL: Peacock, 47–119.

Clay, J. W., & Stuart, A. W. (Eds.). (1987). *Charlotte: Patterns and trends of a dynamic city.* University of North Carolina at Charlotte, Department of Geography and Earth Sciences.

Clay, J. W., & Stuart, A. W. (Eds.). (1990). *Charlotte metro region: Hub of the Carolinas.* University of North Carolina at Charlotte, Department of Geography and Earth Sciences.

Clay, J. W., & Stuart, A. W. (Eds.). (1992). *Charlotte: An analytical atlas of patterns and trends.* University of North Carolina at Charlotte, Department of Geography and Earth Sciences.

Cochran, M. (1987). The parental empowerment process: Building on family strengths. *Equity and Choice, 4,* 9–23.

Cochran, M. (1988). Between cause and effect: The ecology of program impacts. In Pence, A. R. (Ed.), *Ecological research with children and families: From concepts to methodology.* New York: Teachers College Press, 143–169.

Cochran, M., & Woolever, F. (1983). Beyond the deficit model: The empowerment of parents with information and informal supports. In Sigel, I. E., & Laosa, L. M. (Eds.), *Changing families.* New York: Plenum, 225– 245.

Cole, M., & Bruner, J. (1971). Cultural differences and inferences about psychological processes. *American Psychologist, 26*(10), 867–876.

Coleman, J. S. (1987). Families and schools. *Educational Researcher, 16*(6), pp. 32–38.

Coleman, J. S. (1988). Social capital in the creation of human capital. In Winship, C., & Rosen, S. (Eds.), Organizations and institutions: Sociological and economic approaches to the analysis of social structure, *American Journal of Sociology, 94* (Supplement 1988), S95–S120.

Coleman, J. S. (1990). *Equality and achievement in education.* Boulder, CO: Westview Press.

Coleman, J. S., Campbell, E. Q., Hobson, C. J., McPartland, J., Mood, A. M., Weinfeld, F. D., & York, R. L. (1966). *Equality of educational opportunity.* Washington, DC: U.S. Government Printing Office.

Coleman, J. S., & Hoffer, T. (1987). *Public and private high schools: The Impact of communities.* New York: Basic Books.

Collins, R. (1990). Some comparative principles of educational stratification. In Dougherty, K. J., & Hammack, F. M. (Eds.), *Education and society: A reader.* New York: Harcourt Brace Jovanovich. pp. 39–59.

Comer, J. P. (1984). Home-school relationships as they affect the academic success of children. *Education and Urban Society, 16*(3), 323–337.

Comer, J. P. (1986). Parent participation in the schools. *Phi Delta Kappan,* *67*(6), 442–446.

Conn, R. (1986, March 27). Apathy rated Piedmont Courts' top problem. *The Charlotte Observer,* p. 3D.

Consortium for Longitudinal Studies (1983). *As the twig is bent—Lasting effects of preschool programs.* Hillsdale, NJ: Lawrence Erlbaum Associates.

Cook, T. D., & Campbell, D. T. (1979). *Quasi-experimentation: Design and analysis issues for field settings.* Boston: Houghton Mifflin Company.

Cowen, E. L., Dorr, D. A., Trost, M. A., & Izzo, L. D. (1972). Follow-up study of maladapting school children seen by nonprofessionals. *Journal of Consulting and Clinical Psychology, 39*(2), 235–238.

Cowen, E. L., Weissbert, R. P., Lotyczewski, B. S., Bromley, M. L., Gilliland-Mallo, G., DeMeis, J. L., Farago, J. P., Grassi, R. J., Haffey, W. G., Weiner, M. J., & Woods, A. (1983). Validity generalization of a school-based preventive mental health program. *Professional Psychology: Research and practice, 14*(5), 613–623.

Crane, J. (1991). The epidemic theory of ghettos and neighborhood effects on dropping out and teenage childbearing. *American Journal of Sociology, 96*(5), 1226–1259.

Cremin, L. A. (1978). Family-community linkages in American education: Some comments on the recent historiography. *Teachers College Record, 79*(4), 683–704.

Cummins, J. (1986). Empowering minority students: A framework for intervention. *Harvard Educational Review, 56*(1), 18–36.

Davidson, B. P., & Jenkins, P. J. (1989). Class diversity in shelter life. *Social Work, 34*,(6), 1989, 491–495.

Davies, D. (1978). *Patterns of citizen participation in educational decision making.* (Report No. EA 012 794.) Washington, DC: National Institute of Education. (ERIC Document Reproduction Service No. ED 1888 338)

DeAdwyler, T. (1985, October 19). A rougher world within a city: Piedmont Courts housing project bustles with children, steeps in crime, poverty. *The Charlotte Observer,* p. 1A.

DeAdwyler, T. (1985, December 6). City pledges safety, help for complex. *The Charlotte Observer,* page 1B.

Dedicate new church house: Seigle Avenue Presbyterian congregation has ceremony in building. (1946, April 15.). *The Charlotte Observer*, p. 3B.

Delgato-Gaitan, C. (1990). *Literacy for empowerment: The role of parents in children's education.* New York: Falmer Press.

Delgato-Gaitan, C. (1991). Involving parents in the schools: A process of empowerment. *American Journal of Education, 100*(1), 20–46.

Dembeck, M. (1972, January 20). Woman tenant put on Housing Board: Maintenance, upkeep will be her targets. *The Charlotte Observer*, pp. 1B, 2B.

Denzin, N. K. (1978). *Sociological methods* (2nd ed.). New York: McGraw- Hill.

Deutsch, M. (1963). The disadvantaged child and the learning process. In Passow, A. H. (Ed.), *Education in depressed areas.* New York: Teachers College Press, Columbia University, pp. 163–179.

Dickens, E. (1989, April). Seigle Avenue Co-op: Planting seeds for future growth. *The Crier*, pp. 32–33.

DiMaggio, P. (1979). Review Essay: On Pierre Bourdieu. *American Journal of Sociology, 84*(6), 1460–1474.

Dimensions for Charlotte Mecklenburg (1974). *What SHOULD the future be? Proposed goals with essays on community life and activities.* Charlotte, NC: Observer-Craftsman.

Donofrio, A. F. (1976). Parent education vs. child psychotherapy. *Psychology in the Schools, 8*(2), 176–180.

Dougherty, K. J., & Hammack, F. M. (1990). *Education and society: A reader.* New York: Harcourt Brace Jovanovich.

Drumming and Dancing (1992, September 9). *Mecklenburg Neighbors*, p. 25.

Dunst, C. J., & Trivette, C. M. (1988). A family systems model of early intervention with handicapped and developmentally at-risk children. In Powell, D. R. (Ed.), *Parent education as early childhood intervention: Emerging directions in theory, research and practice.* Annual Advances in Applied Developmental Psychology, Volume 3. Norwood, NJ: Ablex.

Dunst, C. J., & Trivette, C. M. (1990). Assessment of social support in early intervention programs. In Meisels, S. J., & Shonkoff, J. P. (Eds.), *Handbook of early childhood intervention.* New York: Cambridge University Press, pp. 326–349.

Durlak, J. A. (1979). Comparative effectiveness of paraprofessional and professional helpers. *Psychological Bulletin, 86*(1), 80–92.

Edelman, M. W. (1989). Children at risk. *Caring for America's Children: Proceedings of the Academy of Political Science, 37*(2), 20–30.

Edelman, M. W. (1986). *Families in peril: An agenda for social change.* Cambridge, MA: Harvard University Press.

Everhart, R. B. (1977). Between stranger and friend: Some consequences of "long term" fieldwork in schools. *American Educational Research Journal, 14*(1), 1–15.

Fetterman, D. M. (1988). Qualitative approaches to evaluating education. *Educational Researcher, 17*(8), 17–23.

First public housing resident is named to Housing Authority (1972, January 21). *The Charlotte Observer,* p. 3B.

Fischer, J. (1983, July 7). Elderly get tuna, crackers; thieves dining on turkey, beef. *The Charlotte News,* p. 1A.

Foster, M., Berger, M., & McLean, M. (1981). Rethinking a good idea: a reassessment of parent involvement. *Topics in Early Childhood Special Education, 1*(3), 55–65.

Fordham, S. (1988). Racelessness as a factor in black students' school success: Pragmatic strategy of Pyrrhic victory? *Harvard Educational Review, 58*(1), 54–84.

Fordham, S., & Ogbu, J. (1986). Black students' school success: Coping with the "burden of 'acting' white". *The Urban Review, 18*(3), 176–206.

Fotheringham, J. B., & Creal, D. (1980). Family socioeconomic and educational-emotional characteristics as predictors of school success. *The Journal of Educational Research, 73*(5), 311–317.

Freakley, E. (1967, January 27). While agencies fight, Charlotte's poor suffer. *The Charlotte News,* pp. 1A, 16A.

Freire, P. (1990). *Pedagogy of the Oppressed* (M. B. Ramos, Trans.). New York: Continuum. (Original work published in 1973.)

French, J., & Raven, B. (1959). The bases of social power. In D. Cartwright (Ed.), *Studies in social power.* Ann Arbor, MI: Institute for Social Research.

Frisby, C. L. (1992). Issues and problems in the influence of culture on the psychoeducational needs of African-American children. *School Psychology Review, 21*(4), 532–550.

Furstenberg, F. F., Jr., Brooks-Gunn, J., & Morgan, S. P. (1987). *Adolescent mothers in later life.* New York: Cambridge University Press.

Furstenberg, F. F., Jr., Brooks-Gunn, J., & Chase-Lansdale, L. (1989). Teenaged pregnancy and childbearing. *American Psychologist, 44*(2), 313– 320.

Gabarino, J., & Sherman, D. (1980). High-risk neighborhoods and high-risk families: The human ecology of child maltreatment. *Child Development, 51*(1), 188–198.

Gardner, E. (1992, September 27). *Putting our past in perspective: Psalm 124.* Unpublished manuscript.

Garfield, K. (1992, May 4). Where blacks, whites worship together: Charlotte church is example of harmony in racially troubled times. *The Charlotte Observer,* pp. 1A, 8A.

Garfield, K. (1992, December 20). Religion a daily reality of life in the Bible Belt: Newcomers grapple with focus on faith. *The Charlotte Observer,* pp. 1A, 8–9A.

Gaultney, J. (1979, July 28). Church 'believes in kids': New experiences a treat at Seigle Presbyterian. *The Charlotte News,* p. 9A.

Getzels, J. W. (1978). The communities of education. *Teachers College Record, 79*(4), 659–682.

Gibson, M. A., & Ogbu, J. U. (1991). *Minority status and schooling: A comparative study of immigrant and involuntary minorities.* New York: Garland.

Giroux, H. A. (1983). Theories of reproduction and resistance in the new sociology of education: A critical analysis. *Harvard Educational Review, 53*(3), 257–293.

Glasser, B. G., & Strauss, A. L (1967). *The discovery of grounded theory: Strategies for qualitative research.* NY: Aldine De Gruyter.

Gold, R. L. (1958). Roles in sociological field observations. *Index of Social Forces, 36,* 217–223.

Goodson, B. D., & Hess, R. D. (1975). *Parents as teachers of young children: An evaluative review of some contemporary concepts and programs.* (Report No. PS 009 247.) Stanford, CA: Stanford University. (ERIC Document Reproduction Service No. ED 136 967)

Goodson, B. D., & Hess, R. D. (1976). *The effects of parent training programs on child performance and parent behavior.* (Report No. PS 009 152) Stanford, CA: Stanford University. (ERIC Document Reproduction Service No. ED 136 912)

Gordon, I. J. (1969). Developing parent power. In Grotberg, E. (Ed.), *Critical issues in research related to disadvantaged children.* Princeton, NJ: Educational Testing Service.

Gordon, I. J. (1970). Reaching the young child through parent education. *Childhood Education, 46*(5), 247–249.

Gordon, I. J. (1978). *Continuity between home and school: Aspects of parental involvement in Follow Through.* Paper Presented at the Biennial Southeastern Conference on Human Development (5th, Atlanta, GA, April 17–29, 1978). (ERIC Document Reproduction Service No. ED 154–931)

Gordon, I. J. (1979). Effects of parent involvement on schooling. In Brandt, R. S. (Ed.), *Partners: Parents and schools.* Alexandria, VA: Association for Supervision and Curriculum Development. (ERIC Document Reproduction Service No. ED 177 700)

Gordon, A. M., & Browne, K. W. (1985). History of early childhood education. In *Beginnings and beyond: Foundations in early childhood education.* Albany, NY: Delmar, pp. 10–28.

Goslin, D. A. (1990). The functions of the school in modern society. In Dougherty, K. J., & Hammack, F. M. (Eds.), *Education and society: A reader.* New York: Harcourt Brace Jovanovich, pp. 29–38.

Gottlieb, N. (1992). Empowerment, political analyses, and services for women. In Hasenfeld, Y. (Ed.), *Human services as complex organizations.* Newbury Park, CA: Sage.

Gould, S. J. (1981). *The mismeasure of man.* New York: Norton.

Gray, S. W., & Wandersman, L. P. (1980). The methodology of home-based intervention studies: Problems and promising strategies. *Child Development, 51*(4), 993–1009.

Greenwood, G. E., Breivogel, W. F., & Bessent, H. (1972). Some promising approaches to parent involvement. *Theory into Practice, XI*(1), 183–189.

Ground broken for church. (1948, November 9). *The Charlotte Observer,* 11A.

Gutierrez, L. M. (1990). Working with women of color: An empowerment perspective. *Social Work, 35*(2), 149–153.

Gutierrez, L. M. (1992). Empowering ethnic minorities in the twenty-first century: The role of human service organizations. In Hasenfeld, Y. (Ed.), *Human services as complex organizations.* Newbury Park, CA: Sage.

Hale-Benson, J. (1986). *Black children: Their roots, culture, and learning styles* (Revised ed.). Baltimore: Johns Hopkins University Press.

Halpern, R. (1988). Parent support and education for low-income families: Historical and current perspectives. *Children and Youth Services Review, 10,* 283–303.

Halpern, R. (1990). Community-based early intervention. In Meisels, S. J., & Shonkoff, J. P. (Eds.). *Handbook of early childhood intervention.* Cambridge, MA: Cambridge University Press.

Halpern, R., & Larner, M. (1988). The design of family support programs in high-risk communities: Lessons from the Child Survival/Fair Start Initiative. In Powell, D. R. (Ed.), *Parent education as early childhood intervention: Emerging directions in theory, research and practice.* Norwood, NJ: Ablex, pp. 181–207.

Hansen, D. A. (1988). Schooling, stress, and family development: Rethinking the social role metaphor. In Klein, D. M., & Aldous, J. (Eds.), *Social stress and family development.* New York: Guilford.

Harman, D, & Brim, O. G. (1980). *Learning to be parents: Principles, programs, and methods.* Beverly Hills, CA: Sage.

Harmon, C., & Zigler, E. (1980). Parent education in the 1970s: Policy, panacea, or pragmatism. *Merrill-Palmer Quarterly, 26*(4), 439–451.

Hasenfeld, Y. (1987). Power in social work practice. *Social Service Review, 61*(3), 469–483.

Henniger, M. L. (Comp.). (1979). *Parent involvement in education: A bibliography.* (Report No. PS 010 780) Washington, DC: National Institute of Education. (ERIC Document Reproduction Service No. ED 174 352)

Herman, J. L., & Yeh, J. P. (1980, October). *Some effects of parent involvement in schools.* (Report No. CG 015 402) Paper presented at the Annual Meeting of the American Educational Research Association, Boston, MA. (ERIC Document Reproduction Service No. ED 206 963)

Hess, R. D. (1969). Parental behavior and children's school achievement: Implications for Head Start. In Grotberg, E. (Ed.), *Critical issues in research related to disadvantaged children.* Princeton, NJ: Educational Testing Service.

Hess, R. D., & Shipman, V. C. (1965). Early experience and the socialization of cognitive modes in children. *Child Development, 36,* 869–886.

Hess, R. D., & Shipman, V. C. (1966). Maternal influences upon early learning: The cognitive environments of urban, pre-school children. In Hess, R. D., & Bear, R. M. (Eds.), *Early education: Current theory, research, and action.* Chicago: Aldine, 91–103.

Hidlay, S., & DeAdwyler, T. (1985, December 2). Gunfire linked to drugs: Uzi gun confiscated at Piedmont Courts. *The Charlotte Observer*, pp. 1A, 6A.

Hill, R. B. (1972). *The strengths of black families.* New York: National Urban League.

Hillery, G. A. (1955). Definitions of community: Areas of agreement. *Rural Sociology, 20,* 111–123.

The History of Piedmont Presbyterian Chapel: 1941 - 1946. (Circa 1946). Unpublished manuscript.

Hobbs, N. (1978). Families, schools, and communities: An ecosystem for children. *Teachers College Record, 79*(4), 756–766.

Hold service at sanctuary: Cornerstone of new building is laid by Seigle Avenue Presbyterian Church. (1949, June 13.) *The Charlotte Observer*, p. 10B.

Holley, H., & Arboleda-Florez, J. (1988). Utilization isn't everything. *The Canadian Journal of Program Evaluation, 3*(2), 93–102.

Honig, A. S. (1982). Parent involvement in early childhood education. In Spodek, B. (Ed.), *Handbook of research in early childhood education* (pp. 426–455). New York: Free Press.

Housing Authority, City of Charlotte, North Carolina (1941, January 1). *From bad houses to good homes: A year of progress toward better living conditions in Charlotte* (Second Annual Report). Charlotte, NC: Author.

Housing Authority, City of Charlotte, North Carolina (1947, April 4). *Better homes for better citizens and a better city* (Sixth Annual Report). Charlotte, NC: Author.

Housing Authority, City of Charlotte, North Carolina (1960). *Providing homes for our senior citizens* (Report: April 1, 1958 - April 1, 1960). Charlotte, NC: Author.

Houts, A. C., Shutty, M. S., & Emery, R. E. (1985). The impact of children on adults. In Lahey, B. B., & Kazdin, A. E. (Eds.), *Advances in clinical child psychology.* New York: Plenum.

Hunt, J. McV. (1961). *Intelligence and experience.* New York: Ronald, 1961.

Hunt, J. McV. (1967). The psychological basis for using preschool enrichment as an antidote for cultural deprivation. In Hellmuth, J. (Ed.), *Disadvantaged child* (Volume 1). New York: Brunner/Mazel, pp. 255–299.

Irvine, D. J., Horan, M. D., Flint, D. L., Kukuk, S. E., & Hick, T. L. (1982). Evidence supporting comprehensive early childhood education for disadvantaged children. *Annals of the American Academy of Political and Social Science, 46* (May), 74–80.

Iscoe, I. (1973). Sociopragmatic objectives in social intervention research. In Kraft, I. A. (Ed.), Critical Human Behavioral Research in Social Intervention Programs. *Annals of the New York Academy of Sciences, 218,* 14–20.

Jablow, P. (1966, September 8). Chance to shine: Slum 'underground' gets major surgery. *The Charlotte Observer,* pp. 1B, 4B.

Jason, L., Clarfield, S., & Cowen, E. L. (1973). Preventive intervention with young disadvantaged children. *American Journal of Community Psychology, 1*(1), 50–61.

Jencks, C. (1972). *Inequality.* New York: Basic Books.

Jensen, A. (1969). How much can we boost IQ and scholastic achievement? *Harvard Educational Review, 39*(1), 1–123.

Johns, R. L., Morphet, E. L., & Alexander, K. (1990). Human capital and the economic benefits of education. In Dougherty, K. J., & Hammack, F. M. (Eds.), *Education and society: A reader.* New York: Harcourt Brace Jovanovich.

Jorgensen, D. L. (1989). *Participant observation: A methodology for human studies.* Volume 15, Applied Social Research Methods Series. Newbury Park, CA: Sage.

Kagan, S. L. (1987). Home-school linkages: History's legacies and the family support movement. In Kagan, S. L., Powell, D. R., Weissbourd, B., & Zigler, E. F. (Eds.), *America's family support programs: Perspectives and prospects.* New Haven: Yale University Press, pp. 161–181.

Kagan, S. L., & Shelley, A. (1987). The promise and problems of family support programs. In Kagan, S. L., Powell, D. R., Weissbourd, B., & Zigler, E. F. (Eds.), *America's family support programs.* New Haven: Yale University Press, pp. 3–18.

Karnes, M. B., Teska, J. A., Hodgins, A. S., & Badger, E. D. (1970). Educational intervention at home by mothers of disadvantaged children. *Child Development, 41*(4), 925–935.

Kieffer, C. H. (1984). Citizen empowerment: A developmental perspective. *Prevention in human services, 3*(2/3), 9–36.

Keith-Lucas, Alan. *Giving and taking help.* Chapel Hill, NC: The University of North Carolina Press, 1972.

King, V. C. (1954). *Story of the origin of the city of Charlotte.* Charlotte, NC: Anderson Press.

Kohn, M. L. (1963). Social class and parent-child relationships: An interpretation. *American Journal of Sociology, 68*(4), 471–480.

Kratt, M. N. (1992). *Charlotte: Spirit of the New South.* Winston-Salem, NC: John F. Blair.

Kusserow, R. P. (1991a, January). *Services integration for families and children in crisis.* (Report No. OEI-09-90–00890) Washington, DC: Department of Health and Human Services, Office of Inspector General.

Kusserow, R. P. (1991b, January). *Services integration: A twenty-year retrospective.* (Report No. OEI-01–91–00580) Washington, DC: Department of Health and Human Services, Office of Inspector General.

Laosa, L. M. (1982). School, occupation, culture, and family: The impact of parental schooling on the parent-child relationship. *Journal of Educational Psychology, 74*(6), 789–827.

Laosa, L. M. (1983). Parent education, cultural pluralism, and public policy: The uncertain connection. In Haskins, R., & Adams, D. (Eds.), *Parent education and public policy.* Norwood, NJ: Ablex Publishing Corporation, pp. 331–345.

Laosa, L. M. (1991). The cultural context of construct validity and the ethics of generalizability. *Early Childhood Research Quarterly, 6*(3), 313–323.

Lareau, A. (1987). Social class differences in family-school relationships: The importance of cultural capital. *Sociology Education, 60*(2), 73–85.

Lareau, A. (1989). *Home advantage: Social class and parental intervention in elementary education.* Philadelphia: Falmer Press.

Larsen, J., & Juhasz, A. (1986). The Knowledge of Child Development Inventory. *Adolescence, XXI*(81), 39–53.

Lawrimore, E. (1966, June 23). Cites Meredith: Guns won't produce civil rights—Shriver: Urges all to break poverty's 'Iron Rule.' *The Charlotte Observer,* p. 1A.

Lawrimore, E. (1966, August 7). Seigle Ave. Church: Where 'church-going' takes on a new and wider meaning. *The Charlotte Observer,* p. 1C.

Lazar, I., & Darlington, R. (1982). *Lasting effects of early education: A report from the consortium for longitudinal studies.* Monograph of the Society for Research in Child Development, Serial No. 195, *47*(2–3).

Leach, D. E. (1976). *Progress under pressure: Changes in Charlotte race relations, 1955–1965.* Unpublished master's thesis, University of North Carolina at Chapel Hill, NC.

LeCompte, M. D., & Goetz, J. P. (1982). Problems of reliability and validity in ethnographic research. *Review of Educational Research, 52*(1), 31–60.

Lee, V. E., Brooks-Gunn, J., & Schnur, E. (1988). Does Head Start work: A one-year follow-up comparison of disadvantaged children attending Head Start, no preschool, and other preschool programs. *Developmental Psychology, 24*(2), 210–222.

Leichter, H. J. (1975). Some perspectives on the family as educator. In Leichter, H. J. (Ed.), *The family as educator.* New York: Teachers College Press, 1–43.

Leichter, H. J. (1978). Families and communities as educators: Some concepts of relationship. *Teachers College Record, 79*(4), 567–659.

Leichter, H. J. (1984). Families as environments for literacy. In Goelman, H., Oberg, A. A., & Smith, F. (Eds.), *Awakening to literacy.* Exeter, NH: Heinemann Educational Books.

Levenstein, P. (1970). Cognitive growth in preschoolers through verbal interaction with mothers. *American Journal of Orthopsychiatry, 40*(3), 426– 432.

Lewin, K. (1951). *Field theory in social science.* (D. Cartwright, Ed.). New York: Harper & Brothers.

Lewin, K. (1948). *Resolving social conflicts.* (G. Lewin, Ed.). New York: Harper and Row.

Lewis, O. (1968). The culture of poverty. *Scientific American, 215,* 19–25.

Lincoln, Y. S., & Guba, E. G. (1985). *Naturalistic inquiry.* Newbury Park, CA: Sage.

Logan, S. M., Freeman, E. M., & McRoy, R. G. (1990). *Social work practice with black families: A culturally specific perspective.* New York: Longman.

Lombard, A. D. (1981). *Success begins at home: Educational foundations for preschoolers.* Lexington, MA: Lexington Books.

Long Range Planning Committee, Seigle Avenue Presbyterian Church. (1983, March 18.). *Final Draft.* Unpublished manuscript.

Lubeck, S. (1985). *Sandbox society: Early education in black and white America.* Philadelphia: Falmer Press.

Marsh, M. (1966, June 23). Shriver: Poverty was stemmed from church. *The Charlotte News,* p. 6A.

Martin, B. (1970, July 27). Should tenants have say in public housing? *The Charlotte Observer*, p. 6D.

Martin, B. (1972, January 1). City Housing Board picks old-new team. *The Charlotte Observer*, pp. 1B, 5B.

Martin, E. (1985, October 2). Piedmont Courts to get facelift. *The Charlotte Observer*, pp. 1B, 2B.

Martin, E. (1988, October 27). Piedmont Courts begins again, 47 years later. *The Charlotte Observer*, pp. 1B, 2B.

Martin, E. (1986, November 30). 1 year later: What's become of Piedmont Courts? *The Charlotte Observer*, 1A, 14A.

Martin, E. (1987, March 23). Piedmont Courts Undergoes Rebirth. *The Charlotte Observer*, pp. 1B, 3B.

Maschal, R. (1986, May 4). Architects hope repairs improve tenants' lives. *The Charlotte Observer*, pp. 1A, 9A.

Matthews, D. (1987, November). Seigle Avenue Co-op: League's newest project gives children hope for the future. *The Crier*, pp. 47–48.

McAdoo, H. P., & McAdoo, J. L. (Eds.). (1985). *Black children: Social educational, and parental environments*. Newbury Park, CA: Sage.

McCall, R. B. (1983). Environmental effects on intelligence: The forgotten realm of discontinuous nonshared within-family factors. *Child Development, 54*(2), 408–415.

McClain, K. (1986, September 21). Church workers know quick fixes won't change lives. *The Charlotte Observer*, pp. 1A, 20A.

McClain, K. (1987, August 25). Davidson College chaplain to head church. *The Charlotte Observer*, p. 1C.

McClelland, D. C. (1973). Testing for competence rather than for "intelligence." *American Psychologist, 28*, 1–14.

McGill, D. A. (Mrs.). (Circa 1948). Women's Auxiliary History: Seigle Avenue Presbyterian Church, 1947–48. Unpublished manuscript.

McKay, A., & McKay, H. (1983). Primary school progress after preschool experience: Troublesome issues in the conduct of follow-up research and findings from the Cali, Colombia study. In *Preventing school failure: The relationship between preschool and primary education: Proceedings of a workshop on preschool research held in Bogota, Colombia, 26–29 May 1981*. Ottawa, Canada: International Development Research Centre, pp. 36– 41.

McKinney, J. (1978). Study of parent involvement in early childhood programs. Early Childhood Evaluation Unit Report No. 7912. (ERIC

Document Reproduction Service No. ED 206 963). Philadelphia: Philadelphia School District.

McKinney, J. (1980). Evaluation of parent involvement in early childhood education programs 1979–1980. Technical Summary, Report No. 8130. (ERIC Document Reproduction Service No. ED 204 388). Philadelphia: Philadelphia School District.

McKnight, J. L. (1987a). *The future of low-income neighborhoods and the people who reside there: A capacity-oriented strategy for neighborhood development.* Evanston, IL: Center for Urban Affairs and Policy Research, Northwestern University.

McKnight, J. L. (1987b, Winter). Regenerating Community. *Social Policy, 17*(3), 54–58.

McKnight, J. L. (1989, January-February). Why servanthood is bad. *The Other Side, 25,* 38–41.

McKnight, J. L. (1980). A nation of clients? *Public Welfare, 38*(4), 15–19.

McKnight, J., & Kretzmann, J. (1990). *Mapping community capacity.* Evanston, IL: Center for Urban Affairs and Policy Research, Northwestern University.

Mehan, H. (1992). Understanding inequality in schools: The contribution of interpretive studies. *Sociology of Education, 65*(1), 1–20.

Miles, M. B., & Huberman, A. M. (1984). *Qualitative data analysis: A sourcebook of new methods.* Beverly Hills, CA: Sage.

Mellnik, T., Minter, J., & Morell, R. (1985, December 3). Crackdown at Piedmont Courts ordered. *The Charlotte Observer,* pp. 1A, 16A.

Miller, S. (1983). *Children as parents: A study of childbearing and child rearing among 12– to 15–year-olds.* Child Welfare League of America.

Minter, J. (1985, December 4). Focusing on Piedmont Courts: Police overreacted, some residents say. *The Charlotte Observer,* pp. 1B, 6B.

Minter, J. (1990, May 15). Women's reading group blooms into support group. *The Charlotte Observer,* pp. 1C, 3C.

Mistry, V. R. (1983). Fostering readiness for primary grades: Innovative action programs with municipal schools in India. In *Preventing school failure: The relationship between preschool and primary education: Proceedings of a workshop on preschool research held in Bogota, Colombia, 26–29 May 1981.* Ottawa, Canada: International Development Research Centre, pp. 93– 102.

Moock, P. R. (1974). Economic aspects of the family as educator. In Leichter, H. J. (Ed.), *The family as educator*. New York: Teachers College Press, pp. 92–104.

Moock, P. R. (1978). Education and the transfer of inequality from generation to generation. *Teachers College Record, 79*(4), 737–748.

Morell, R. (1985, December 4). Officer wounds man at Piedmont Courts. *The Charlotte Observer*, pp. 1A, 12A.

Morell, R. (1986, November 9). Students from project often find success elusive. *The Charlotte Observer*, pp. 1A, 13A.

Morrill, J. (1986, August 3). A cycle of disrepair: Project's maintenance a continuing battle. *The Charlotte Observer*, pp. 1A, 8A.

Morrill, J., & Paddock, P. (1986, March 30). Project's early hope fades to despair. *The Charlotte Observer*, pp. 1A, 10–11A.

Moynihan, D. P. (1965, March). *The Negro family: The case for national action*. Washington, DC: Office of Policy Planning and Research, United States Department of Labor.

Myers Park's involvement with Seigle Church: A more than twenty-year sister relationship (1974, May). *Christian Outreach, 1*(1), p. 1.

Neighborhood medical clinic to become reality in July (1975, May). *Christian Outreach, 2*(1), p. 1–2.

Nichols, R. C. (1975). Schools and the disadvantaged (A summary of the Coleman Report). In Bronfenbrenner, U., & Mahoney, M. A. (Eds.), *Influences on human development* (2nd ed.). Hinsdale, IL: Dryden Press, pp. 468–471.

Noblitt, B. (1966, June 23). Charlotte public housing rapidly going all-Negro. *The Charlotte News*, pp. 1A, 9A.

Northen, H. (1988). *Social work with groups* (2nd ed.). New York: Columbia University Press.

O'Brien, K. (1992, December 9). No progress on school plan: Board unlikely to make requested changes. *The Charlotte Observer*, pp. 1C, 2C.

Office of Policy Planning and Research, United States Department of Labor (1965, March). *The Negro family: The case for national action*. Washington, DC: U.S. Government Printing Office.

Ogbu, J. U. (1974). *The next generation: An ethnography of education in an urban neighborhood*. New York: Academic Press.

Ogbu, J. U. (1978). *Minority education and caste: The American system in cross-cultural perspective*. New York: Academic Press.

Ogbu, J. U. (1990). Social stratification and the socialization of competence. In Dougherty, K. J., & Hammack, F. M. (Eds.), *Education and society: A reader*. New York: Harcourt Brace Jovanovich, pp. 390–401.

O'Neill, T. (1985, December 5). Officer shot man in self-defense, assistant DA rules. *The Charlotte Observer*, p. 1C.

Paget, K. D., & Bracken, B. A. (Eds.). (1983). *The psychoeducational assessment of preschool children*. New York: Grune & Stratton.

Parker, F. L., Piotrkowski, C. S., & Peay, L. (1987). Head Start as a social support for mothers: The psychological benefits of involvement. *American Journal of Orthopsychiatry, 57*(2), 220–233.

Patton, M. Q. (1989). A context and boundaries for a theory-driven approach to validity. *Evaluation and Program Planning, 12*(4), 375–377.

Patton, M. Q. (1990a). Humanistic psychology and humanistic research. *Person-centered Review, 5*(2), 191–202.

Patton, M. Q. (1990b). *Qualitative evaluation and research methods* (2nd ed.). Newbury Park, CA: Sage.

Peshkin, A. (1988). In search of subjectivity—One's own. *Educational Researcher, 17*(7), 17–22.

Piedmont Courts housing project to get $6 million renewal (1985, October 2). *The Charlotte News*, pp. 1A, 3A.

Pinderhughes, E. B. (1983). Empowerment for our clients and for ourselves. *Social Casework, 64*(6), 331–338.

Piven, F. F., & Cloward, R. A. (1971). *Regulating the poor: The functions of public welfare*. New York: Vintage Books.

Plomin, R. (1989). Environment and genes: Determinants of behavior. *American Psychologist, 44*(2), 105–110.

Plomin, R., Loehlin, J. C., & DeFries, J. C. (1985). Genetic and environmental components of "environmental" influences. *Developmental Psychology, 21*(3), 391–402.

Powell, D. R. (1987). Methodological and conceptual issues in research. In Kagan, S. L., Powell, D. R., Weissbourd, B., & Zigler, E. F. (Eds.), *America's family support programs: Perspectives and prospects*. New Haven: Yale University Press, pp. 311–328.

Powell, D. R. (1988). Client characteristics and the design of community-based intervention programs. In Pence, A. R. (Ed.), *Ecological research with children and families: From concepts to methodology*. New York: Teachers College Press, pp. 122–142.

Radin, N. (1972). Three degrees of maternal involvement in a preschool program: Impact of mothers and children. *Child Development, 43*(4), 1355– 1364.

Raim, J. (1980). Who learns when parents teach children? *The Reading Teacher, 34*(2), 152–155.

Rappaport, J. (1981). In praise of paradox: A social policy of empowerment over prevention. *American Journal of Community Psychology, 9*(1), 1–25.

Rappaport, J. (1985). The power of empowerment language. *Social Policy, 16*(2), 15–21.

Rappaport, J. (1987). Terms of empowerment/Exemplars of prevention: Toward a theory for Community Psychology. *American Journal of Community Psychology, 15*(2), 121–148.

Raspberry, W. (1992, December 18). The secret is spirituality: It's the one thing successful social programs have in common. *The Charlotte Observer*, p. 17A.

Reimler, K. (1966, April 2). Charlotte women leave comforts of home to wage battle on the fields of poverty. *The Charlotte News*, p. 8A.

Rickel, A. U., & Smith, R. L. (1979). Maladaption of preschool children: Identification, diagnosis, and remediation. *American Journal of Community Psychology, 7*(2), 197–208.

Rickel, A. U., Smith, R. L., & Sharp, K. C. (1979). Description and evaluation of a preventive mental health program for preschoolers. *Journal of Abnormal Child Psychology, 7*(1), 101–112.

Robbins, D. (1991). *The Work of Pierre Bourdieu: Recognizing Society.* San Francisco: Westview Press.

Rose, S. D. (1974). Group training of parents as behavior modifiers. *Social Work, 19*(2), 156–162.

Rossman, G. B., & Wilson, B. L. (1985). Numbers and words: Combining quantitative and qualitative methods in a single large-scale evaluation study. *Evaluation Review, 9*(5), 627–643.

Rowe, D. C., & Plomin, R. (1981). The importance on nonshared (E_1) influences in behavioral development. *Developmental Psychology, 17*(5), 517–531.

Ryan, S. (1974). *A report on longitudinal evaluations of preschool programs. Vol. 1: Longitudinal evaluations.* (DHEW Publication No. OHD 75–24.) Washington, DC: Office of Human Development, Children's Bureau.

Ryan, W. (1976). *Blaming the victim* (Revised ed.). New York: Vintage.

Saleebey, D. (1992). *The strengths perspective in social work practice.* New York: Longman.

Savickas, D., & Whisnant, M. (1973, April 28). *Charlotte Housing Authority scattered sites study: Piedmont Courts.* Unpublished manuscript.

Scarr, S. (1981). Testing *for* children: Assessment and the many determinants of intellectual competence. *American Psychologist, 36*(10), 1159–1166.

Scarr, S., & Weinberg, R. A. (1976). IQ test performance of black children adopted by white families. *American Psychologist, 31*(10), 726–739.

Scarr, S., & Weinberg, R. A. (1978). The influence of "family background" on intellectual attainment. *American Sociological Review, 43* (October), 674– 692.

Scarr-Salapatek, S. (1975). Unknowns in the IQ equation: A review of three monographs. In Bronfenbrenner, U., & Mahoney, M. A., (Eds.), *Influences on human development* (2nd ed.). Hinsdale, IL: Dryden, 78–91.

Schaefer, E. S. (1972). Parents as Educators: Evidence from cross-sectional, longitudinal and intervention research. *Young Children, 27*(4), 227–239.

Schlossman, S. (1978). The parent education game: The politics of child psychology in the 1970s. *Teachers College Record, 79*(4), 788–808.

Schultz, T. W. (1961). Investment in human capital. *The American Economic Review, 51*(1), 1–17.

Schwartz, K., & Wildman, J. (1982, August 25). City's prevention efforts rarely succeed. *The Charlotte Observer,* pp. 1A, 6A.

Schweinhart, L. J. (1987). Can preschool programs help prevent delinquency? In Wilson, J. Q., & Loury, G. C. (Eds.) *From children to citizens. (Vol. 3: Families, Schools, and Delinquency Prevention).* New York: Springer-Verlag, pp. 135–153.

Scott-Jones, D., & Turner, S. L. (1990). The impact of adolescent childbearing on educational attainment and income of black females. *Youth & Society, 22*(1), 35–53.

Seigle Avenue Presbyterian Church completes their lovely new sanctuary. (1949, December). *The Mecklenburg Presbyterian, IX*(3).

Seigle Avenue Preschool Cooperative. (1992, April 8). *Seigle Avenue Preschool Cooperative Program Description.* Unpublished manuscript.

Seigle Church observing 25th (1970, May 2). *The Charlotte Observer*, p. 5A.

Seitz, V. (1987). Outcome evaluation of family support programs: Research design alternatives to true experiments. In Kagan, S. L., Powell, D. R., Weissbourd, B., & Zigler, E. F. (Eds.), *America's family support programs*. New Haven: Yale University Press, pp. 329–342.

Seitz, V., Rosenbaum, L. K., & Apfel, N. H. (1985). Effects of family support intervention: A ten-year follow-up. *Child Development, 56*(2), 376–391.

Session Annual Statistical Report. (1985, December 31). Unpublished manuscript.

Shires, W. A. (1966, August 1). Moore-Sewell split began as a minor conflict. *The Charlotte Observer*, 3A.

Shirley, D. (1986). A critical review and appropriation of Pierre Bourdieu's analysis of social and cultural reproduction. *Journal of Education, 168*(2), 96–112.

Shriver: No stigma to clinic tests. (1966, June 23). *The Charlotte News*, p. 1B.

Simpson, R. (1979, May 5). Seigle Ave. Church marches ahead: It changed with the neighborhood. *The Charlotte News*, p. 6B.

Slaughter, D. (1988). Programs for racially and ethnically diverse American families: Some critical issues. In Weiss, H., & Jacobs, F. (Eds.). *Evaluating family programs*. NY: Aldine De Gruyter, pp. 445–476.

Smith, G. (1985, December 8). Public housing's legacy of problems. *The Charlotte Observer*, pp. 1A, 12A.

Spindler, G. D. (1974). The transmission of culture. In Spindler, G. D. (Ed.), *Education and cultural process: Toward an anthropology of Education*. New York: Holt, Rinehart and Winston, Inc., pp. 279–310.

Stack, C. B. (1974). *All our kin: Strategies for survival in a black community*. New York: Harper & Row.

Strom, R., & Johnson, A. (1974). The parent as teacher. *Education, 95*(1), 40–43.

Swann v. Charlotte-Mecklenburg Bd. of Ed., 91 SCT 1267; 402 US 1.

Swartz, D. (1990). Pierre Bourdieu: Culture, education, and social inequality. In Dougherty, K. J., & Hammack, F. M. (Eds.), *Education and society: A reader*, pp. 70–80.

Tarr, B. (1991, spring). A Christian community in Charlotte. *Davidson Journal*, pp. 34–35.

Taylor, K. W. (1967). *Parents and children learn together.* New York: Teachers College Press.

Todd, T. M. (1986). *A report of the Mayor's Task Force on Piedmont Courts.* Charlotte, NC: City of Charlotte.

Tompkins, D. A. (1903). *History of Mecklenburg County and the City of Charlotte from 1740 to 1903.* Charlotte, NC: Observer Printing House.

Trotter, H. (1947, August 15). Minister and wife move into church. *The Charlotte Observer*, p. 1B.

Tulkin, S. R. (1972). An analysis of the concept of cultural deprivation. *Developmental Psychology, 6*(2), 326–339.

Valentine, J., & Stark, E. (1979). The social context of parent involvement in Head Start. In Zigler, E., & Valentine, J. (Eds.), *Project Head Start: A legacy of the War on Poverty.* New York: The Free Press, 291–313.

Valentine, V. (1991, August 24). Residents pulled together to improve Piedmont Courts. *The Charlotte Observer.* p. 1B, 5B.

Vanderslice, V. (1984). Empowerment: A definition in process. *Human Ecology Forum, 14*(1), 2–3.

Vaughn, J. (1986, July 20). A child's story: Boy dreams of a better life amid realities of poverty in project. *The Charlotte Observer*, pp. 1E, 8E.

Washington, J. M. (Ed.) (1986). *A testament of hope: The essential writings of Martin Luther King, Jr..* San Francisco: Harper & Row.

Watters, P. (1964). *Charlotte.* Special report of the Southern Regional Council. Atlanta: Author.

Webb, N. (1985, December 1). Shooting spree wounds 7, panics Piedmont Courts. *The Charlotte Observer*, pp. 1A, 13A.

Webb, N. (1985, December 4). Focusing on Piedmont Courts: Even on a quiet night at complex, patrolling officer stays on the alert. *The Charlotte Observer*, pp. 1B, 6B.

Weick, A., Rapp, C., Sullivan, W. P., & Kisthardt, W. (1989). A strengths perspective for social work practice. *Social Work, 34*(4), 350–354.

Weinberg, R. A. (1979). Early childhood education and intervention: Establishing an American tradition. *American Psychologist, 34*(10), 912– 916.

Weinberg, R. A. (1989). Intelligence and IQ: Landmark issues and great debates. *American Psychologist, 44*(2), 98–104.

Weiss, H. B. (1987). Family support and education in early childhood programs. In Kagan, S. L., Powell, D. R., Weissbourd, B., & Zigler, E. F.

(Eds.), *America's family support programs: Perspectives and prospects.* New Haven: Yale University Press, 133–160.

Weiss, H. B. (1989). State family support and education programs: Lessons from the pioneers. *American Journal of Orthopsychiatry, 59*(1), 32–48.

Weiss, H. B. (1990). Beyond *Parens Patriae*: Building policies and programs to care for our own and others' children. *Children and Youth Services Review, 12,* 269–284.

Weiss, H. B., & Jacobs, F. H. (Eds.). (1988). *Evaluating family programs.* New York: Aldine De Gruyter.

Weissberg, R. P., Cowen, E. L., Lotyczewski, B. S., & Gestin, E. L. (1983). The Primary Mental Health Project: Seven consecutive years of program outcome research. *Journal of Consulting and Clinical Psychology, 51*(1), 100–197.

Weissbourd, B. (1983). The family support movement: Greater than the sum of its parts. *Zero to Three, 4,* 8–10.

Weissbourd, B., & Kagan, S. L. (1989). Family support programs: Catalysts for change. *American Journal of Orthopsychiatry, 59*(1), 20–31.

Wenig, M., & Brown, M. L. (1975). School efforts + parent/teacher communications = Happy young children. *Young Children, 30*(5), 373–377.

Westinghouse Learning Corporation (1969). *The impact of Head Start: An evaluation of the effects of Head Start on children's cognitive and affective development.* Vol. I-II. Athens, OH: Ohio University.

Who, what, when, where, why? (1985, July 30). *Seigle Avenue Mothers Invention, 16*(12), p. 3.

White, H. (1991, August 8–14). Apartment complex has sense of community for 50th birthday. *The Charlotte Post,* pp. 1A, 2A.

Whyte, W. F. (1984). *Learning from the field: A guide from experience.* Newbury Park, CA: Sage.

Wildman, J. (1982, August 23). Often, crime's a neighbor. *The Charlotte Observer,* pp. 1A, 8A.

Wildman, J., & Schwartz, K. (1982, August 23). Afraid, she's too poor to move away. *The Charlotte Observer,* pp. 1A, 8A.

Willerman, L. (1979). Effects of families on intellectual development. *American Psychologist, 34*(10), 923–929.

Williams, C. (1983, July 11). Hot meals: Church dips into budget to supply food for elderly after thieves hit. *The Charlotte News,* p. 1B.

Willis, P. E. (1977). *Learning to labour: How working class kids get working class jobs*. Westmead, England: Saxon House.

Willis, P. E. (1983). Cultural production and theories of reproduction. In Barton, L., & Walker, S. (Eds.), *Race, class and education* (pp. 107–138). London: Croom Helm.

Willis, P. E. (1990). *Common culture: Symbolic work at play in the everyday cultures of the young*. Boulder, CO: Westview Press.

Wilson, S. (1977). The use of ethnographic techniques in educational research. *Review of Educational Research, 47*(1), 245–265.

Wilson, W. J. (1987). *The truly disadvantaged*. Chicago: The University of Chicago Press.

Wohlford, P. (1974). Head Start parents in participant groups. *Journal of Applied Behavioral Science, 10*(2), 222–249.

Wolcott, H. F. (1980). How to look like an anthropologist without really being one. *Practicing Anthropology, 3*(1), 6–7, 56–59.

Zigler, E. (1978). The effectiveness of Head Start: Another look. *Educational Psychologist, 13*, 71–77.

Zigler, E., & Berman, W. (1983). Discerning the future of early childhood intervention. *American Psychologist, 38*(8), 894–906.

Zigler, E., & Black, K. B. (1989). America's family support movement: Strengths and limitations. *American Journal of Orthopsychiatry, 59*(1), 6– 19.

Zigler, E., & Seitz, V. (1980). Early intervention programs: A reanalysis. *School Psychology Review, 9*(4), 364–368.

Zigler, E., & Seitz, V. (1982). Head Start as a national laboratory. *Annals of the American Academy of Political and Social Science, 46*(May), 81–90.

Zigler, E., & Trickett, P. K. (1978). IQ, social competence, and evaluation of early childhood intervention programs. *American Psychologists, 33*(9), 789– 798.

Zigler, E., & Weiss, H. (1985). Family support systems: An ecological approach to child development. In Rapoport, R. N., (Ed.), *Children, youth, and families: The action research relationship*. New York: Cambridge University Press, pp. 166–205.

Zimmerman, M. A. (1986). Citizen participation, perceived control, and psychological empowerment. *Dissertation Abstracts International, 47*(10), 4335B.

Zurcher, L. A. (1969). Stages of development in poverty program neighborhood action committees. *Journal of Applied Behavioral Science, 5*(2), 223–258.

Index